THE MUTANTS` RISE& HOMO STUPIDLIGENCE` DEMISE

THE MUTANTS` RISE& HOMO STUPIDLIGENCE` DEMISE

The Final Count Down for Us

BENJAMIN KATZ

Library of Congress Control Number: 2024905641
ISBN: Softcover 979-8-3694-1541-2
eBook 979-8-3694-1542-9

Print information available on the last page.

Rev. date: 03/11/2024

To order additional copies of this book, contact:
Xlibris
844-714-8691
www.Xlibris.com
Orders@Xlibris.com
858066

CONTENTS

DEDICATION

This book is dedicated to us, Homo Stupidligence (both intelligent and stupid), who lack the essential virtues of Sapiens; far sight and evolving wisdom, and therefore become increasingly self- destructive. This book is a Wake-Up Call to us.

It is also dedicated to all the wise, inspiring people who try to break away from our confines of them I knew, one of the best specimens of our race: Yael Sekely, who died in January,2024.

I owe my thanks to Mogens Kischi, an artist and an IT wizard, who corrected the text grammatically, and made it more fluent and concise…and contributed with some of his pictures to it.

I owe also thanks to Shai Gabai who took the picture, which is on the book` front cover: The mutant and Homo Stupidligence.

POTENTIAL ADVANCED TIME´ TRAVELER, BEWARE!

Human nature is a fusion of a beast, intelligent animal, and a potential noble/higher being than we are and therefore the four most important questions and answers in our future journey are:

1. Are we destroying life conditions on earth? Definitely: yes!
2. Why do we do this against ourselves? We do it because we lack far sight and wisdom to understand the ill consequences of our actions.
3. Are we not Homo sapiens? Not at all. From our actions throughout history and currently, it is obvious that we are Homo Stupidligence, both intelligent and stupid, constructive, and destructive.
4. What can we do, to save earth as habitat place for life, and ourselves as evolving beings? We must evolve beyond our mental / cognitive constraints and conflicts. There is no other way to help us out of this self- created destructiveness.

We have out- smarted ourselves!
What are we to do next?
Either we´ll evolve/ survive by becoming wiser,
or we`ll degenerate/die out as a species.
Humans are both blessed and cursed.
In attempting our survival` chances to raise,
we must our evolving chances chase.
The time is ripe for Homo Stupidligence
our evolving potentials to embrace…

In this way will our existential conundrum be resolved when we further evolve!

PREFACE

´Call it a new race ´man-Plus`- call it what you will. The people who constitute this new race of men are not of recent arrival; They have been cropping up among men-Homo sapiens, that is-for hundreds, perhaps for thousands of years, but they are trapped in the human environment; they are trapped in the company of men, and they are molded by the company of men and by the human environment... So you see, the process is quite certain`(The Trap: Howard Fast)

Have you ever thought of being other than common so- called Homo sapiens? Have you ever thought of becoming the first unit for ever- evolving, advanced beings, who will be much wiser, more far sighted, longer living and healthier, and more mental balanced than you and us, and who will live sustainably, peacefully, and just on earth and beyond? Have you ever thought of becoming less emotionally gullible, greedy, war monger and self - deceptive for the benefit of future civilization? You should have if you are truly Homo sapiens!

If not, you can still pursue this direction by reading this both auto biographical and universal document, in which I described how I came to conceive our directed evolution as the ultimate meaning of our transcending journey. In this book I describe, how slowly I became a mutant, which means being partly human all the while struggling to overcome my human limitations in my mind, in my thoughts and aspirations... and one day also in my life expectancy and vigor.

There are both an alarming reason and impending necessity for this new direction:

We must evolve beyond sapiens as we are on self- destructive course. We get dumber and more reckless greedy (low IQ tests and our consumption testify for these trends), while global population- pollution- consumption- infotainment, nature catastrophes and wars are all on the RISE!(2024)!

So dear reader:

> ´You stand today in front of a crossroad.
> The first one leads you to your demise.

as it is your semi -automated mind` code.
The other one may evolve you into semi-God!

Because:

The ultimate human Meaning and Must,
is in defying the destiny of animated dust.
Challenging the constraints of life's Animator,
to evolve and ascend, and become a creator`(B.K)

But before you embark on this expanding journey of your mind, you´d better know, what elements do your life story consist of and how they reflect you mind capacity, overview, or lack of them.

1) The venture/journey of your life consists of a core of your personal life story.
2) In your personal life story, the human history supplements the personal one, be it local, national or global. This history becomes a part of your personal life story.
3) In your personal story, the awareness-or lack of it – of the influence of your and other human Nature (with all its contradictions and self- deception), your specific Nurture (how it affected you with conditioned values and convictions) and the collective Narrative you were exposed to as a child and grownup- be them religious, ideological, national- came to color/define your story, making it into either unique, idiosyncratic or unspecified collective (being a part of a human flock).

In most personal life stories, conditioned convictions, norms, and value play a key role as well as self- deception and pretension to ensure our mental security by our servitude to the authorities of these convictions. But there is also the element of rebelling against these conditioned convictions in some personal stories, and on top of it there is the element of aspiring to transcend the fixed role our nature, nurture and narratives destined for us. If we can learn to view our personal story out of the perspectives of our inherent mental/cognitive/ emotional limitations, delusions, and illusions, we may become wiser as to wish to bear the torch of our further evolvement.

To pursue our evolutionary push is the only viable mean to remove from us institutional stupidity and short sight, and thereby open for a future for advanced humans, our progenies, who will inevitably be free of our constantly oscillating between hyper elevation and dark desperation, baseless hopes and viable ones!

INTRODUCTION

Four narratives converge in my life journey towards becoming a mutant. These are as follows:

1) My life story from sapiens into a mutant.
2) Israel`& my kibbutz` story.
3) the human world` story and
4) the history of the evolving humanity beyond sapiens, described throughout this book as insights on the human nature/condition and deep aspirations.

Human:

If you became mentally resigned-ill
and you in your life stands still,
without any defying free will,
then you lose life essential thrill
and death stamps you with oblivion` seal...

You are at best just a flicker of light.
Alone, you are just a vanishing slight.
Unified: you may pursue a purpose
greater than your vanishing light,
as you become an evolving might!

When a person in our time writes about his/herself and his/her life, it revolves most often around events in his/her life, desires, sex, gossip, devaluating other people while promoting ones` own attributes, catastrophes, hardships success, a la; 'I did it my way`, often with false glimmer. He or she will conceal own faults, setbacks and defects and enhance self- glory and success etc. Most the focus on such auto biography is put upon his/her quotidian, transitory life.

Politicians write very often about their lives/deeds in their times as their focus. They reduce negative personal exposure to enhance their self- image (as faultless) and their so-called glamourous distinction in their quotidian world. But to write a story about a life of a man who tried to activate the potential stardust in himself and in us, all- as an ultimate aspiration to lift us up beyond our primitive reckless greed and short sight, war mongering, ecological destructive patterns - is a rare affair indeed. Yet, this is the very essence of this book.

As far as I remember myself as a thinking young adolescent, I was interested in history and world affairs, and I felt attracted to the following vision/mission as stated below:

'Man's dearest possession is life. It is given to him but once, and he must live it so as to feel no torturing regrets for wasted years, never know the burning shame of a mean and petty past; So live that, dying, he might say: all my life, all my strength were given to the finest cause in all the world—the fight for the Liberation of Mankind`— Nikolai Ostrovsky (How the steel was hardened).

'The mark of a noble individual lies his unwavering commitment to doing what is right, rather than being swayed by the countless options available`- Seneca.

I became very early in my life- due to the Holocaust which resulted in the death of my parents` families, wars which I experienced as a child and as an officer (1947-8,1956, 1967 and 1969-71) and deaths of many people whom I knew- aware that knowing history and its roots- human nature- is essential not only to understand the human condition and our current global state, but also to try and find enduring remedy for our short sight/stupidity demonstrated so profusely in our ongoing contrary course-progress-regress and self- destructiveness.

Human beings consist of coarse composites of four elements, three are visible, the fourth is invisible for the eyes of most of us: Spiritual, material, animal...and the fourth is the evolving/ upgrading drive. This last one leads us to our ultimate meaning.

The other three are the sole reason for our fractured/contradiction prone consciousness and view of ourselves and our reality. It is self-evident that the material and animal prone drives are the big trouble makers in our history, but what about the spiritual one?

An example for this taken from the Middle East: The conflict of the Alevi community, the minority that has been ruling for 50 years in Syria, with Sunni Islamic fanaticism is long and even reaches the Middle Ages. The great Syrian halachic sage Ibn Taymiyyah (14th century) ruled that the Alawites (then called Nuzayirs) are infidels 'worse than the Jews and Christians`, that they should not be recruited into the Muslim armies because it is 'like recruiting a wolf into a flock of sheep` and that their devil is death without the possibility of atonement. The Muslim Brotherhood movement, which as you remember, is the parent movement of Hamas, used to quote the infamous halachic ruling in Syria at every opportunity. The Muslim Brotherhood called for the ouster of Hafez al-Assad, the father of the current president, from the day he took power in 1970 on the grounds that it was an illegitimate 'infidel` government. The Islamic rebellion against Assad the elder that took place between the years 1979-1982, ended in a shocking massacre. The Syrian army wiped off the face of the earth entire neighborhoods in the city of Hamat, which was a stronghold of the Brotherhood. In the civil war that broke out in Syria in 2011, Assad Jr. faced an opposition that gradually became increasingly Islamic in character. But this time the rebellion was not focused on one city but spread to the whole country. The Islamic opposition did not only threaten the regime, but openly declared its intention to destroy all ´infidel` Alevis. The Alevis do not forget to this day that in August 2013, during the war in Syria, a coalition of rebel organizations carried out a campaign to destroy members of their community in the Latakia district. The trip took place about a month after the call of the leader of the Muslim Brotherhood in Qatar, Yusuf al-Qardawi, to destroy the Alawites, citing Ibn Taymiyyah. Although the Syrian army repelled the rebels after few days, they managed to commit shocking crimes, including murder and rape, the beheading of an Alevi religious scholar and the desecration of holy places for the community.

Apropos the spiritual drive and its political long- term consequences.

Being under the influence of the above named three drives, we keep creating and nurturing self- destructive divisions in our lives, being obsessed by petty affairs, all the while our current human world become turbulent and out of balance.

´The issue isn´t the limited duration of our lives, it is rather our tendency to fritter away a significant amount of it` were Seneca` words which resounded in my young soul.

Later in my life I read the lines of Bukowski:

´We're all going to die, all of us, what a circus! That alone should make us love each other but it doesn't. We are terrorized and flattened by trivialities; we are eaten up by nothing! `— Charles Bukowski.

This was also my view of reality from early age, contrasted by the insight and experience, demonstrating that working together for a project greater than our own sphere is the medicine for our mental malaise.

The mental malaise was visible: We are bewitched/made stupid by our brain/mind which splits us up into sects and religious/ideological/national warring groups.

in 2004 I published The Fifth Narrative, anticipating a global growing division and chaos, and suggesting a global common vision. I started writing it in 2000. Now as 2024 commences, the global growing chaos is clear to observe.

Already in 2004, I knew for sure, that we, as global citizens were going to aggravate our global demographic, ecological, consuming, polluting and sustainable problems, realizing that humans are much better at denying problems or talking about them, then doing something effective to eliminate them or prevent them. This task become almost impossible if they must sacrifice some of their privileges and comfort.

The only enduring remedy I saw was:
'Only by our evolving fueled by rage,
we can break out of our minds' cage,
which consists of self-interest& triviality
and distorted narratives on our reality`

Therefore, I proclaimed already in 2004 in the spirit of the Roman senator, Catoe -who repeatedly said: 'Carthago delenda est`: Carthago must be destroyed-: Stultitia (folly, stupidity, silliness) delenda est!`

Looking back on my past, the elements, which were woven into my life and brought me to view the future of humanity as I do are:

1) Demanding and varied life experience
2) Robust character building in the kibbutz, Israel and in wars
3) Nurturing from childhood Reflections, life affirming vision/mission based on impending necessities. and not the least: critical thinking.
4. Learning history, human nature, war waging, solidarity, and cooperation.

From childhood up to this time I studied the facts and on the human condition/nature through myriad of experiences. I studied the history of man, the human nature and our psychology including our unfortunate limitations, which are built in our brains and make us destroy ourselves and our life conditions om earth. The outcome of this lifelong endeavor had been my NEW VISION /MISSION for humanity and the process of how I slowly mutated away from the mental cage of human mindset.

Therefore, this book is primarily about Sapiens` ultimate meaning with our existence and, why it has been hidden for us, and how we can bring it into the light and pursue it!

In it I will describe the long way before I made up my mind to transcend Homo Sapiens, and became a chimera, half sapiens and half mutant. Such a person makes himself free from the common way sapiens conceive their purpose and meaning with their lives.

CHAPTER I

CHILDHOOD (1945-1957)

´A man who did not study world history and human nature, cannot follow my story, as his overview didn´t mature`.

Timeline:

The land of Israel has been populated by the Jewish people since 2000 BC, but there were also other ethnic groups. There were other groups living in this vicinity side by side and often both fighting frequently each other and intermixing with each other as well. Here's a timeline, in case you didn't realize that it was the Jewish homeland in the history before 1948 independence war (or as the Arabs call it: Nachaba: Catastrophe).

1900 BC: Abraham chosen by God as the Father of the Jewish Nation.
1900 BC: Isaac, Abraham's son, rules over Israel.
1850 BC: Jacob, son of Issac, rules over Israel.
1400 BC: Moses leads the people out of Egypt and back to Israel.
1010 BC: King David unites the 12 tribes into one nation.
970 BC: King Solomon, son of David, builds the first temple structure in Jerusalem
930 BC: Israel is divided into two kingdoms, the Kingdom of Israel and the Kingdom of Judah.
800s BC: The rise of the prophets, God's messengers.
722 BC: Kingdom of Israel is conquered by Assyrians.
605 BC: Kingdom Judah is conquered by the Babylonians.
586 BC: Solomon's Temple is destroyed by the Babylonians.
539 BC: Persians conquer the Babylonians and take control of Israel.
538 BC: The Jews return to Israel from exile.
520 BC: The Temple is rebuilt.
450 BC: Reforms made by Ezra and Nehemiah.
433 BC: Malachi is the end of the prophetic age.
432 BC: The last group of Jews return from exile.
333 BC: The Greeks conquer the Persian empire.
323 BC: The Egyptian and Syrian empire take over Israel.
167 BC: Hasmonean's recapture Israel, and the Jews are ruled independently.
70 BC: Romans conquer Israel.
20 BC: King Herod builds the "second" temple.
6 BC: Jesus Christ is born in Bethlehem.
70 AD: Romans destroy the temple.

After that, the people were captives to the Romans, Byzantines, Arabs, and Crusaders. Through all this period, the Jewish people continued to live in Israel. There were more or less of them, depending on the centuries, but there was never a time when the Jews didn't live in the land. They stayed, they built their communities, they raised their families, practiced their faith and they suffered at the hands of many outside rulers, but they always kept their faith. It is what sustains them, even now.

The history of my Kibbutz and Israel in the years 1936-1957: Vision, mission, hard work, and wars.

1936: my parents leave their families in Ukraine and wander to Palestine, due to their vision/ mission. As the Nazis invaded Polen and Ukraine and murdered millions of Jews there, among which my family members, I considered myself lucky that my parents left in good time, so I was granted a life of this reason.

12 July 1939: Kibbutz Negba was founded as part of a policy by the Jewish Agency/Zionist institution to inhabit Jews in Palestine. The first settlers were members of Hashomer Hatzair(The young guards` movement) from Poland. It was the southernmost Jewish settlement in Mandatory Palestine.

Kibbutz Negba, located in the south-center of Israel, provided quite a few tense moments in the country's history. From the establishment of Negba as a settlement in 1939, through the bloody battle against Egypt in the War of Independence (1947-8).

September,1939: Discrimination against Jews began immediately after the Nazi seizure of power on 30 January 1933. Violence and economic pressure were used by the Nazi regime to encourage Jews to voluntarily leave the country. After the invasion of Poland in September 1939, the extermination of European Jewry began, and the killings continued and accelerated after the invasion of the Soviet Union in June 1941. On 31 July 1941, Hermann Göring gave written authorization to Heydrich to prepare and submit a plan for a ′total solution of the Jewish question` in territories under German control and to coordinate the participation of all involved government organizations.

20 January 1942: The Wannsee conference: The Wannsee Conference was a meeting of senior government officials of Nazi Germany and Schutzstaffel (SS) leaders, held in the Berlin suburb of Wannsee. The purpose of the conference, called by the director of the Reich Security, Reinhard Heydrich, was to ensure the co-operation of administrative leaders of various government departments in the implementation of the Final Solution to the Jewish Question, whereby most of the Jews of German-occupied Europe would be deported to occupied Poland and murdered. Conference participants included representatives from several government ministries, including state secretaries from the Foreign Office, the justice, interior, and state ministries, and representatives from the SS. During the meeting, Heydrich outlined how European Jews would be rounded up and sent to extermination camps in the General Government (the occupied part of Poland), where they would be killed. Heydrich emphasized that once the deportation process was complete, the fate of the deportees would become an internal matter under the purview of the SS. A secondary goal was to arrive at a definition of who was Jewish.

This Conference legitimized the mass murder of my family and 6 million Jews in Europe and it meant that I knew from the time I could think/reason, how deep beastly humans can be and why, we Jews have to be ready to cut off the heads of this human medusa, whenever it wakes up..

The conference and the genocide formed my life view of what Sapiens could do of evil reverberated and settled down in my mental spine. It sits as epigenetic burning mark in most Israelis` and its message is: Never Again! The enemies of Israel should note it if they insist on destroying it, that such act will surely result in their own destruction, by all means, including nuclear devices. Arabs, Iranians, and Turks who are often being carried away by their inflaming rhetoric, should know that Israel will take all of them down, if it will come so far!

17.10.1945 – I was born. In the beginning, in the very beginning I was born in Palestine, an English dominium at that time. I was born shortly after the end of World War II, shortly after the Holocaust, which meant the death of all my family members and a third of the Jewish global population. My parents who immigrated to Palestine, were the only survivors of their big families. I was born shortly after two American Atom bombs destroyed two Japanese cities and killed and maimed hundreds of thousands of civilians, women, and children. This was the world into which I was born. Luckily, I did not grasp the magnitude of these disasters and the impact they had on my parents and their comrades who left both Ukraine and Poland just three years before Hitler invaded Poland. Was it luck or coincidence…or a burning faith which my parents nourished in a vision of establishing a Kibbutz and a Jewish state, granted me my life?

Conflicts between Arabs and Israelis

In February 1947, Great Britain, a declining empire, gave up control of Palestine to the United Nations. On November 29, 1947, the General Assembly of the United Nations voted to partition Palestine, providing both Arabs and Jews with their own land.

Who decided to partition Palestine?

In 1947, the UK turned the Palestine problem over to the UN. After looking at alternatives, the UN proposed terminating the Mandate and partitioning Palestine into two independent States, one Palestinian Arab and the other Jewish, with Jerusalem internationalized (Resolution 181 (II) of 1947).

The partition plan was rejected out of hand by Palestinian Arab leadership and by most of the Arab population. Meeting in Cairo on November and December 1947, the Arab League adopted a series of resolutions endorsing a military solution to the conflict.

Fighting broke out after the partition plan was announced and continued well into the following year.

On May 14, 1948, David Ben-Gurion, Israel's first Prime Minister, read the Israeli Declaration of Independence to the public. The following day war erupted when Egypt, Transjordan, Iraq, Syria, and Lebanon sent their armies to invade the nascent state.

War of Independence:

Syrian and Lebanese troops moved into the north of Israel, while Iraqi units and Transjordan's Arab Legion focused their attack on Jerusalem. Other Arab units were deployed to Jewish settlements in the Jordan Valley and later in the Galilee. Jerusalem was a highly contested territory, and the battles for it were costly for the Haganah, the new Israeli army. By the second United Nations truce on July 18, much of the Negev was still controlled by the Egyptian army.

1948 War. Negba become a front. We were evacuated away from the kibbutz and our parents for half a year.

The Battles of Negba were a series of military engagements between the Israel Defense Forces and the Egyptian army in the 1948 Arab–Israeli War. Negba, a kibbutz founded in 1939, had a strategic position overlooking the Majdal – Bayt Jibrin road, and was a target of two major assaults by the Egyptians in June and July 1948.

On June 2, the Egyptians attacked the village from the south with a battalion reinforced with armor, artillery, and aircraft, and were beaten back by 140 defenders, who were assisted by motorized Negev Brigade forces. The second attack took place on July 12, when the Egyptians staged diversionary assaults on nearby positions and surrounded Negba from all sides, again with a reinforced battalion. This attack was also dispersed, and Negba remained in Israeli hands, serving as a forward base for attacks against Egyptian forces up to Operation Yoav.

1947:

Does Human nature change, at all?

Partition Divides India and Pakistan Along Religious Lines. Many millions are being dislocated and over one million people die in the conflict.

1948

Heads of state from Italy, Sweden, Switzerland, and other countries meet to discuss the Marshall Plan's rebuilding of Europe after World War II. The United States Helps Rebuild Postwar Europe Through Marshall Plan. Creation of Israel Divides Middle East.

1949: Back to the old human division`′ mentality and politic.

NATO Offers Western Europe Security Amid Cold War.

Detonation of First Soviet Atomic Bomb Sparks Nuclear Arms Race. Chinese Civil War Brings Communists to Power in Beijing. Block politic and rivalry is now cemented.

1950–1953: Back to war again!

Korean War Leaves a Peninsula Divided.

1950s–1960s: Progress/regress in the world:

U.S. Civil Rights Movement Kicks Off Decades of Protest, Reforms.

1954: First Successful Organ Transplant Advances Lifesaving Medical Technology.

1955 – 1975: United States and Soviet Union Wage Proxy War in Vietnam.

1956: British troops invade Egypt and oil installations burn at Port Said, north of the Suez Canal, on November 10, 1956. 1956. Suez Crisis Becomes Flashpoint in Cold War.

1950s–1970s: Space Race Sends Cold War Competition to New Heights.

My story:

Before the war erupted in 1947, the kibbutz was surrounded by Arab villages and caravans on the way to Jaffa and back to Gaza passed by. In the ever-trot and quiet like a distant dream, they moved through the desert while the camel's silver bells tinkled: ling, long, ling, long. It is life's eternal song. I was barely three years when Egyptian forces encircled the kibbutz and bombarded it from the surrounding hills. The carnage was huge, and the bombs hit the children houses shortly after the children had—in the cover of darkness—been evacuated. This evacuation I had some reminiscence. I remembered the violent sobbing as parents, who had to stay back in the kibbutz to defend it, waved goodbye to their children. My mother lifted me up and handed me to a woman, who took me into the darkness of an armored personnel carrier, where she put me on a cold and hard metal bench. It was pitch-dark, and I could not see anything, only hear sniffling children around her, who were scolded if they cried loudly. My legs were too short to reach the floor, so my feet dangled in the air. I was afraid of falling into the dark abyss and of the weeping adults outside, and I wanted to cry, but I should not as my mother told me. We had to cross the Arab lines, and therefore, we had to be quiet. The cars with the kids started moving with extinguished lights, and there was someone who held my hand in the darkness. I thought that this row of cars looked like a camel caravan, only without the bells ringing ling, long, ling, long. The only sound that could be heard was the motor humming. Some children sniffled quietly, but the engine humming sound blurred their sobbing. I wondered who was the woman that held my hand in hers.

And then I fell asleep. It was the same night the children houses were razed by the Egyptian artillery, but I slept soundly in the armored car that brought the kibbutz children northward. For a second time I was saved without knowing it, maybe by sheer luck, coincidence, or providence. The day after, I woke up in a small bed in a large house, with the other children around me in their small beds. Wey cried a bit, and I asked where we were living now. ′We have traveled to a foreign country! ` a big boy said to me. One girl asked if her parents could find her in this foreign country when they came to pick her up. ′They will neither come today nor tomorrow. They may never come again. They must fight against the evil Arabs, ` said the big boy before he turned around and walked out. I and the others lay in our beds and wept until we had to get up and eat our first breakfast in ′the new foreign country.'

I had lively and magic fantasy from the very start and could create some fantasies.

Somebody taught me and the other kids in those days a lullaby, a song for falling asleep. The song describes how the dark night falls, the wind is blowing on the treetops, a star up in the sky is twinkling, and the little child in his bed tries to fall asleep. The burning candle beside him had to be put out. And it continues in the following fashion: On this very night, three murderous horsemen are on the way to you, the child. Sleep sweetly, sleep deeply, my child, they are on their way toward you. The first horseman was killed by a beast, the second horseman was killed by a sword, and the third horseman, sleep sweetly, my child, had forgotten your name. And so, the lullaby ends. And you, as a little child must deal with the fact that three murderous horsemen wish to hurt you, and the third one who had survived may one day remember your name—and then what?

The first thing I recalled when I came out of the big house in Nes Ziona was a lighted tunnel opening in front of me on the other side of the dusty road. It flashed between the dusty trees on the other side of the square, just behind an empty water basin. A glimmering ray of light penetrated the leaves and beamed at the tunnel exit. And the light burst forth and filled the tunnel with fluid of gold. I stood on the stone steps to the big house belonging to a rich Arab man who left it when the war had started, and the light flowed down the stairs, down my bare feet, and to the dusty path. From the edges of the circular pool filled with clear water that lay in the middle of the dusty square, small bright dots of light like colorful diamonds flashed and sparkled. I walked gingerly down the stairs, along the dusty road, and over to the grove, which enclosed the lighted tunnel. My small legs trudged through the deep, soft, and warm dust. The sunlight heat penetrated down to the dust and burned my toes, so I jumped a few times out to the roadside, where the undergrowth and the hard crust were cooler to walk on. I heard a woman's voice behind my back far, far away. ′Benjamin where are you going? ` But I went directly inside the lighted tunnel, so I could not listen to her or to the rest of the world. For now, I listened only to myself. And yet I imagined that soon, within a moment, I would hear the heavy, regular steps behind me—this encroaching world—and that a panting, breathless woman would pick me up and carry me back to the house, which was filled with coolness, deep shadows, and ordinariness. But nothing happened, perhaps because I was invisible in the light tunnel. I jumped from one tuft of grass to another and could feel that I was going out on a great journey. Suddenly, I stood in a large clearing, which I vaguely recognized. In one corner stood three white-painted wooden houses, surrounded by large eucalyptus trees that shaded the flowing golden light. In the shadows at the entrance to one of the houses stood a small bed, and I knew immediately that something was strange about it. In the bed lay a boy under a light blanket with his head resting on two large white pillows and with big brown eyes that followed me with a suspicious gaze. I was not sure if he knew the boy. It seemed to me that my mother had once told me about a boy who could not get out of bed. ´Why can't he get out of bed? Does he have no legs to walk on? ` I asked my mother. ´Yes, he has two legs, ` my mother said, laughing, ´but he is sick, so he is too weak to go. `

What did it mean to lie in bed and to be too weak? I did not understand it. When I woke up in the morning, I jumped just out of bed as easy as a light feather. I approached the boy who watched me gloomily and concentrated and I became frightened by his tired old man's expression. The boy leaned on his elbows and looked at me while he coughed violently. We looked at each other for a while without saying anything. The boy would soon die, but neither of us knew it yet. ´Who are you? ` asked the boy. ´Benjamin, ` I whispered. ´Why do you whisper? Are you sick in your throat? ` the boy asked with a terrible laughter. I did not answer but just kept staring at him, knowing that the light from the tunnel protected me. ´Who are your parents? ` the boy interrogated. ´What's the name of your father and mother? ` This question I could not answer. I knew my father as a father and my mother as a mother, and my father was also a great hero who fought somewhere else, and that was about all I knew. I looked at the sick boy and grimaced. ´Can you whistle? ` the boy asked me.

I tried to whistle but failed. Now the boy smiled, and his face looked like a bird of prey. I came to think of the birds of prey my father had once in a cage and one day had escaped and flew away. ´Have you seen a big black bird of prey? ` I asked the boy. ´I have seen many. It's the big birds that catch small mice and other small animals. They can catch a pup or a kid. I have a picture where you can see them all, ` the sick boy replied. ´I have a great bird of prey, which my father had caught and put in a cage, and we and it is so big. ` I showed it with my hands. ´You are full of lies. Get out of here! ` shouted the boy excitedly. ´Why do you cough all the time? You do not look like a real child,` I said ´Go your way! You're full of lies! Go away! ` I was angry that the boy did not believe that I had a monkey and a bear. I turned to the boy and shouted, ´You are full of lies! I will go out and catch more monkeys and bears, and you will not be allowed to see them! ` I turned my back on the sick child and went back to the hot, dusty path and toward the lighted tunnel.

Sometime later—and I did not know how long—I was told by some older children that the adults had thrown the sick boy into the trash can. He had been coughing a lot and made lots of rotten carrot-colored poo, and finally, he died and was thrown into a large garbage can. Now he was gone, and therefore, he would never get to know that I had a monkey and a bear. I stood in the sun on the sidewalk with children` toy horse's harness on me and helped play the horse role, as the small children should always be horses, and I was wondering what the coughing boy was doing down in the trash can.

A grown-up made for us some colorful kites, and one of them flew away and disappeared. I thought that it flew to find the little boy who had just died (at the time, I understood that death was like a hiding game). I thought that the little boy had hidden himself in the garbage container since he was not in his bed any longer, and I was not certain whether he had gotten something to eat in the garbage container. I knew that cats got something to eat from the container. But the colorful kite left us to look out for the boy and find him in his hiding place. But neither of them came back home, so I learned that as things disappear, they may never come back again, so there was no reason for endless brooding. Sorrow—yes, even heartbroken tears, but there was nothing I could do about things or people who were gone once and forever. Yes, I could make a new kite, nicer than the former. I could get hold of new things instead, and I could get new friends and close relations. I learned that if I add my little light, the road becomes friendly as to walk on it safely. There was no reason to brood too much on life premises. It was muddy from the very start. The only thing worth focusing on was the light from the tunnel and the road that it followed.

We, the children came back to our ruined kibbutz and mourning members who had lost many of their family members and friends in the war. in 1949 Living in the countryside, with armed Arab infiltrators roaming in the south part of Israel and attacking civilians, with barbed wire around the kibbutz, mines in the fields (the result of the which just was over), and with guards guarding our children houses, with lots of wild dogs howling from the nearby hills and without any grown-ups in the night in our children house and surroundings, (we grew up in children houses), just a guard who passed by once or twice, I was sometimes scared. And who would not be scared under these circumstances?

And as to make things worse, I would not accept my parents who sent me away. Upon returning to Negba, I rejected my parents. I was very angry at them and run away from them, few times almost into the mine fields. I was particularly angry with my mother and would not obey her but ran away. I could crawl through the barbed wire and come out to the open fields, among the stray dogs and the exploding mines. My mother yelled at me and ran after me (My father was away from the kibbutz, in a teacher seminar), but I was so good at running that she could not catch me, calling a male neighbor to chase me and grab me. As my father was in the seminar, so I had nothing to fear from this quarter.

The war first ended when the United Nations Security Council called for a permanent armistice on December 29, 1948. The Arab states still refused to negotiate directly with Israel.

The population losses exceeded 6,000, and the War of Independence took on mythic proportions in Israeli culture. Its combatants were seen as new Hebrew warriors. The Canaanite movement, a small group of artists and thinkers in the post-independence era, was extremely effective in juxtaposing the tanned, tall, and strong sabra or native Israeli Jew, to the weak, downtrodden Diaspora Jew. I and my comrades became a part of this new Jew: a courageous warrior, the children of the SUN.

The Law of Return & Population Growth

On July 5, 1950, the state of Israel passed the Law of Return. Its opening line read: "Every Jew has the right to immigrate to the country." The law created an influx of Jewish immigration to Israel. The large numbers of Holocaust survivors (almost 1 in 3 Israeli citizens by1949) had difficulty settling into the new country; tensions were high between members of the Yishuv (pre-state inhabitants) and the survivors. It was no easier for Jews from Arab lands.

The population of the State of Israel more than doubled in its first five years. Half of the national budget went towards immigrant resettlement, with military spending coming in a close second. In 1950 the Jewish Agency began a program of building low- cost crowded camps equipped with tents and few modern facilities.

The new settlement program also coincided with 'Operation Ezra and Nehemia,' which airlifted more than 100,000 Jews from Iraq in 1950-1951. In 1954, as the Moroccan population in Israel grew, the government devised a way to allow these new immigrants who fled the Arab countries to be sent to villages and development cities throughout the country.

Economic Development

By the middle of the decade, Israel's real income–meaning money the nation earned rather than was granted–was climbing, with production rates of goods and quality of life rising. However, large numbers of immigrants, mainly Sephardim from Arab Lands, were still living in poor conditions in development cities.

Sinai Campaign:1956

In the 1950s, the Arab world attempted to pressure Israel through economic sanctions; Israeli ships could not use Arab ports, and Israeli airplanes could not use Arab air space. In 1955, Egypt purchased large amounts of weapons from the Soviet Union and Czechoslovakia. The next year it announced the nationalization of the Suez Canal.

These actions, combined with increased terrorist attacks across the border and Egypt's massive military build-up, prompted Israel to join Great Britain and France in attacking Egypt on October 29, 1956. The British, French, and Israeli combined military action was successful, but the United Nations set up forces in the Sinai to ensure that it would not be repeated.

We grew up with this strange cocktail of being heroic-we stopped the Egyptian military advance in my kibbutz- and building a new land. We grew up with defiance-Israel prime minister put it forcefully then: 'It does not matter much what the other nations say. It is important what the Jews do! ` with the death of many kibbutz members in Independence war, with the death of 6 million Jews in the holocaust, and with great faith that we can change the world and humans for the better, started my life story.

As you see, I was born in an exceptional historical juncture: The great tragedy for the Jewish people-the Holocaust-took place and two doom Atom bombs hit Japanese towns, obliterating them in the cruelest war in human history just before I was born. During this enormous tragedy, my parents and their comrades were pursuing two visions/missions- starting a collective and just society in a kibbutz and creating a homeland for the persecuted Jews. On top of all these tragedies, the war of Independence, which started by the invasion of Arab troops into the new land, meant devastations of my kibbutz and the loss of many members. We the children escaped death just by one day, as the Egyptian troops bombed the children house 24 hours after our evacuation. It is obvious that with these lessons of human bestiality, I could not come to believe any longer in the goodness-kindness and love of humans as a stable, irrefutable virtue.

I grew up on the so called 'diet` of Jewish warriors, where ' Never again` we would let others slaughter us as sheep, that 'Never again` we would let our enemies to plot such a sinister plot as the Nazis did, without them risking annihilation. The Holocaust taught me a lesson on the complexity and duality of human nature, which seems rather resistant to change. As a child I understood from my parents and other grownups in the Kibbutz that there was a devilish man named Hitler, and he had evil troops called Nazis and they killed 6 million Jewish people, including 11 family members, just like they were sheep. This story made me understand the following lesson too: There are lots of evil people, lots of collaborators and opportunists in this world and they will be there as long as human beings are what they are. If you wish to survive, you must become strong as to be able to defend yourself. You must become also tough and hardened mental warrior, brutal and rough when needed, because human nature is not going to change out of the blue as Mashiach is not going to come out of the blue. These are but collective illusions on the verge of delusions.

Another lesson was, that humanity will always face crisis, challenges and dangers, all triggering impending necessity, which we must learn to face head on-not hiding our heads in the sand- and that such necessity can best be faced, by being evolutionary and motivated by evolving vision/mission in our approach to human life.

My father was forced to be a teacher in history and literature and at a certain time, the principal of the regional school in our kibbutz. He wanted to work with bees, but in the Kibbutz, you could not decide your occupation. Impending necessity ruled the day.

Lesson number three which I was taught was that in hard times and in a struggle for survival, solidarity, self-sacrifice, robustness, focus, determination, empathy, compassion, and unity constitute the right medicine.

Lesson number four: Never become a brain washed useful idiot in the service of humans, religions, or ideology. Never admire humans as they are above all human` limitations, as semi gods. It is enough with respect if they prove of deserving it. Keep entertaining your critical mind and remember that humans are but human, and even reaching this state they fail sometimes

My father was a brainy man but also a blind idealist, to the point of becoming a useful idiot. He believed in Stalin and his gang and Communism to the point of uncritical admiration, so when Stalin died in 1953, I saw him in tears for the first time in my life, and when his crimes were exposed in 1956, he suffered of existential crisis. The end of his blind devotion to communism came when I fought as a young officer in 1967 war the Arabic united armies, which were supplied with the weapons by Russia. This, that Russia turned against us and against Israel′ existence, made him give up his adoration.

Lesson number five was: Be as close to nature and healthy lifestyle as possible as a ′healthy soul can best dwell in healthy body and vice versa`, we were taught.

My father was a heavy smoker, like most males in the kibbutz. He smoked up to 60 filter free cigarettes daily and would not stop, even after I pleaded with him to stop when I grew up. I did not stop and died smoking. Two years before dying in 1977 of heart attack-66 years old-he started believing in God.

It was alright with me. He needed -like most of us- to believe in something greater than our -often fickle and petty life- and his God faith was a good substitute for his old faith in communism and Stalin.

His generation worked hard and tried to live up to their lofty ideals with such zeal, fighting both enemies and each other-due to different ideologies -with such a ferocity, as Jews can possess, that they were consumed by their own fire. Most of the men in my Kibbutz died in the middle of their 60eeth.

My father: More of what I learnt of him.

I had fine relations with him but not very close or open ones. He was too rigid as to gain my trust in personal matters. From my father I picked his analytical and scholarly capacities, interest in history and the idea of striving to accomplish something greater than ordinary life can offer and the need for enduring meaning giving vision/mission in life, instead of being self- focused. I was fortunate as to learn to appreciate history. History together with my learning of the human nature-via both my mother and later my study and my practice with people as a psychologist- helped me predict very often both personal, national and global trends and directions. I call this capacity: Psychohistory. Asimov coined this expression, which helps not only to predict but also to think of solutions for the human condition beyond our perpetual/repetitive solutions. An illustrative example for our dubious progress is technology and modern lifestyle, both create new problems as destroying our life condition on earth and lots of lifestyle ailments, demonstrating that our left hand doesn`t know what the right hand does and vice versa, all due to our conflicting and contradictory human nature.

My mother:

My mother was very loving, open, and demanding towards me. She was proud of me, and not so much of my sister and my little brother-as I realized later in my life-, because I was popular and did well in school, social life, in sports and had good brain. My sister who was born in 1939 did not get the same care and love as I did and was placed in a group as the youngest of them all. Suffering of kind of dyslexia-as my little brother also suffered of- and being very shy, she had tense relations with my mother all throughout my mother` life. My brother did not seem to suffer too much of her possessive attitude, but when she died in 1994, he did not seem to be sorry. I was the only one who really mourned her departure.

My mother was opportunistic and could get easily in contact with all kinds of people, virtues, or attitudes- if you will-which I possess. She did not like kibbutz life and would rather leave it but my father rejected the idea. She was a good organizer/leader and remarkable cook. She had leader jobs very often in the kibbutz and outside. She was a sharp human's knower but focused mainly on people` weaknesses and futility and very rarely saw the positive in them. My parents were very different, and it was obvious that my mother was disappointed of my father` lack of political ambitions. She criticized him often and he got angry, but they kept being married to his last day.

From my mother I picked a sound, down to earth reasoning, opportunism, practical attitude to problem solving, context and critical thinking, distance to dogmatism, charm and social ability and interest for understanding people, but without her pronounced negativity.

I started my young life being introduced both verbally and practically with: First and foremost — work with your hands. The huge gap which most people accept in their behavior between what they say- Talk-and what they do-Walk- was a shame I my upbringing. ´What you promise to do-you do! ` was a motto in my young life, saving me the ill effects of boasting, show off and futile exposure so common in the West.

As a child I was introduced to David Ben Gurion` saying- he was Israeli first and legendary prime minister-who stated that it is not important what the non-Jews say about Israel internal affairs, but very important what the Jews do self. There was defiance and pride in this attitude but also stress that actions are weigh much more compared to declarations. Later in my life I realized how common is it for people to make the Talk, but neither the Walk or the Work to achieve the goal.

We grew up with respect for those who were engaged in manual labor, and we had daily day practical chores from very early age, whether it was feeding our animals in our zoo, cleaning after meals or washing floors in our dormitories or helping in the kibbutz fields.

These life view and practice helped me later in my life to persist on doing what I found needed and worthwhile, regardless of what others meant on my deeds, as long as I did not hurt anybody! This gave me later the mental backbone to design my global vision.

The Bustan: 1950

Once when I was around five-6 years old, my father asked me if I knew how to tend a Bustan, which is the Arabic word for "orchard." He was good at tending trees, flowers, and honeybees. He explained to me that in a blooming Bustan, there are many different trees, and one must water them in hot climate like ours. He asked me whether the trees needed more. I said that they needed manure since I saw him spread chicken manure in a ditch under our trees around the house. He asked me whether there was more one could do. I shrugged my shoulders because I did not know. Well, he said that there must be reasonable distance between the trees; otherwise, they could not get enough nourishment and sunlight and would wither. If you plant them very close, only the strongest will survive, and their fruits will be tasteless. ′Is there more? ` he asked. I did not know what to answer. He said that in a Bustan, the gardener had to uproot the weeds all the time; otherwise, they would strangulate the trees. A good gardener will do this weeding all the time if he wished for a healthy and prosperous Bustan. And he said lastly something that saddened me; That tree got sick and old like us, humans. A gardener had to care for them, heal them if it could be done, but when there was no hope, he had to uproot them and plant new ones instead. ′Do they have to be uprooted, ` I pleaded. ′Yes, ` he said. ′This is important to keep a Bustan healthy and ever evolving.'

What was this Ever Evolving? He explained me that it meant that the Bustan` trees will keep improving and bettering as to face new challenges, through the efforts of the tireless Gartner. At the time he uttered it, I only wondered, but later, this theme came to resound in my mind, especially in regard to us, humans, and our future venture...

The kibbutz was still surrounded by a large black barbed wire fence, and the area was full of anti-tank obstacles and landmines, which occasionally exploded in the fields when a dog or a fox ran over them, and there were some members from the kibbutz, who lost their legs as they hit them with their tractors.

I was afraid of the big, stray dogs that roamed close to the houses and sometimes I together with the other kids helped our own dogs in the fight against the starving dogs from the abandoned Arab villages.

It was very hot in the summertime.

Desert wind brought sometimes the stabbing and piercing grit with it. It blew a day or two and then headed south and stopped, after which a devouring Hamsin (very hot days) broke out. The air was quivering hot, heavy, and suffocating, and at nights, it felt as if the darkness was engulfed in an invisible and corrosive fire. The summer was hard, and Hamsin felt endless. It was perhaps for this reason that my first meeting with the Bustan seemed so overwhelming for me. I was almost five-six years old when my father came one early morning in the beginning of the summer and woke me in the children's home and helped me get dressed and brush my teeth. And we two went through the fields towards the hills in Morth West. It was the first time I was allowed to go on such a journey with my father. When we had gone a long way through the scorched fields in the fresh morning air, we hit a dusty road.

The hills were covered with blood red, lemon yellow, and white flowers, and there were so many of them that it looked like a huge blanket. ´See, father! ` I cried, elated. ´See all the wildflowers there! ` All of a sudden, I saw the most beautiful blanket of colorful flowers I had ever seen. My eyes, accustomed to the desert gray and yellow colors and its barren nakedness, could not be satisfied by the colors of this giant floral mosaic. ´Come, my son! We must tread the hill! ` shouted my father and started to go up with large, measured steps. I started running after him. I caught up with him halfway and continued past him. When I reached the top of the hill, it was as if a bolt of lightning struck me. I gasped so loud that my father looked at me anxiously. On the slope to the west was still a thick carpet of glowing red and purple anemones, and a little further away, behind a low cactus fence with red ripe, pungent fruits, lay the Bustan.

Many years later, as a young man, I saw the film about Kaspar Hauser, talking about a boy who spent his first sixteen years in a deep, dark cellar or cave. Somebody took care of him and taught him rudimentary language. One dark night, he was carried away by this mysterious man and brought up on top of a hill. Morning broke out, and he saw for the first time in his life the sun rise and colorful creation/miracles: lush green fields that flashed in the sun, golden yellow cornfields, forest with its green trees, and clear blue sky.

This was similar for the experience I had had with my father at the entrance to the Bustan. The Bustan was cradled in gentle sunlight as an indescribably beautiful mosaic of all shades of green, bloodred pomegranates, red-hot poppies, almond trees, white and pink flowers, and vines with bunches of green and red grapes, lemon trees, orange trees, and mulberry trees with deep red, juicy, and fragrant fruits, all enveloped in a sense of intoxicating fragrance. I heard the soporific hum of bees, and the world went merry-go-round. I closed my eyes and pressed my small fists against the eyelids. When the movement stopped, I opened my eyes again, and now I saw a number of ancient, gnarled, and wrinkled olive trees that stood by themselves. The world around me stood still; it trembled a little bit still, but the dizzying movement had stopped. I moved my eyes to the north, where the cactus fence framed three magnificent mulberry trees with branches heavy with pink, black-red, and white-yellow juicy berries.

I decided to climb on one of them. I got hold of a branch and pulled myself up against it. My legs were fighting in the empty air to reach the branch, and after a major effort, I succeeded in beating my legs around the branch and rise. From there, it was not difficult to reach the tree's crown. I sat on a thick branch and headed out carefully after a bird, which gave a small sharp peep from its throat and now, flew down to the ground. Just before it hit the ground, it flew up again and disappeared among the olive trees.

'And what do you want? ` I asked myself. 'I want this orchard! ` I replied promptly. And ever since I was enchanted by the idea of blooming Bustan, sustainable and ever evolving on the verge where the fertile land meets the desert

--

In December,1950 my little brother was born. I stood outside the flat where my parents made a little reception for the guests who came to bless the newborn child and wish my parents the best. I was angry and cursed my parents out loud. At last, my father who got impatient with me, sprang out of the window, and started chasing me. He got me after some running and gave me a blow on my behind and carried me sobbing back to the flat. This was the first and the last time he or other people hit me. But it was enough as I learnt my lesson at the very spot.

But there were new, great horizons opening for me, besides the Bustan. I learnt two new songs from my father, which were full of heroism, promise for a great future and a struggle to realize it, all of them appealing to my young fantasy of warrior fighting with velour to free the enslaved people in the world.

Special impression on me made The International with its mobilizing spirit and solidarity, which were often sang by the kibbutz members in our festivities:

> 'Arise ye workers from your slumbers
> Arise ye prisoners of want!
> For reason in revolt now thunders
> And at last, ends the age of can't.
> Away with all your superstitions

Servile masses arise, arise
We'll change henceforth the old tradition
And spurn the dust to win the prize.

So, comrades, come rally
And the last fight let us face
The International unites the human race.
So comrades, come rally
And the last fight let us face
The International unites the human race.

No more deluded by reaction
On tyrants only we'll make war
The soldiers too will take strike action
They'll break ranks and fight no more
And if those cannibals keep trying
To sacrifice us to their pride
They soon shall hear the bullets flying
We'll shoot the generals on our own side.

No savior from on high delivers
No faith have we in prince or peer
Our own right hand the chains must shiver
Chains of hatred, greed and fear
E'er the thieves will out with their booty
And give to all a happier lot.
Each [those] at the forge must do their duty
And we'll strike while the iron is hot.'

It was great to grow up in in international solidarity where all the workers of the world were good people and the capitalists from USA were bad boys, and we, in our Kibbutz, together with the enslaved workers were keen on changing this world and make it and people better.

There was great passion, great goals, bad and good, emotional catharsis in fighting the evil forces and a noble cause. What did a child who grew up on the stew of wars and sacrifices, need more?

1953: I was happy, very happy; it was springtime, and we should celebrate Pesach. I got my neat blue pants, and my mother filled my pockets with nuts and showed me how I could break them. For Pesach, kibbutz families and their friends and guests gathered on long tables in the dining room. Our kibbutz was not as high up in Pesach religious ceremonies but more in the meaning behind Pesach story, the history of the Jewish slaves emancipating themselves from slavery and migrating toward the ′promised land‵ as free people. We ate however in eight days the party lasted, only unleavened bread, matzo. Abraham's father claimed that it was stone-aged diet that they ate in these days—lots of vegetables, nuts, meat, and fish. On the first evening, Seder, we ate too bitter herbs and green herbs, which we dipped in salt, egg, and a puree of apples, nuts, and cinnamon, which was to create the illusion of the clay, as slaves in Egypt sled with, and they placed a Seder dish on the table with those things as well as a burned lamb bone. The salt water symbolized the slaves' tears; the bitter herbs, the bitterness of slavery; and the green herbs and egg, spring and rebirth. And we read from Haggadah, the story of the Exodus, in the kibbutz version. I loved the story and its exotic scent but was also very concerned about the drama of moving from bondage to freedom; for me, Pesach was the yearning and aspirations to, and struggle for, freedom, where we celebrated not only that the Jews were free people now but also as a reminder for ourselves of the duty to work for the freedom of all people in the world. I loved to hear Moshe, a kibbutz member with a beautiful baritone singing on the podium the traditional song among others on Moses, who struck the water out of the rock when the Jews wandered in the desert and were close to die of thirst. I closed my eyes and listened, enchanted to Moshe's velvety baritone that filled the dining room with its magical tale. ′ And Moses smote the rock so that water came leaping forward. And the water filled up the water vessel, by a miracle, a great miracle. ‵

The culmination of the celebration occurred when the kibbutz large choir went to the podium and loudly and polyphonically sang a song that made me shudder. ′Get up you wanderers of the desert. ‵ I was as enchanted by the song's magic: ′Arise, wanderers in the desert. The road is long and the war is not over. You have walked a long time. But before you come to your destination, a long and wide road is awaiting you. 40 years of wandering in the mountains and in the desertsand will cost the lives of six hundred thousand of your brothers. Do not let their corpses hold you back for those who died, in bondage they died. Let us walk past them! Let them lie there and rot along with their slaves' belongings, which they took with them from Egypt, the slavery land. Let us forget the slaves who could not uproot the slavery from their hearts, who could not live without their daily onion, garlic and meat. Maybe the desert wind will today or tomorrow cover them with sand or they will be prey for the vultures. ‵

He thought while listening to the choir singing it that it must be so; a journey away from slavery and toward a promised land is bound to great suffering and cost many lives and that six hundred thousand slaves lives was the price for the many who became free people as the case was with his parents, who had left East Europe in 1936 to fight for a Jewish homeland, and the price for establishing the state of Israel, a refuge for the Jewish people, was staggering yet necessary. Six million Jews who lost their lives under Second World War. Otherwise, the nations of the world would not allow such state to be established, he was told.

1954:

On the first of Maj, we stood in a long line on the football field, children in front and the adults behind, all of us in white shirts and blue shorts. I listened with my comrades under a blazing sun to long speeches as party leaders held for the adults, and I felt both drowsy and dizzy. After the first speaker came another speaker, and they went on and on indefinitely. I became impatient and began shifting weight from one leg to the other. The air quivered with heat, and I only waited for the time all of them would sing the ′International, ` and then the ′International` tractor would come from the dusty field to the scene. I was pleased to see the ′International` this time really moving, gasping and coughing up against the dining hall at its tracks to lead us to the final victory over the fat, greedy, and complacent capitalists who shamelessly exploited the working class in the big cities, which I, my father, and all the kibbutz members and children also belonged to. I could not understand all the words from the hymn but thought that the song was great and electrifying. The magic event occurred finally, at long last, when three accordion players played for, and four hundred people sang the song with solemn and full voices: ′ Arise ye workers from your slumbers Arise ye prisoners of want for reason in revolt now thunders and at last ends the age of can't…`

During the song, I wondered what it meant to be condemned, how the kibbutz members became a slave army, and who suppressed them here in the kibbutz. Now I remembered that my father had told me that the kibbutz was the proletarians, not slaves, that we fought against the great capitalists who would oppress us as slaves, and that the International would lead us into this decisive battle, but where was this International that was supposed to lead us? The song was over, I thought in panic, and the International had not showed up yet. I peered toward the kibbutz garage, which some of its back was visible through the eucalyptus trees, and waited for the red-painted tractor, called International, to come rolling, coughing, and snorting, but why did it not come? It would lead us to the nearby religious kibbutz, where we, the proletarians, would start the revolution against the blinded God believers who would not let diaspora mentality vanish and could not live one day without praying to their god who, according to my father, was a mere figure of the imagination and the opium for the people. I also thought about mammon. What did it look like? I believed that a lot of large gold coins piled up in a dark basement or scattered all over the floor in a deep cave was mammon and that on top this heap of gold sat a fat capitalist and looked at them with greedy eyes.

When the ceremony was over, and the tractor did not show up went to my mother and asked why the International would not come and lead us to the war against the capitalists. ′What kind of international tractor are you talking about? ` asked my mother. ′I talk about the red caterpillar in the garage! ` I said. ′Father can just start it and drive it out. I saw it yesterday in the garage. ` ′Why should it come up now? ` my mother asked, bewildered. ′This International shall lead us to a revolution! ` I replied. ′How does it look like? ′ asked my mother, smiling. ′I said it before. It's the red tractor with caterpillars, which stands in the garage. We can put a big machine gun up on it, for it will frighten the capitalists and make them run away. ` My mother began to laugh uncontrollably. I started crying and beating her with my small fists, and then she stopped laughing and gave me a hug. I stopped sniffing, and she explained to me that the tractor was not the right International. The right International was an association of proletarians in the world who would gather and march against the enemy. It was the right International.

On the evening before I was sent to the children's house, my mother read a story for me about a girl named Sleeping Beauty, who had fallen asleep and slept for one hundred years and only woke up when she was kissed by a prince. ′Can you sleep so long without eating and drinking? ` I asked. ′No, I cannot, but the story is not a real story. It's an adventure, where you tell something that is not true to say something else that can be true, ` said his mother. ′Why? Can't you just say what it really means? ` I asked. ′I can also sometimes, but in a fairy tale, there is always something more to understand than what is being said, something you have to imagine and understand. In Sleeping Beauty, it is about a beautiful young woman who is brought to life by a handsome prince. I think that the hidden point was that many people sleep throughout their lives but hope that someone will get them to wake up and feel alive. It does not happen in life! ` ′Why will they rather sleep? ‘I asked. ′They can play. They can travel, work and have fun . . . instead of sleeping . . .` ′It is because they are afraid that they cannot do well in life, and they are afraid of making mistakes, if they try to do something that they want, and then they will fail. So, they dream their lives away. ` ′Dream life away? ` ′Yes, they fantasize, for example, that there will come a prince and help them to have a better life. That was what our parents had done in Ukraine. They dreamed that God would save them from the Nazis. One should never daydream. We fight instead! ` ′It is too hard stuff for him, ` muttered my father, who was sitting with a newspaper. ′I don't think so, ` replied his mother defiantly. ′We can teach him to dream less and instead do something without waiting for miracles. It's the difference between us and the others. We create and struggle to change, and they talk and talk for no avail. ` ′Is Stalin also a man who does things without talking so much? ` I asked my father. ′Yes. Without him and the Red Army, the world would have been lost to Hitler,` said my father gravely. ′Why do you confuse his mind with Hitler and Stalin? ` my mother asked angrily. ′I don't confuse him at all. I say to him that there are people who daydream and that there are people who accomplish meaningful things, and there are those who just live their lives, and then there are those who accomplishes things like us. The final words on Stalin's huge impact on the world we live in, have not been yet said,` concluded my father. ′You and the sun of all nations, Stalin! ` my mother hissed. ′You go too far! The child needs some concrete examples so he can relate to and not some sinister mass murderer as a model. ` ′Can't you stop arguing! ‘I shouted. ′Yes! ` replied my mother. ′Tomorrow we will read about some great people for you. If you want to be great, you have to know how to become one! ` ′Can children become great people? ` I asked. ′No! ` said my father. ′But they can possess abilities and creative power, which can cause them to become great one day if they will work hard for it.` ′I will work for it!` I said. ′I will cultivate the most beautiful Bustan on earth! ` I thought that I could be both a gardener in a Bustan of my own and a prince kissing beautiful princesses simultaneously.

1955: The winter was rainy and stormy, and the kibbutz dusty roads transformed quickly into thick mud traps, so the tractors that had tracks constantly had to pull the other tractors out of the mud when they got stuck in the mud pool. At that time, a gang of Palestinians from Gaza attacked a nearby kibbutz, killing and wounding many people, after which the Israeli armed forces avenged the attack by killing seventy people from Gaza, and so the conflict rolled on and on. I was told by my father that this conflict would continue for a long time, maybe one hundred years, because the Israelis would not give up the areas they had conquered during the war, which the Arabs had lost, and the Arabs would not give up their dream of going back to their old places. ′So, the war will continue? ` ′Yes! We must realize that we will live on our swords for a long time, ` he said. My mother, who overheard the conversation, exclaimed, ′Why on earth you tell a ten-year-old boy that the war will continue indefinitely? What are these murky perspectives you draw for him? He is a child, so let him enjoy his childhood! ` ′I tell him about our reality, and I will not fool him with a tale of paradise on earth. He might as well learn that people are not able to establish peace on earth and that there is no reason to trust them. What did the Second World War had taught us? We were about to disappear from the face of the earth, while other nations were either indifferent or played their cynical game. We must be the strongest in all conflicts, and the others should fear us. That's what I will teach my son! ` ′Do you need to emphasize this day and night? I wonder if you have not already made your point. See him, Shika, David, and the other boys run around with their wooden swords and their bows and arrows and constantly play war. Enough is enough! We have the right to a peaceful life once in a while, ` sobbed my mother. My father gave her a light hug, and she turned and walked sobbing into the apartment. I looked puzzling at my father and asked what it was that made her sad. ′The girl from your class who has been sick for a long time died today, and your mother has just visited her family. Her friend Miriam died last year, and the girl from your class was also named Miriam. I think it is therefore. ` I breathed deeply. I did not know that my classmate had been so ill, and now another funeral means three days mourning without music and song. I had learned to cope with it when adults died, but I thought it was unbearable when death hit children and young people. After the girl's funeral, we were supposed to hold three mourning days, but then it was fortunately Chanukah for eight days, and it was my best holyday after Pesach because it was a festival of lights in the middle of the winter darkness and because we celebrated the happening of a miracle, and I was fascinated by miracles caused by the invisible hand of both nature and man. I knew the story of Chanukah by heart. Man celebrated an event that took place around the year 165 BC, when Israel was occupied by the Greeks, whose leader was called Antiochus Epiphanes, who forbade Jews to read and study the Torah and to lead a religious life. Judah Maccabi led a rebellion, where the Jews managed to free the country from Greek oppression and to recapture the temple, which had been desecrated and filled with Greek statues of gods. Worse still, the Greeks had left the flame that always should burn in the temple as a reminder of God's eternal covenant with the Jews, which went out. But the Jews were lucky. They found a spare container with enough oil for one day and sent scouts to find more oil, but they were delayed and did not come back after eight days, but a miracle occurred, so the oil that was meant for a day burned in all eight days. I loved to revive Chanukah story along with the other children. We were playing that we were fighting in the mountains with spears, bows and arrows, and swords against the heavily armed Greek soldiers, and I was delirious when the big boys chose me as Maccabaeus. In the rain and mud, the two-armed forces battled back and forth until the Maccabees finally took the temple, which was marked with a chalk circle on the ground and lit the lamp again. When my mother came to fetch me home for tea and cake at four o'clock, I was elated and happy, covered with mud from head to toe, but it meant nothing. The fight had been riveting and was ended fairly, and I had forgotten all about the death and grief of the girl from my group. It was there I almost intuitively found out that when I was fighting for a just and great cause, world's sorrow vanished out of my mind.

1956: The great people in history: My father asked me one day if I knew the word ′sublimation.‵ ′Our whole kibbutz′ project is based on the idea of sublimation‵ said my father and explained that the kibbutz is based on the idea that there is an energy called libido, which is the energy that makes all animals wish to procreate, but the kibbutz members channeled it toward the higher goal as to build a kibbutz and a new life for the Jewish people. It was this sublimated libido of the people that made the creation of Israel possible. ′It is the energy that refines the people and improves the world! ‵ my father explained. ′And what happens to the fertility of man when you sublimate the libido? How do you get children? ‵ I asked.

′You can still make children. It's like bees make honey from the flower's nectar while life in the hive continues, and they constantly get new bees. You move just some of the libido energy to another area where you can work for some other goals such as improving the world and man instead of using all the energy to make new babies, ‵ said my father. ′Is it only us in the kibbutzim who can sublimate like this? ‵ ′No! This is done in many kibbutzim and in Russia and in China and in many other countries. Where the proletariat controls the historical events, they sublimate to become better humans. ‵ ′Did Stalin, do it? ‵ ′Of course, he did it. He worked only for the revolution and for a better society. He is a symbol and an ideal for all of us, regardless of what his hater write about him. But in the capitalist countries, people live just to live well and consume as much as they can, and they believe in Greed, Gold and God! ‵ ′And God cannot sublimate them? ‵ I asked. ′Not at all! God exists after all only in the believers' imagination, and they fill themselves with illusions about life after death instead of focusing on making this world a better place to live for all of us, ′ concluded my father. ′Why do they do that? It's ridiculous! ‵ I exclaimed. ′They do it because there are many people who find it easier to disappear into a fantasy or wishful thinking than to work hard to realize an ideal. 'Mundus Vult Dicipi' is a Latin proverb that means that people will be deceived because they wish to be deceived. Therefore, people are deceiving themselves and others. They do this all the time, but since they often believe their own lie stories, they forget that they are deceiving themselves, ‵ my father concluded. ′What did you call this in Latin? ‵ I asked. ′**Mundus Vult Dicipi**: the world wants to be deceived, and therefore, it is being cheated′ ′**Mundus Vult Dicipi . . . Mundus Vult Dicsipi**. . .‵ I repeated these magical words.

As some girls from my group began to develop small breasts, our teacher told us about the changes that would happen in us, both girls and boys, and how the sublimation of our instincts would help us to be better youngsters and afterward adults contributing socialists. Although we- both boys and girls- still went in the common bath together and continued to sleep together in the same bedrooms, we had to prepare for a life with impulse control, for what was a real socialist without self-control and the will to delay the need for love and procreation? To postpone needs and desires and to channel the libido at large and life-affirming goals. I took this very seriously because I then would be able to accomplish much greater things than the common capitalist young people who were controlled by their desires. I practiced postponing my needs and built up a steely character by putting a piece of chocolate that we got once a week in front of me, fasten my eyes on it, and waited at least one hour before I ate it, and besides, I trained hard in all sports to be strong and persevering. I wanted to be a great orator like Demo stones or Trotsky, so I went on practicing speeches with two smooth stones in my mouth. This was the way I trained my voice to the day when the great and significant events would be an inseparable part of my life. "Through hardships to stars" my father always said and it became my noble ambition. I swore to myself that it was the path I would try to pursue in my life beside tending my Bustan.

1957: Laika:

I remember the time (1957) the Russians launched their rocket named Sputnik with a dog named Layka in it. Sometimes we children seemed to hear Layka barking up in the star filled night sky. After long contemplation we who had some knowledge of ballistic rockets, jet motors, horsepower etc. decided to take the communists' challenge up and send our home-made Kibbutz rocket up to the heavens.

The mission had three main purposes; two practical and one metaphysical, but all with an ideological flavor:

- To save Layka's life and free her from captivity (practical).
- To transcend the force of human gravity. As a child, I was much fascinated by Daedalus′ and Icarus' bold attempt to break away from the bonds of earthly, dusty life. To defy and challenge our humane mental and physical "Straight jackets" became in my childish mind the true extension of ′Great deeds and challenges are what make people great` (practical).
- To figure out, once and for all, whether or not God dwelled up in heaven, and if God did, whether He had a better vision than our human made one. In my childhood it was socialism (metaphysical).

A friend and I studied the basic construction of space rockets intensely. Another friend stole a substance called carbide, which when mixed with water gave us the required horsepower to lift the rocket.

From the kibbutz kitchen we ′borrowed` two big and empty conserves tins. The first one had contained green olives, the second one salted cucumber.

The next step was to find appropriate candidates for our space mission.

We seduced and caught four candidate astronauts, all cats, by using the heads of slaughtered chickens.

The first cat was quickly disqualified, being too big and heavy compared to our rockets' ballistic capacity.

The second one was - to be honest - either dumb or debilitated, without the slightest sense for technical skills.

The third astronaut was somewhat queer. After a short investigation it turned out to be a hedgehog and was likewise disqualified.

The last cat was the darling of our schoolmaster. Its name was Ben-Gurion. Since Ben-Gurion did not protest too noisily over its destiny, we proceeded to the next stage. In the bottom of the olive tin we laid some old cotton clothes. This tin served as Ben-Gurion' sleeping and eating chamber, and also as the Instrument Navigating System of the craft.

In the cucumber tin we put the carbide next to a dish filled with water. The two elements would be mixed in the Count-Down- Phase. We made a little hole in the bottom of the cucumber tin and threaded a little rope which we ´borrowed` from the cowshed through the hole. We soaked the rope in petrol, which we also ´borrowed` from a tractor motor.

Now all was ready for the Count-Down. We put Ben-Gurion, who at the last moment became a little apprehensive and protested by scratching the instruments in his chamber. We mixed the carbide with the water, and lit the rope.

With great excitement we watched as the little flame moved slowly into the cucumber tin.

Many years have passed, but I still remember vividly the almost intolerably hard beating of my heart as the flame reached the Combustion Room, the gas in the cucumber tin exploded and up into space our rocket flew. It was a magical moment.

Everything in the rocket functioned perfectly. In a few seconds the rocket reached the height of our house windows (it was a one-story house), and the first stage of the rocket departed as scheduled. The only thing on which we hadn't planned was the fire it started in a nearby field.

The olive tin kept on flying higher and higher towards the vastness of the Universe, but as it came closer and closer to the roof of the house, it became apparent to us -the experts- that its original speed was dramatically reduced. At that very crucial moment I became a bit uncertain: would our rocket break free of gravity? The rocket shot upward, reaching an altitude a little bit higher than the roof and then another explosion occurred. It was not as big as the first one, but the smell was much fouler.

Our spaceship fell on the roof of the house next to the water container. Shortly afterwards, our astronaut emerged out of his space ship, healthy and in fine shape but a little bit blackened and sooty. He looked at us with a mixture of contempt and indifference, stretched his body in a typical cat movement and crawled down the water pipe and back to earth. We looked at each other, pretending not to care, and went home.

As one might expect there was a final act for this event. The kibbutz fire brigade captain, who had extinguished the fire in the nearby field, exploded in an impressive tantrum. The school master was also a bit dissatisfied once he found out that his cat had lost its lust for mouse catching and instead looked for salted cucumbers all the time. But all this was nothing compared to the feeling that we did not accomplish any of our three aims and that I had to lay aside my career as a rocket scientist.

Time went by, and the dreams of a child were aborted by the harsh reality of life. In the following years, many friends and acquaintances perished in the wars between Israel and its Arab neighbors. This blood shedding was seen everywhere throughout the 20th century.

Yet I did not give up my lofty aspirations. I still wished to remind people when I became grown up, what many of them once knew as children: That much of life's essence is in keeping ′launching rockets upward` and in thereby passionately helping Icarus' dream of ascending and transforming ourselves.

1957:

Last meeting with the Bustan: From the kibbutz's large, red-painted iron gate, twisted to the west was a wide, dusty road around the graveyard, where all those who died in the war were buried. The dusty way ploughed through the cornfields on the big orchard of almond trees on the small round hills in the horizon. There was autumn in the air, and the dust on the road was soft and warm. Now I ran toward the arbor, where the guard kept looking for unauthorized guests who tried to steal almonds and watermelons. Two months before, the scent of the blooming almond flower could reach all the way to our house at night, when the west wind from the sea stroked the landscape. After school and the compulsory work in the fields, I ran along the road past these thousands and thousands of fragrant, graceful trees on the way to my destination. Sweaty and out of breath, I ran up the winding road while I admired the view despite the fact that there was something disturbing in this uniform landscape. The many trees that stood in long, straight rows as tightly disciplined soldiers and sumptuous unit felt completely wrong, but I did not know why. Soon, the farmworkers from the nearby cities would arrive, eager to shake the almonds into the cloth covers that were spread out under the trees. The guard with his big dog, his rifle over his shoulder, and his salt cartridges in a glittering belt around the waist was also there. I and the guard knew each other well as I often ran past the hut. Even the vicious dog now could like me and contented himself with some controlled growling at the sight of me. I slowed down when the dog approached with wagging tail. Amin stood outside the arbor in the process of repairing the south flank of the hut with some old white-yellow flour sacks. I yelled at the dog, which came rushing, and sniffed at him while I stroked it gently on the neck and back. It was big and black, a cross that resembled a German shepherd and a Doberman. It was proud and majestic in its ritualized movements, assertive, and war experienced. One day I saw it fight with two dogs at once, and it was as slick and stupendous as Jack London's ′wolfhound` when it was at loggerheads with the surrounding dogs. We went toward Amin, the dog in front, and I was moving behind. I shook hands with the tough, sinewy Bedouin and was welcomed into the hut, where there was shade and cool. I saw the steaming water jars, with the precious drops of refreshing water. Since I was a little kid, I had been fascinated by these clay pots, and thought that the water there was the best you could get. In the corner of the hut, there were lying a couple of big ripe watermelons and an elongated ammunition box made of wood, and beside the mattress, my eyes and nose caught some fragrant and warm Arabic flatbread that Amin had just taken from the oven. Next to it, on a white plastic plate lay three fresh onion and some hard-boiled eggs, and then there was a large glass with black olives. Amin belonged to El Uzaiel tribe from the northern part of the Negev desert. I breathed heavily while the sweat on my face and shoulders slowly began to cool. ′Want to taste the watermelon? ` Amin asked and I nodded. Amin bent down after a big butcher knife that lay under the mattress. ′Amin` I asked, ′can a camel fall in love with a human? In the cowshed, there is a cow that has fallen in love with me. Do not laugh at me! Don't you believe me? It's true, although I do not have much sense of how a cow falls in love with a human. The workers workers in the cowshed are laughing at me all the time when I come by. Have you bewitched it, they keep asking me? When she sees me come up against the stall, she runs up to me and wants me to pet and scratch its head and between the shoulder blades. She licks my hands with its rough tongue and looks so sad at me with its big, gentle eyes that it hurts. It must be an expression of love, although many believe that cows can't really attach themselves to people, such as dogs do. ` ′I do not think that you can expect love from a camel, but it obeys you,` Amin said, giving me a big, juicy, and red slice of watermelon. I put my teeth into the juicy, ripe fruit, so the juice ran down my cheeks and chin and onto my gray, sweating and dusty undershirt. The dog looked at me with an expectant gaze, and its eyes were almost golden colored by the strong sunlight. Amin sighed deeply and looked at me. ′You run very well! There was a time when I could run in the same manner. Like a wolf. I could run away from our camp and to the well, a distance of ten to fifteen kilometers, fill water containers, and run home again. We have good runners in our tribe, boys at your age, twelve years. They want to run a race with you when you come to visit us one day. When your father came to visit us after the Great War, he was also good at running. We ran even in a race, which he had arranged, but times have changed, you know, and from tomorrow, you do not have permission any longer to run on this road through the almond trees, said my boss. You have to find another place to run. ` ′What does that mean, Amin? Do you think that I steal? ` ′Do you think that I suspect you, my friend's friend, as to steal? Do you consider me as a shallow person? ` the Bedouin raised his voice in anger. ′No, ` I answered, while the dog raised his head and looked at us. ′Do you see, my friend! You have been able to visit the Bustan all these years, my friend. You were able to visit your Bustan all the years I've been here, but you cannot anymore. Boss prohibits this. ` ′But why does he prohibit? ` I asked with anger in my voice.

′Tomorrow morning, the bulldozers will start razing the Bustan and all the area around it. The boss and his thick buddies from Tel Aviv believe that the Bustan is good for nothing today. It is a waste of good, fertile soil. That is how he thinks. ` ′Good for nothing? What kind of idiot is he? ` I shouted tearfully. ′What does this obese swine know about what is useful? His kinds have gradually destroyed everything beautiful because it is good for nothing. Look at this uniform landscape around us, and now my Bustan? ` ′Ben, the Bustan is not yours as the soil here is neither yours nor your kibbutz. It now belongs to the state, which rents it out at will for Mammon's sake. ` ′Yes, but it is mine, no matter what you think! ` I shouted. The dog stood up but lay immediately down again as Amin called it to order. He patted me on the shoulder and said, ′Ben, you are a young boy with a violent temper, fiery, I would almost call it. No one can bear an old Bustan on his back all alone! You can plant it, cultivate it, enjoy its fruits and shade until the day it is time for it to die out, but it can always be yours in your heart. When the time comes, you will be able to cultivate a different Bustan but not similar to the one here! Don′t cry! ` Amin said, his voice breaking as he clasped me on my head while the I was weeping silently, ′But though! But you know very well that everything we humans have here on earth is transitory. ` He tried to console me.

Amin glanced at the dusty road on which the hot air was corrugated in soft, transparent dance movements. Everything about time is money in the new world, thought the Bedouin. The air dances in the heat, and it restores my childhood dreams and adventures, and here stands a boy with a broken heart because of a Bustan. And he sees things in the dancing air that was there and that were my precious, but which have now faded away as if by magic, leaving only dump heartache. He sees things that should be here, but they are first to come many years from now. My tears have long since dried up, and this young boy who does not yet know the brutal demands of life has to build up a shell, a solid shell around his heart if he wishes one day to establish a real Bustan. He must understand that he will have to transcend our reality if he wishes to establish an enduring Bustan. A Bustan in our reality will flourish and wither and flourish again as long as human stupidity is enduring. He looked around. The dog lay on his back and rubbed in an attempt to get rid of his fleas. A cloud of dust rose in the arbor, and the Bedouin kicked his dog in the belly, which hurriedly rolled to the entrance with a plaintive howl. I felt the dry dust in my throat. The dog, I thought, is like many people, a slave most of the time but can become a terrible tyrant. What the hell! The dog does not concern me. They will cover my Bustan with soil and plant on it even more of their almond trees in long, straight rows. My childhood country, what are they doing to you? All the mysterious, enigmatic, unpredictable, and untamed places in you, they cover away under their effective products ′Sit down now, ` said Amin. ′The sun is high up in the sky. It is too strong yet! ` ′No, thanks, Amin. I would like to see the garden for the last time, for I will not come again. ` 'You are angry, my friend, ` said the Bedouin. 'I can remember the day when we let our sheep and goats graze around here after the Great War, ` 'At my home, in the kibbutz, there is no one who is interested in my Bustan. My father calls it my obsession. ` said Abraham. 'Only Allah the Great knows where all this leads. Maybe people's self -destruction will lead to a new epoch? Only the almighty knows the direction of the evolving human caravan. ` Amin stood and walked toward me and hugged me softly. I waved to the Bedouin and started running on the dirt way. I kept on running. I did not look back. When I came up on top of a hill, I stopped. The Arbor, Amin, and the dog were gone. The world around me began to spin around like a carousel. What is happening to me? I thought. Little by little, the carousel slackened and finally stood still. I was still dizzy and sat on a large white limestone and lay then on the parched earth. I lay on the fertile, warm earth of the Bustan. I closed his eyes, and then it came back. The world began to spin but this time more slowly. It was as if my head rose above my body and floated freely, so I could see the azure sea as a giant whirling. I opened my eyes, and there stood my Bustan in its splendor, endearing and completely quiet. Man, oh man, what's happening to you? I thought. All the plants, trees, and flowers in straight, long, disciplined rows: almond trees; the kibbutz cottonfields with their sweet, intoxicating, toxic pesticide odor; and wheat fields. The land is swallowed, flattened, cultivated, but its soul is gone. People are so effective in their actions, and their hearts are so effective, but is there a soul in an effective heart? Why can't they see the soul in a Bustan? It was true what Amin had said that all things passed away and that one must not bind himself too much to the perishable, but he had also said that an evolving Bustan don't die as it keeps evolving and transforming. It was a comforting thought and balm for the crushing pain that would not entirely disappear but knowing that Bustan could not die comforted me and gave me hope.

The reddish green succulent figs hanged from low branches. I wanted to savor them one more time to remember their sweetness, to remember everything. I plucked a few pieces and lay down under the tree. The coolness of the shady haven mingled with the salty sea breeze. I filled my nostrils with the air, closed my eyes, and tasted the figs. I ate them slowly and let the sweet juicy pulp fill my mouth and taste buds, and recollections of an indescribably wonderful feeling surfaced from my early childhood. I could feel the storm inside me now was subsiding. A strong gust of wind rustled suddenly through the Bustan, so it shook and rattled in the leaves. I turned my back and left my Bustan. I continued running as fast as my legs could carry me, and only when I reached the hills, I dared to stop to catch up my breath. The sun's last rays gilded the landscape around me. When I ran toward the kibbutz fields, away from the Bustan and the hills that kept it safe for a long time, I felt a slight breeze that cooled my sweaty forehead. The disappearing sunrays mixed with velvety colors and the scent of the wheat and sweet whispers, which came from somewhere invisible for me. When I went through the gate of the kibbutz, the sweet murmuring disappeared, and the world became pitch-black. I walked into the cone of the electric light from the projector at the fence and was overwhelmed by the feeling of having left something behind me. And then I knew it was my childhood that ended there, and I could not see what was to come instead, or where the road now would lead me to, and how I would ever find an evolving Bustan to work for and dwell in.

CHAPTER II

ADOLESCENCE: 1957-1964

Historical events: Quo Vadis, Mundus?

1957:

Israel hands over the Gaza Strip to UN forces.

USSR launches Sputnik.

International Atomic Energy Agency established.

Great Britain explodes a thermonuclear bomb.

In 1957, President Eisenhower sent Congress a proposal for civil rights legislation. The result was the Civil Rights Act of 1957.

1958: The Great Chinese Famine begins in 1958 and ending in 1961 causing the death of nearly 30 million.

1959: Fidel Castro comes to power in Cuba after Revolution.

United States Vice President Richard Nixon and the Soviet Union's Premier Nikita Khrushchev engage in an impromptu debate.

The Dalai Lama and tens of thousands of Tibetans flee to India after China Invades Tibet.

The Luna 2 spacecraft crashes into the Moon.

First Pictures of Earth from Space Taken By Explorer 6.

1960:

1. OPEC (Organization of Petroleum Exporting Countries) is formed.
2. Soviet missile shoots down the US U2 spy plane.
3. The United States announces that 3,500 American soldiers are going to be sent to Vietnam.
4. Construction on the Aswan High Dam in Egypt began.
5. President Dwight D. Eisenhower signs the Civil Rights Act of 1960 into law.
6. The first televise U.S. Presidential debate takes place between Kennedy and Nixon.
7. John F Kennedy wins presidential Election.

1961:

1. US Cuban Exiles and CIA mount unsuccessful attempt to overthrow Castro known as the Bay of Pigs.
2. Yuri Gagarin becomes the first human in space.
3. East German Authorities close the border between east and west Berlin and Construction of the Berlin Wall begins.
4. U.S. President John F. Kennedy establishes the Peace Corps.
5. President John F. Kennedy advises American families to build bomb shelters.
6. IBM introduces the Selectric typewriter Golfball.

1962:

John Glenn becomes the first American to orbit the Earth in February of 1962.

Cuban Missile Crisis when USSR plans to deploy Missiles in Cuba brings the world to the brink of world war.

President Kennedy proposes a "Consumer Bill of Rights."

Marilyn Monroe is found dead on August 5 after apparently overdosing on sleeping pills (The era of the drug abusers)

Oral Polio Vaccine developed by Albert Sabin given to millions of children to combat Polio.

1963:

1. John F. Kennedy assassinated on Friday, November 22nd, 1963, in Dealey Plaza, Dallas, Texas.
2. Beatles Release I Want To Hold Your Hand/I Saw Her Standing There and Meet the Beatles
3. The United States Senate approved ratification of the Partial Nuclear Test Ban Treaty.

4. The Sabin oral Polio Vaccine which is taken with a lump of sugar is given nationwide in US and UK.
5. Members of Ku Klux Klan dynamite Baptist Church in Birmingham, Alabama.
6. The United States and the Soviet Union agree to establish a "hot line".

1964:

1. Three North Vietnamese torpedo boats attack the US Destroyer Maddox in the Gulf of Tonkin.
2. The Civil Rights Act of 1964 is signed into law by President Johnson.
3. Dr. Martin Luther King, Jr receives the Nobel Peace Prize.
4. President Lyndon Johnson declares a War On Poverty Campaign.
5. The most powerful earthquake in U.S. history at a magnitude of 9.2, strikes South Central Alaska.

My story:

My first lesson/insight as a youngster was, that most humans are dedicated experts in making the Talk without the Walk if the efforts demand sacrifices and self- sacrifice from them, unless they have too much to lose, not acting.

Later, I understood that this common pattern is a kind of subconscious pretension to look better than they were. It is a kind of show off, which makes them feel good about themselves.

Such behavior was not at all encouraged in my kibbutz. If you were to be trusted and to gain status, your words were to be backed up with appropriate actions. We just did not like the bragging/cheating types. We considered them, with our black -white terminology as parasite.

In the kibbutz and Israel at the time we had both pressing, impending necessities: to build a Jewish state and our kibbutz, and these vision and a mission related to working physically/ manually for achieving this purpose ...This attitude demanded hard and dedicated work, often to the point of some self- sacrifice.

I learnt to pursue as an adolescent three directions simultaneously: conformity, non-conformity, and the ever-evolving mission.

It was obvious for me that foundation of Israel and the kibbutz belonged to the last direction, evolutionary push which was channeled to accomplish these goals.

In the kibbutz we were staunch conformists regarding the ideas, values, lifestyle sketched by our vision. On the same time, we were nonconformists in the eyes of the outside society and the world around us. We tried to realize a vision which failed so often in the history of man regarding collective commitment and engagement, solidarity, simple life, free of greed and working to better both man and humanity. This was clearly an attempt to evolve away from other political systems and human self- interest.

And there was the reminiscence of the Bustan: One day, I returned to my Bustan, although as I knew it was gone. As I came nearer, I could see the felled logs and overturned roots. For a moment, I pondered whether it had only been a dream because the bulldozers had leveled even the small surrounding hills. Within a few years, long rows of almond trees were planted in the Bustan's place. Times had changed. Now it was all about profit. The age of efficiency painfully dawned upon all of us. Today the kibbutz is surrounded by the well-known plane fields and regulated plantations. There is a plastic factory, and the trees must work overtime through the pesticides they are being exposed to that have slowly seeped into the kibbutz groundwater.

Already in my youth I realized the price of what we consider profit prone progress: There is no remedy for such progress, then changing the distorted minds of people who push it forward, poisoning our life conditions in their eagerness to maximize their profits.

This was how my youth story started, which is also partly the sad story of our current humanity destroying our earth-Bustan.

The faint trace of a rebel?

At the age of 13, In the feast of the lights-Hanuka- we, the children, were supposed to light one of the candles in the kibbutz dinning hall, which could accommodate 400 people. Upon lightening this candle, we were supposed to recite some text dedicating the candle to the memory of Jewish people who died in wars. I, on impulse, decided to change the text into a joke and said something different and stupid. The silence in the dinning hall was deafening as hundreds of people watched this with disbelief. Right on the spot I realized that I messed it up and became very shameful. I went to our dormitories, hid in my bed under the blanket and heard my comrades comment my stupid comment and laughing at me. There was no place, mercy, or acceptance for such folly. I, the popular guy became suddenly, a pariah (mostly in my own eyes). I wanted the earth to open and swallow me right on the spot.

The day after, lying still in my bed in the afternoon, my father came up and told me in a stern voice, that I did something unforgiveable, and I had to bear both the shame and responsibility of my utterings. I bore this shame almost four-five years, from the age of 13 up to 18, but then I came to think of, why my father had said these words without offering me a mental outlet. He could have tried to explain to me, his teenager′ son something like: ′Alright, you said something inappropriate, but it was not the end of the world. Everybody says once in a while some dumb things, yet if you did not hurt people on purpose, let us not make it into such a terrible thing`. He was a teacher but not a psychologist, so he did not know how to talk with me about things like this. I don′t remember what my mother said, but something to the extent that this was not the end of the world, was likely of her to utter.

What came out of this incidence? It was the last time I felt such shame, not because I stopped breaking the conventional rules but because I did not do it on purpose to hurt. This measure became my moral principle: if I don´t hurt with purpose, I can sleep alright and be in peace with my consciousness, while learning of the experience. I can be outspoken and express sometimes sharp meanings, if I feel irritated by the dumbness of my opponents, but don't regret it afterwards. This feelings of guilt and shame, which dwelled in my mind for some 4 years, after the incident, exhausted itself and died out, as I never broke my own rule of not harming anybody on purpose, not even in my wars.

When I was 14 years old, I read the novel on Till Uglespiegel, a young man living in Flandreau in the 15th century, where the Spanish Inquisition ruled brutally the people. Till` mother was burned down by the Spanish Inquisition accused of being a witch, and he dedicated his whole life to fighting against the Inquisition ´ inhuman and bestial suppression of his folk and for the idea of liberty. Till could not get older or die as he was the immortal incarnated spirit of liberty.

Ever since reading this novel, this narrative of Till´ relentless struggle against the human beast and liberating the people from it, played an essential role in my imagery of what should be a worthwhile and meaningful cause in life to struggle for. Fighting for liberty, including removing the mental shackles of our minds became an essential issue in my life.

I was afraid when I grew up in my kibbutz, Negba. I was afraid of Palestinians´ terror groups who invaded Israel from Gaza in the fifties, attacking the kibbutzim in the Southern part of Israel, very close to Negba, and killing many people in them. Their attacks resulted in Israeli troops attacking Gaza Palestinians, revenging their blood, and a circle of violence was thus established.

I was afraid of the wild dogs roaming freely in our fields and wilderness around us. Very often I had to go in the dark night, at the age of thirteen, from my parents` house in the kibbutz to our dormitories and school, one kilometer outside the kibbutz, through dark, dirt way, while the second generation of wild dogs were barking and growling in the fields just beside this dirt way. I would equip myself with a big thick stick and ran this way, hoping to avoid them, or if not, to fight them.

Two years later, at the age of 15, I was elected as a spider guide for children in the nearby city. Although I got money to travel by bus, some twelve kilometers away, I chose often to run all the way in the afternoons, to spare the money for a little ice cream. On the way home, when it was dark, I took the bus to the nearby station and then had to run some four to five kilometers in the darkness again to reach the kibbutz. Again, there were these coyotes running around in the fields in gangs, some infected by rabies, so this nightmare repeated itself. Haunted by them and my imagination and equipped with a big stick, I ran alone dutifully each week for almost one year.

As a scout and spider leader I had to harden my character and not show hesitation and fear. Yet I was bloody afraid of climbing up our water tower, on an open ladder, 15 meter high (without a protective structure around it). But we had to do it, and facing shame if I stalled, I did it, as I did, using the Omega rope from a top of a high tree down to earth, again without any protective measures. I was afraid of the dentist, being treated by such one at the age of five. I was afraid of injections (they were very big in the eyes of a child) after being treated for pneumonia at early age with a Serie of seven of them in my buttocks. There were so many reasons to be afraid of, that I got immune against anxiety and depression, paradoxically as it sounds, probably because I faced ahead on all my fears.

In the kibbutz and in Israel we had a certain talk style at that time: we called it: Tachles, which means: Come to the point. Stop going around the bush and say clear and concrete what you mean. The opposite to this so- called military style, was what we dubbed as brain masturbation, where doubt and too many deliberations bring one nowhere. Endless scholastic talk like the rabbinical Jews used in the diaspora: Pilpul (a kind of disputation and discussion without any concrete point) was this kind of brain masturbation. What counted for us was planning what we wanted/needed to do and then execute this without all the superficial verbiage which characterized most of the communication between people in the modern human world, as we were taught to think.

We put much stress on being useful and performing productive tasks in our communities and secondly on clapping ourselves on our own shoulders for being such avant-garde for humanity. Yes, there was some stench of spiritual/visionary superiority, which I found later, was a virus most people in social setting are infected by.

Life experience, hard and dedicated work, courage and being a good, combat soldier in the Israeli armed forces, and not loose, high flying talk, were what counted for us and me at the time: What you said had to match what you did!

We were working in the fields, in the orchards, with animals, in the kitchen, and cleaning our dormitories from seventh grad. The kibbutz in these years was based entirely on the community` work and was almost self- reliant regarding food production. We were pretty proud of this independence. Such a farm economy was our ideal.

We learnt from childhood the basic truth on human mutuality` Quid pro quo: Rights come with obligations. Talk less – do concretely more. If you do nothing and just talk, you are a parasite from our point of view, unless, of course, if you are sick or handicapped. This attitude was gone with the wind in the European societies later, as social welfare ensured decent lifestyle even for the parasites. I still think that this principle of Rights- obligations` quid pro quo is the right fundament upon to build a constructive, active, and decent human being.

Being exposed to culture, good films, literature, poetry, classical music, and other kinds of music (but not to the over-pumped and over sentimental Western one) we grew up to appreciate the classical cultural world.

Physical activities, even strenuous and demanding, pre-military training was routine in this kibbutz life. I was very active, worked hard and ran in the fields to develop speed and endurance.

I felt great attraction towards performing something great for the benefit of mankind and read diligently about people who excelled in achieving great feats by working alone or together. It was probably due to our sexual sublimation, the fact that we were not allowed to have sexual relations before being married, that I turned my focus on this form for excellence. Sublimation of the sexual drive was a must in our Kibbutzim, so in my case it worked fine, as I concentrated on becoming knowledgeable and wise and dreamt on Heroism, self- sacrifice to raise myself over ones ′ordinary life, all the while that I was soaking in it by daily day life!

My adapted brother-one out of four whom my parent adapted because their parents stayed away from them in the cities- came from Russia to us in 1957, at the age of 12 years old with his comrades who were born either in Polen or Russia. He had a different experience with sex and love making. He and his comrades were much more lenient regarding this matter than we, the original kibbutzniks, the children of the sun.

In my teenager period, I heard the Hebrew song on the combatant who looked forward for Tomorrow, because all promises and surprises were awaiting me there. The text started to make sense to me in a peculiar way:

The combatant is looking for tomorrow:

Here, the evening is already falling on the desert,
But we'll tell until the late hours of the night,
How the combatant looks forward for tomorrow,
How he for tomorrow longs.

This day he walks in smoke and fire,
And he remembers the battles he went through,
But with the falling evening,
before the battle will resume -
he is always thinking of tomorrow.

He is looking forward for tomorrow,
And he will find it for sure!
from the remote area, from the desert,
It will come, it will come suddenly!
because he longs for it without ceasing…

I thought then that seeking after a red rose opening its delicate petals for me tomorrow is not enough for such one as me as it may or may not come through. In the kibbutz we learnt not to wait for miracles to come but to gestalt them by focused and determined effort. We detested all the Jews who was waiting for their Mashiach riding to save them on his white donkey. My grandparents and their families and millions other Jews believed in God and his messenger and were slaughtered. Ergo we could form this wishful tomorrow, but it costs sweat, hard labor and blood.

And who but a new breed of Jews, warriors and vision bearing hard workers can bring force such tomorrow?

I read a note Mark Twain wrote in 1899 about the Jewish People, which revibrated in my mind:

'If the statistics are right, the Jews constitute but one percent of humans. It suggests a nebulous dim puff of star dust lost in the blaze of the Milky Way. Properly the Jew ought hardly to be heard of, but he is heard of, has always been heard of. He is as prominent on the planet as any other people, and his commercial importance is extravagantly out of proportion to the smallness of his bulk. His contributions to the world's list of great names in literature, science, art, music, finance, medicine, and abstruse learning are also away out of proportion to the weakness of his numbers. He has made a marvelous fight in the world, in all the ages; and has done it with his hands tied behind him. He could be vain of himself and be excused for it. The Egyptian, the Babylonian, and the Persian rose, filled the planet with sound and splendor, then faded to dream-stuff and passed away; the Greek and the Roman followed, and made a vast noise, and they are gone; other peoples have sprung up and held their torch high for a time, but it burned out, and they sit in twilight now, or have vanished. The Jew saw them all, beat them all, and is now what he always was, exhibiting no decadence, no infirmities of age, no weakening of his parts, no slowing of his energies, no dulling of his alert and aggressive mind. All things are mortal but the Jew; all other forces pass, but he remains. What is the secret of his immortality? `

I did not buy his idea of immortality, but the Jewish stubbornness, enduring and both irritating and inspiring spirit I could identify myself with.

These tributes are partly genetics, partly Epi genetic and due to much stress on learning and learning on how to survive. But already in the end of the fifties in Israel, a certain form for muddy normalcy settled down on my people and have been changing and diluting slowly the Israelis 'never again` warrior mentality. as I write these lines (2024) Jews/Israelis resemble in the many aspects modern westerners -individualism, self- focus indulgent minded) yet, the old habit of discussing and fighting among them, they have kept alive and therefore risk vanishing into historic history oblivion if they``ll keep on their compassion for ceaseless infighting.

In the kibbutz, we did not strive to be neither self- indulgent individuals, nor genius or exceptional. You were appreciated alright, if you were loyal, hardworking, responsible and decent. I think that I was a bit of an exception, nurturing some ambitions/aspirations beyond this profile.

Kibbutz members worked long and hard.

They worked around 48 hours a week on top of voluntary jobs. Saturday was supposed to be the only free day, but even on it, members have some tasks to perform like milking cows, feeding the chicken, serving in the common kitchen, working in the nursery, and plucking fruits in the kibbutz orchards etc. Such working regime could amount to no less than 54 hours of work a week.it was tough life but power monger′ bosses! We, the children had also chores, which we had to attend. After school day and lunch in the school dining hall, we worked in the fields, orchards, with cows, chicken etc. 2 ½ hours each day, sometimes including Saturdays.

Coming back from the fields at around 16 in the afternoon, we got some tea and bread with watered jam in the common children dining hall, and thereafter washed ourselves in the common shower-this time boys and girls separately- made lectures and had after supper different cultural, sport and spider activities up to 21.30. Since the ideal of becoming synthesis-orientedhuman was promoted and I was very open towards ideas of becoming better and more educated young man, I was engaged in both sports, cultural activities, local politics in the school and writing to the school newspaper.

I also read a great deal. Both literature, politic and history. Two books made great impression upon my mind: Thyl Eulenspiegel. It was a modern retelling of the Eulenspiegel story. It was the Legend of Thyl Ulenspiegel and Lamme Goedzak, by Charles De Coster (1867). The author transferred the character to the period of the Reformation and the Dutch Revolt. It was a book of both fighting for freedom and yet, wandering around and keep being ever young.

The second book′ title was: How the Steel Was Tempered or The Making of a Hero by Nikolai Ostrovsky (1904–1936). With 36.4 million copies sold, it was one of the best-selling books of all time. The story follows the life of Pavel Korchagin, including his fighting in and aftermath of the Russian Civil War. Korchagin fought for the Bolsheviks during the war and was injured. The novel examines how Korchagin heals from his wounds and thus becomes as strong as steel.

One citation from the book made great impression on me: "Man's dearest possession is life. It is given to him but once, and he must live it so as to feel no torturing regrets for wasted years, never know the burning shame of a mean and petty past; So, live that, dying, he might say: all my life, all my strength were given to the finest cause in all the world—the fight for the Liberation of Mankind"

— Nikolai Ostrovsky

And there was a bit desert in Ain Rand as she aspired also for the greatness of the human soul.

Ain Rand did not attract me with her superhuman model who was supposed to be selfish, but with her principles regarding attaining the best in ones` self as: Rationality, independence, integrity, honesty, justice, productiveness, and pride. If you put these seven virtues into action in your lifework, you have fair chance of succeeding in at least some of your endeavors for the sake of humanity, I reasoned then ...

My models at this time were great men who achieved something for the benefit of humans and, like albert Sweitzer, Madam Kuri, Newton, Salk, Darwin, great orators, and philosophers which ideas I tried to read.

The book Cola Brugnon was also a model to identify with ; He was my down to earth counter balance to these great men. He was a carpenter, enjoyed life a great deal and was full of life joy, even though life was not always easy.

Yes, there was place in my mind for both great deeds and practical work, struggle for liberty and joy and merriment. Colas Breugnon is a 1918 novel by Romain Rolland, a nostalgic look at his hometown of Clamecy through the eyes of the eponymous sixteenth-century old carpenter. Written as his diary, it chronicles the local goings-on, from wars through plagues to brigandry, through his optimistic and joyful eyes, the optimism undying even when struck with personal tragedy or unlucky love. A mostly light-hearted book.

Being old by now- coming close to 80- I see many young people now adays-2024- choosing to show off, to invest their energies in Maj flies` self- promoting, exhibitionistic and shameless narcissism prone celebrities as a role model. Most of these celebrities and influencers are literally dumb, without any rea and varied life experience or cultural, educational background. Their showoff is their brand. Most of them will never get older and wiser as their minds are distorted, and their bodies/brains are abused by drugs and booze and pornography. Sooner than later, many of them die before getting old, and then the mass media describe their merits and tragic lives beyond the false glamour. For me, both these sweet nothing models and their admirers are people who live like Maj flies, unaware as they waste their lives away for a bit a passing attention or distracting political trends like GBT.

I went already as an adolescent for the slogan:

A healthy soul
in a healthy body
serve one best to pursue
our ultimate life goal!

So, I kept living a healthy lifestyle, being physical active, slim and agile, read a great deal history, politick, ideas expressed by great men and of course I was also all the school pensum and lots of literature on science, medicine, hygiene, wars and utopia, as my motivation was to become wiser as to be good at helping the split up humanity.

I often listened to classic music. I learnt to play accordion and sang in the school chore as tenor. I nurtured also daydreams of becoming a real good middle-distance runner.

Singing to change mood and reduce fear

I mentioned it before that when we, as small children, were evacuated from our besieged kibbutz to a safer place in the center of Israel. There was this low sound of the motor of the armored car, and there was this thick darkness all around me. We, the children, and our caretakers sat on hard bunch in the truck. I was afraid because I could not see a thing and could not reach the floor with my small feet. I searched for the comforting hand of my caretaker. She whispered to me not to be afraid. I could even sing silently a song. What kind of song should it be in this immense and impenetrable darkness, crossing the lines of the enemy (this fact I did not understand; we just had to be silent and not cry). So, I chose to sing a song which I learned lately, about the children of Israel, a courageous generation, all are going in the darkness in a long row, and they carry in their hands lighted torches and candles. They carry the light, which disperses the darkness. And suddenly, the armored car was lit up by all these torches and candles. Ever since I was granted this revelation, I sort of learned how to sing myself into any desirable states of mind. As my father and my older sister liked to sing and taught me many songs, I learned the joy of singing together and alone.

As teenager I could run singing, walk singing. I could remove melancholy or disappointment singing. Probably due to many reasons but also singing all the time, I did not in my adolescence and thereafter considered life to be unbearable and I never considered suicide. Singing, sport, being clean from drug abuse and due to my social status and the aspiration to become wise and accomplish something useful and great- on top of having robust mind- became my motivators and protectors against apathy and resignation.

Later, as a psychologist, working for decades with burdened people who were captives of their bad moods, I encouraged many of them to learn how to sing to themselves, be it a lullaby, a nature song, a melancholic one, a march, whatsoever. This capacity of singing to yourself out loud or silently I in these teenager period, nurtured to the point of refined mood changer. It is a precious gift, and in my view, it is at least as potent as yoga or meditation and physical exercise at the same time and much more pleasant and easy to practice.

In the kibbutz society at that time there were no criminals, thieves or drug addicts. People had equal rights, and there were no rich or poor. There was no violence and hardly any suicide. Material consumption was modest and the spirit of mission and achieving something big- high. We contributed with the best soldiers in the armed forces and was reputed for being honest and reliable. It was a little society, all together 500 people (Today-2024- there are around

270 kibbutzim), which functioned much better and just than any other societies in the world. No wonder that we were proud of our society as teenagers. We felt that our parents made a decision-pursuing a great vision- which gave us both our life and turned out to become a great social success.

I read about Two Jews who discussed for about 120 years ago the Jewish problem/dilemma- long time before the Holocaust- which was a choosing between being people without a country and nationhood or fight for national home in Palestine, and as good Jews are often, they disagreed. One focused on the existing Jews who settled down in America and elsewhere and who lived with their culture and common language, Yiddish. The other was advocating, creating a Jewish national home in Palestine, and reviving the Hebrew language. When they could not agree, the one who advocated a national home in old Israel, said, 'All right, let us agree to share it all between us two. You take all what already exists of Jewish life, and I take that which does not yet exist. With other words, all the real and concrete must be yours, and all the aspirations, dreams, and efforts to create such reality will be mine! The land of Israel and a modern Hebrew language does not exist yet, so I take them.

I thought regarding the moral of it. Both the state of Israel and modern Hebrew languages became realities, and our daily day reality is mudded and the conflict with Arabs became a fact of life, yet without my parents pursuing the second alternative, I and all the people I love and cherish would not be alive, so sometimes it is more meaningful to nurture a viable vision than to accept passively the existing.

Without a great vision of the future and fighting spirit to turn dreams into realities, stagnation is the destiny of those who cling themselves to the present alone. Historical development and progress are always being driven by aspirations, dreams, and active, goal-oriented efforts, I concluded.

Pesach and Moses` narrative being imprinted in me

There are lots of big and small narratives telling people what the meaning of their life is or should be. For me, belonging to the Jewish folk, the one supreme narrative- The exodus of the Israelites from Egypt- formed my life view as an adolescent. The Jews who were enslaved in Egypt land were coerced by Moses talk to leave their slavery and journey to a promised land. As a teen ager I could grasp that its ultimate meaning was to transcend the state of human slavery into being new and liberated folk. This meaning wandering to the Promised Land was a meant to transform us to become better and wiser than we are at our current stage, as my parents, their comrades and we tried hard in our kibbutz.

I grasped that the story of the Exodus is an evolutionary tale, full of faults by both man and God. As a young socialist bent on critical thinking and careful not to end up as my father- in blind admiration to people- I had no problem finding faults in both humans and God.

I could accept that the desert generation had to die as they were with them all their belonging from Egypt, died first, before even coming halfway, as they could not cut off their bonds to their slave mentality.

Moses who led them all the forty years this voyage took, died too before entering the Promised Land. The children, who were born in the desert came into the Promised Land, supposedly untainted by the marks of slavery. Yet, when they came into the Promised Land, they, too became corrupted within two generations and acted as all the people around them. There was a trap in this exodus, I reasoned. Unless the exodus is not a part of one's life, people become corrupted.

Here I found God` short sight. God should have made them wander over 400 years, not 40 years, if they` should get a fair chance to transcend human′ coarse core, and hold them to the fire of exodus, I concluded later in my life. But at the age of 14-15 I could only see half success-half failure in this epoch to free man of his mental bonds.

The narrative was great and instructive, but the strategy to transform the people failed miserably, I concluded.

Therefore, I adopted only its essential: As Moses got his calling from God through the burning bush, the lesson must be!

> From the eternal Burning Bush
> Keeps flowing the evolving call
> of our ultimate meaning:
> ′Keep on your evolutionary Push!'

My two voices in a dialogue:

The time flew by, and I learnt to have a silent dialogue with myself once in a, imagining different scenes. I told myself that I belong not only to my kibbutz or to the Jewish people but to all of humanity. This is what my father told me for the last ten years. Be solidary with humanity. ′I just think that there are many Jews and Arabs and Bedouins and people from England, USA, France, and many other countries that are in the group they are born into and grew up in even if they move to another place, but it is not so with all people. There are some people who have a larger wingspan and have been blessed to go beyond the ordinary human narrow sense of belonging. These people are there for humanity as a whole and belong to its dreams and aspirations . . . Therefore, you should do it without expecting any personal gain, fame, or others' adulations` my voice told me. ′Moses died before he could enter the Promised Land. He had trouble with his people, which you have read about, and he was sometimes disappointed and angry, but he undertook his obligation, and it made him into a great man. He could have deserted his obligation, but he chose to carry out his mission, without going into the Promised Land`. I knew that there were people like Moses, not many, who wished to work for the sake of humanity, and I wished to join them one day.

The other voice in me took over: 'You can still choose to live a life like the great majority of people without such burden! Such life, ordinary one, can be joyful and engaging as well ''The life I am talking about`-came the first voice in- 'is a completely different one from the ordinary life. It is transforming people and their lives and social intercourse and leaves enduring mark on where the journey of us as wiser and more benign beings will bring us to. ` 'I do not understand what you are talking about!` said my conform voice. 'What is it that you do not understand? Ordinary life is like reading children's adventure throughout people's lives without ever accomplishing something significant and enduring for the sake of humanity, but life can become a journey towards a Promised Land for all of us when some of us receive the grace to show some enduring direction. It is not everyone who has the opportunity to choose such endeavor, but the ones who have been attentive to this Promised Land symbol, may have granted this aspiration…

My far sighted, aspiring voice said: 'Old people told that after God had created the world and the people who would live in it, he had two lumps of clay left. Of the first one, he created a camel and with the other one- a palm tree with sweet dates. On their way in their life mind desert, thought God, people would be able to search for a Promised Land for their mind subjugated and suffering humanity. God was wise and He knew that people who are well fed and fat, lack incentives to pursue such a journey. In our age, boys dream much about girls and what boys can do to them, but luckily, we learnt to sublimate so we may find a way to accomplish such great feat

Daydreaming I came to think of another story which I heard, which sketches the difficulties of transforming people` minds, as to wish to pursue a Promised Land.

There was a river that flowed through different landscapes, and each time it met an obstacle, it forced its way by sheer force. But one day it came to a landscape that it could not penetrate or pass by, and therefore, it could not continue its course. Then it heard a voice. 'If you continue to press on as usual, you end up as a quagmire or a mud pool.' 'But in such a way, I have always dealt with all difficulties on my way,' the river said. 'What should I do instead?' 'You can let the warm wind sucks you up and carry you over the desert and the mountains and then let you fall down as rain and start a new life,' whispered the voice. "'I can't do this since I will lose myself!' said the river. 'You will only lose a part of yourself that is causing you problems, but your core will follow, and it is the most important,' whispered the voice. And after much hesitation did the river just that and realized that rebirth can only occur along this way.

Melancholy:

But sometimes I felt sort of melancholy. Great thoughts cannot nurture you all the time, as well as sublimation is not always easy to bear. On top of all that, the slow bloom of a non-conformist in me could not see a clear outlet, in kibbutz, where ideological uniformity was the rule.

I thought I missed something. We sang: 'Beauty blooms up and withers away while I daydream without doing a thing.'

I was a teenager in love, but it was forbidden and regardless how much work and sport I did and how much I nurtured great ideas and even held speeches in the school, I felt sometimes the pangs of sadness . . .But then something came out of the blue and lifted me up. We were preparing a large play, where most of the students in the school's- more than one hundred students- participated. The play was called the Lush green meadow and focused on the black Americans interpretations of the stories in the Old Testament. There were scenes from the stories of Adam and Eve and the serpent in paradise, Cain and Abel, Noah's Ark, Moses who led the Israelites from their bondage in Egypt Land to the Promised Land, and several other stories. I was offered the role of Moses and went enthusiastically into learning the texts by heart. I had also been chosen to sing in the chore of angel's gospel songs, which were added to the play. When I did not play my role as Moses, I dressed out with white garments and white wings. I saw in playing this piece a great opportunity to learn English and was very excited about the gospel texts and songs. I spent many nights rehearsing my role as the reluctant Moses who God had chosen and assigned to lead his folk, the Israelites towards the Promised Land. I was greatly moved by the scene where Moses led his people out of Egypt for forty long years, wandering in the wilderness, knowing that all the people who had lived under slavery, including Moses himself, were to die in the desert. I got tears in my eyes and had to try not to let my feelings overwhelm me when the choir sang: 'When Israel was in Egypt's land. Let my people go. Oppressed so hard, they couldn't stand. Let my people go. Go down, Moses, way down in Egypt's Land. Tell old Pharaoh to let my people go. Thus spoke the Lord, Ball Moses said; Let my people go. If not, I'll smite your firstborn dead. Let my people go. Go down, Moses . . . The Lord told Moses what to do. Let my people go. To lead the children of Israel through. Let my people go. Go down, Moses . . .` After I eventually died as Moses on the scene, I ran backstage and changed into an angel costume again and was ready for the next scene, where Joshua led the Israelites seven times around the walls of Jericho as they blew their trumpets until the walls collapsed. There I stood, erect and solemn among the group of tenor singers, and saw Joshua continues my mission and conquer the land from their local residents. It was obvious to me that this was the right thing to do, and I sang in a loud voice and with much enthusiasm the song: 'Joshua fit the battle of Jericho, Jericho, Jericho. Joshua fit the battle of Jericho, and the walls came tumbling down. Hallelujah. You can talk about the men of Gideon. You can talk about the men of Saul. But there're none like good old Josha at the battle of Jericho Up to the walls of Jericho with sword drawn in his hand Go blow the horns, Josha cried. The battle is in my hands`.

The play was so successful that we came to play it five more times for full houses for audience from nearby kibbutzim. All this long period was my spirits high and elevated.

The gospel songs alleviated mt melancholy, so I went singing them to myself for a long time: `My Lord, what a morning / My Lord, what a morning / My Lord, what a morning / when the stars begin to fall. You'll hear the trumpet sound / to wake the nation's underground / looking to my God's right hand / when the stars begin to fall. You'll hear the sinner moan / to wake the nation's underground / looking to my God's right hand / when the stars begin to fall`.

It helped me also to make climbing the water tower to more routine than a nightmare, by repeating the climbing.

I was not born with a sense of rhythm in my feet. I had tried to learn couple dances, but my legs which were good at running, jumping, and walking would not quite follow rhythm, so I gave up but not without a pang of envy toward my comrades who could dance.

While I climbed upward one night, I could suddenly smell smoke from the nearby grove. There were probably some of the oldest students who baked potatoes on a fire and talked about the upcoming military service and perhaps about love and sex. There were probably some of the beautiful girls whom I secretly was infatuated by. When my favorite platonic love, a fourteen-year-old girl, came close to me I looked at her on the sly, and I could feel my heart beating a few extra strokes, but when she looked back, I removed hurriedly my glance and pretended I was busy with something else. The idea of loving openly made me sad and longing, but it helped me quell my anxiety climbing up the water tower. How, I thought, it would continue day after day, year after year, slowly and tiring, and I would never have the courage to look her in the eye and declare my feelings for her. I began to sing a sad Russian song for myself when I finally approached the top of the tower: ′Day after day, year after year, as words without melody . . . long dark nights and the rain that pours endlessly, and all my days disappear as smoke . . .` While occupying me with something else which can attract my attention, I could overcome my fear, I reasoned. For example, think how beautiful the sky is or how incomprehensible and magical space is. I would think more what science meant to me and figured out that it was greater than love. Love will come when it comes! And if it does not come because I am too shy, what am I to do?

But was I shy? Only in this matter of love. I was popular and likeable boy in school, and there were girls who were interested in me. But somehow, I felt surer following Milky Way than talking to a girl on my feelings. So, I focused on the Milky Way. It is the galaxy that our solar system belongs to. In it, there are perhaps 250 billion suns and many of them like ours, which means that it might teem with life up there. Do you understand what it might mean for us and our self-understanding and life onward journey, my voice asked. Yes, I understand, but why are you concerned with it? I asked the voice. Because it is exciting, more exciting than anything else! If in our galaxy there is a million developed and organized civilizations, it will be possible one day to get in touch with them, learn from them, transform us, fight diseases that kill us, learn how to avoid wars and famines . . . So, you think then that if we send them a message in the morning, we must wait six hundred years to get a return message? I asked. Yes, but it will, of course, be worthwhile if they can help us with anything, which they are better than us, said my second voice… There is a Chinese proverb that says, 'When you look at the moon, you yearn to get close to it without being sure whether it can ever succeed, but your longing can give you a focus, which can help you to pull your boots out of the mud!' It was well said! I chuckled. It occurred to me on the way up here, so now I can go around, free of thoughts of love or death. I would rather think about a possible meeting with other intelligent life that can teach us something about life so that we may one day be able to settle us on other planets, which will be hospitable to such some stunted fools as we, sapiens seem to be!

Young Guardians:

I joined the ′ Young guardians` movement in the sixth grade through a ceremony where we were wearing blue shirts with red leash on the collar. We swore allegiance to both the pioneering spirit and the socialist vision, along with accepting ten specific commandments, which were the pillars of the movement. After joining the movement, we met with a counselor once a week to acquire and discuss the ideas in the vision and to undergo paramilitary training and character hardening, which included shooting at targets, navigations in the nights, courage and endurance demanding exercises, and talks dealing with introspection and motivation to live up to the ideal of the Guardian.

In our classroom hung a large blackboard, and on it hang the ten commandments: The Young Guardian: 1) is a truthful man who defends the truth. 2) is an inseparable part of the Jewish people and retains strong ties to the state of Israel, has deep roots in the country's culture, and supports Judaism and Zionism. 3) is engaged in his work and struggles to create a life where work is a productive expression of human creativity and freedom. 4) is politically active and dedicated. He works for freedom, equality, peace and solidarity. 5) is a loyal friend who works with his comrades to achieve progress and to spread the movement's values in the world. 6) develops and maintains free and honest relationship to the members of his group and assumes the responsibility to provide for their welfare. 7) respects and takes good care of nature. He acquires knowledge of it and lives and acts in accordance with the principles of sustainability. 8) is brave, independent, enterprising and critical thinking. 9) builds up a strong character and strives for physical, mental, and spiritual balance. 10) is guided by reason, taking responsibility for his actions, maintains sexual purity, and strives to set an example for the others.

I thought that sexual abstinence was a very big challenge since we slept two boys and two girls in the same room, but even harder was that we had to be happy all the time. We sang a particular song almost every time we met to get into this mood of enduring happiness. ′The young guardians are a happy bunch. None of them gives up and complains. Our group is prepared for any task! `

It worried me because I occasionally would sigh and was not happy all the time. I certainly was not sure if I was ready for any task granted me, and so I stood there also in the commandments that I also had to be independent and critical, and I was not sure whether I followed, without any doubt the socialistic dogma. During the last year, I had grown up almost sixteen centimeters. My voice had come in transition, and there was growing black hair under my armpits and in the groin, and I cut himself often on the razor blade while trying to remove the sprouting stubble on my chin, and I was plagued by constant and bothersome erections. But there were also uplifting moments. I was a talented, focused, and teachable student in school, popular, respected, and well-liked.

I often thought about what I could talk to a girl about, when I went with her hand in hand and how I could get my penis to relax. I could maybe start with something about Leninism, socialism, and some of the ideas the kibbutz was based on. It was important to start relations with a girl with some well-chosen topics, but I could not really get started because I could not talk to anyone about my feelings. They were forbidden.

When I turned fifteen years old, I and the other group members were ready to be introduced into the tough issues that created the framework for our lives in the kibbutz: Marxism/ socialism, Zionism, and Judaism. Because of my good memory and focus, I learned quickly all the important concepts and embarked on a career as an amateur journalist for the school newspaper, where I wrote enthusiastic articles for the youth.

As a youngster, inexperienced, you can be tempted to follow black-white convictions and ideologies/faiths, but if you don′t change them later with more contextual and nuanced views -you have become a fool! I was aware of this danger, as my mother taught me indirectly the art of opportunism, not on account of others, but on account of risking to end up as useful idiots in the service of manipulating others.

Luckily, I worked by now-1960- three hours every day after school in the cowshed, where I looked after the cows and milked them and sometimes helped get the pelt of a dead calf. When I finished the day's work at four o'clock, I trained running in the fields, hoping to qualify for the Olympic Games in 1964. As I was good to gather the youth and keep them engaged and to hold speeches, I was elected as a scout leader for a group of children of ten to twelve years in Ashkelon City. Once a week, I and a girl from the group, Nili, took the bus after school to Ashkelon City, twelve kilometers away from the kibbutz. In the city, we met young children in the street, and our task was to introduce them to the movement's spirit. Often, we had to deal with fifty to seventy children from the city's poor neighborhoods and organized games, excursions, and cultural events for them. It was the first time in my life that I had received money from the kibbutz to pay for the bus ticket. In the kibbutz, they did not use money. Although we almost spent two hours waiting for the bus and driving back and forth on the bus, which had many stop stations on the way, and we spent additional three hours with the kids, we did not get any money to buy neither food nor drink. I soon found out that if I saved the bus ticket to the city, I could buy an ice cream for the money and feel truly spoiled. I only needed to run the twelve kilometers along the traffic road, past some small villages and to the town, and it was no big deal for me. Inside the town, I met with Nili, and when our activities with the children was over, we went back home on the bus. When we got off the bus, 5 kilometers away from the kibbutz, it was pitch-dark, and there we had to go on foot back to the kibbutz because there was no bus going to the kibbutz in these hours. We went on a road between fields and orchards, and we felt both scared and insecure in the dark, but we were, of course, the brave guardians who learned not to give in for fear. For safety's sake, I found a thick stick, so I was prepared- if I should have to- to defend ourselves. We were afraid of wild dogs, which dwelled around the hills and hunted on the fields at night. Some of them suffered from rabies and could attack a passerby. There were some from the kibbutz who had been bitten and had been through a painful and prolonged treatment. To make the agony with the five kilometers in the dark shortest possible, I suggested to Nili that we could run back to the kibbutz. It was there on the dark road that I learned that you cannot chase away the darkness with a stick but that you can defend yourself with it. So, I was prepared to defend ourselves against what could threaten us in the darkness, thereby feeling more ready and less afraid.

I knew by now, that most people live their lives from day to day and think mostly on their personal and social challenges like earning enough money, fulfilling their needs and to live as enjoyable and convenient as possible, and it is this mind-set and focus which determines what they find challenging and significant in their lives. I did not criticize living an ordinary life. In the kibbutz, we were proud to be ordinary and work with our hands as sometimes the ordinary people were the salt of the earth, I thought to myself. But I wished to be more than ordinary man. Is it a vanity or a high motive? So, I was in love with, and I sublimated my urges, and I should be ordinary, but I felt a quest for something extra ordinary, and it was springtime of my life, and I felt frustrated by this inner struggle. I often listened to "Summertime" as my heart flooded with grief, pain, and sweetness without knowing why.

Once a week, the group met with the scout movement supervisor, who was about twenty years old, to talk about how the group members were doing, and at one point, the debate revolved around all the precious and constructive energy that young people waste on sex and eroticism and which we conserved through our sublimation to be useful and constructive for the common good of the community. The supervisor explained what a great chance it was to be able to help improve the world at a young age instead of wasting time trying to get inside each other pants. It sounded convincing to me but not to another young fellow in the group, who thought it was not ′natural. ` ′Look at the sheep, the donkeys, the camels, the horses, and people. It works by itself, completely without all the sublimation hysteria! `, one fellow, coming from the city, insisted. He, who grew up in the city and joined the group later, believed that they were on their way into a monk's order and declared that he had no intention of wasting any chances. During one of the meetings, the fellow sent me a small note, saying; 'If we do not release our libido's drives, we will get pain in the balls and a brain which is fried! I laughed but could not share the secret of my infatuation with a certain girl with him. He was still a stranger, not growing up on a kibbutz, and I should be a model for him.

Having spent three meetings discussing every possible aspect of the topic, all members of the group had agreed to transform their libido into cultural, social, work-related, revolutionary, and missionary activities, and each had to identify the areas that they burned most for and would throw themselves into. We promised that sex and love were postponed until the day we had attained sufficient maturity as to be able to understand the depths of love, as our supervisor had expressed it.

Afterward, when we met outside, the city fellow whispered to me: 'I now intend to limit myself to pretending. For me, it is all very simple. It's about touch and penetration, and the rest is just some ideological distortion! We can be both engaged in our lives and in love making.'

I nodded smiling, as part of me was pragmatic/opportunistic and the other part; idealistic. These two parts lived in peace with each other, though.

The city fellow told me: 'There are three things that are insatiable: the human eye that wants to see more and more, the desert land that can never get enough rain, and the woman's desire for a man. This is how people are in their core regardless of all their sublimation. Man is driven by his drifts, so I consider this a perversion`, he proclaimed. I laughed again thinking that there was common sense in what he proclaimed, but I can wait some years... I was already slowly maturing into being both conformist and nonconformist, without having trouble containing these opposites. But I was not clear to revolt. I thought I ought to follow the collective decision. The fellow continued to tease me, saying that what one does under the blanket, can always be denied. I still believed that this so-called sublimation cure, could also be used to sublimate crazy people, sinners, dreamers, and not the least, the many fanatics who plant crazy ideas in young children' souls. To sublimate to steer drifts and fanatism and too much emotionality, still made sense to me.

My mother had had her own special prejudices, and as all people are contaminated by them, hers were not the worst, as she blended them together with some acute and perceptive observations. Since she grew up as a Jew in Poland and Ukraine, she strongly felt the pervasive Polish/Ukraine anti-Semitist attitude and resented it and all these people strongly. She had her views of Polish people's collaboration with Nazi Germans, and I could not blame her for this as her whole family perished in the gas chambers on Polish soil. She considered the Polish people to be vain, profane, and overblown proud, as she considered the Arabs living in Israel and abroad to be black animals. She told me the story of a Polish dragon officer who enjoyed the night with a hooker, and when he had to leave, he took his shining uniform on and uttered some farewell words. The hooker looked astonished at him and inquired, ´What about the paying ?` upon which he slammed his boots against each other, saluted, and declared,:´ A Polish officer does not accept payment.` Oh, foolish pride! How often it makes us act foolishly or being caught in the most impossible situations, I thought.

Two of Russia's greatest poets, Pushkin and Lermontov, I learnt by reading their biographies, were killed in duels because they felt obliged to fight officers who had provoked them to duel on purpose. They went into their certain death because they had believed that their pride was more significant than their lives (or what they viewed as life in dishonor).

This very day people sacrifice their lives for not being "dishonored" as their reference group had taught them from early childhood. That is what our neighbors the Arabs often do, while we, the Israelis, fight back but put much stress on the value of our lives here and now. This honor attitude is for the most stupid because people pride/vanity and automatism come always in first place without analyzing who the offender is, what the circumstances are, or if one can manage the situation in a better way, I thought then. Every time people show automatic reaction patterns in accordance to collective values and religious/ideological conditioning, I felt that what they demonstrated was sheer stupidity, a parrot` replications in words and deeds. Learning to know ones´ self can never be built on such automatism.

I identified myself in these years fully with Till Uglenspiegel, who had a good life appetite. Till was funny, cheerful, and in love with life, although the Inquisition had killed his mother and filled his life with grief. He was always hungry and thirsty. He fought ceaselessly against the Inquisition and for his people's freedom. But the most important thing in his life was the love to his childhood girl, Nele. And his Nele, who turned to be my secret love, went with me through the golden cornfield, smiling as a warm sun and was so pretty that my heart was about to burst. And she sang to me of freedom and love, both immortal, and I listened to her echo that rolled across the field and disappeared into the horizon, and my heart was crying of happiness and longing.

In my lively imagination, I and She joined the struggle to free the oppressed people, breaking their shackles of human stupidity, pretense, materialism, and shortsighted greed. We fought for a new humanity, which should stand up and move toward a future full of comforting and warming light, progress, and transformation. I and her flew up as we were wearing wings and came to hover over the fields and forests, hills and deserts, mountains, and valleys, with a message that a new world has been created for the oppressed masses. I had transformed myself into Till, and I was the bearer of the message of the very last hymen of liberation, though I did not quite know what this hymen was about, but I knew that it existed. I, my secret love and some friends walked around to inflame people to rise against their oppressors. We just lacked

Lama Goedzak, the good natured and loyal dumpling, which was Till's friend, but there was a thick and good-natured boy in my school, so we could take him with us, my fantasy told me.

We walked around and fought all kinds of inquisitors, and although they were many, we could win over them. We stopped occasionally in a tavern; filled our stomachs with thick and smoked sausages, ham, and delicious bread; and washed it all down with red wine from our motherland vineyards and supplemented it with fried chicken and apples and pears, which we stole from the rich peasants. We were going out to meet our troops which had revolted against the Spanish Inquisition, and we fought and defeated the Spanish troops, who fled back to their country. Then I pulled out of the story with my friends and sent Till Uglenspiegel back on stage again to be united with his Nele. ′That is how big the love I have for my secret love` I whispered to the wheat field.

How many times I read the end of the story about Till and Nele. I almost knew it by heart. As Nele glanced at herself, she saw that she was naked and rushed to get dressed. She saw that Ulenspiegel also was naked, and she tried to put his clothes on him, but since he did not wake up, she was gripped by fear and began to cry. ′If I killed him with my magic ointment, I would also die!`. Then she heard bells and saw a group of people with a priest in the lead came towards them and soon came face-to face with her and looked at Ulenspiegel, who was stretched out in the grass. The priest was drooling with delight and said, "The great idiot Ulenspiegel is dead! Thank God and the law! Hurry to dig a grave so we can get him in the ground but take his clothes off first!" Nele protested, saying that he was going to freeze underneath without his clothes on, and wild with grief, she bent over to Ulenspiegel's face and kissed him, sobbing bitterly. The priest chanted, ′The big mother fucker's dead! Blessed be God! ′ So they dug a grave, laid Ulenspiegel, into the grave, and covered him with sand. But suddenly, while the pastor read the prayer for the dead, the sand pit began to move, and Ulenspiegel stood up, shook his sandy hair, and grabbed the priest by the throat. ′You bloody Inquisitor! ` he shouted. ′You put me in a grave while I sleep. Where is Nele? Have you buried her? ` The priest screamed and fled, and Nele came running toward Ulenspiegel, who said, ′Kiss me, my darling! ` The rest of the entourage fled too, and only the mayor and an alderman were so shocked, so they lay down in the grass. Ulenspiegel went and shook them and said, ′Do you really believe that one can bury Ulenspiegel, Flanders's immortal spirit, and Nele, its heart? Also, she can sleep but never die! Come, Nele!` And he went away with her while he sang his song about the struggle for freedom and love, but no one knows where he went, but the song is with us!` And I whispered to myself, ′The last hymn for the struggle for freedom and for love cannot die as long as there are people like Ulenspiegel and Nele, but how does it sound this very last hymn, and how is it different from other songs?` There was something that was invisible for me. I knew that everything on earth was temporary, but this song lives forever, but how is it done?'

I closed my eyes and whispered to myself, ′Sesame, sesame! Shut up and . . . show me the very last eternal hymn!'

The wandering tour in the Negev desert:

There was this bird of prey hovering over the desert with outstretched wings, which flew in circles and then glided downward. I could see on the horizon a hazy gray mass under the strong midday sun. ′It is either a sheep or a donkey. It's hard to see, but it's either dead or on the verge of dying 'I said.

′How can you see it from this distance? I can only see a small, obscure dot! ` said a girl from the group, amazed. ′I can see. I can see that it moves slightly. It is as if the animal's hind legs are quivering and twitching slightly. I think that it is about to die out! 'I said. Three other raptors joined the first, and they circled now as a flock over the place, waiting for the animal to die. ′It is a sheep. Now I'm sure` I concluded as we marched ahead on the rocky path. We were a big group of youngsters, around two hundred scouts, and we went into the desert on a march of five days. It was our third day, and we put about thirty kilometers per day with full packs with food, spare clothes, sleeping bags, cookware, and raincoats. The only thing that we should not bear in these five days hike was water that they got supplied every night when we made a camp. It was a demanding trip, although it was early springtime and the temperature were over thirty-five degrees. I went next to Gili, the fellow from the city who joined the group three years ago. In front of us walked my secret love- Smadar- with another girl. Smadar and Shlomit had shorts on, and I could not remove my eyes from Smadar's nice ass and beautiful legs.

′If you continue that way, it ends up that you will fall over your own feet` said Gili, I chuckled, blushing. ′You walk like a zombie, totally absorbed by her ass! ` whispered Gili so she could not hear us. ′Man would think that you had grown up in a Yeshiva (religious school) and had never seen a woman's ass and a couple of naked girls' legs before! ` ′Hold your mouth shut! ` I snarled. ′I say no more! ` he said, laughing. We walked further along the dry riverbed, where the animal was lying, and the birds now sat, poised to pounce on prey. Now I could see that it was indeed a sheep. ′Gili!` I shouted backward. ′Can you see the sheep lying down there? ` Gili wiped out the sweat from his brow and blew his glasses and looked in the direction that I had pointed. ′Shall I help you carry your pack? ` I asked him. ′No, I can manage it myself,` said Gili peevishly. ′Your back is dripping with sweat! ` I commented. ′And then what? ` retorted Gili. ′It is springtime, and you sweat as it was tropical summer! ` said I. ′The lamb is alive, and they hack into it while it is still alive. We must do something! 'cried Gili.

′There's nothing we can do, Gili. It dies now, and it is numb. This is how nature works 'I said matter of fact. I saw many animals die and not few people and children, so I learnt to distance myself from death around me. Smadar and Shlomit also caught a glimpse of the massacre taking place, and Shlomit asked if we could do anything to save the sheep. ′No, there's nothing we can do. The sheep is done with, 'I said . Smadar looked at me with tears in her eyes, and I shrugged and looked away. At one point, we came to a ledge that we had to help one another down from, and then all jumped into a riverbed. While walking there, we heard a sudden rumbling sound behind us, and turning around, we saw large stones that came rolling toward us. I turned around and listened attentively. ′What is it? ` someone cried.

′Come out of the riverbed in a hurry!" I shouted. ′Quickly out! Run up the cliff! ` The others looked confused at me as I yelled and gestured. I pushed Gili in front of me and grabbed Smadar and pulled her up the riverbed then I lifted Shlomit. The other boys followed suit and helped the girls come up from the riverbed I was shouting to the others who went in front of us, oblivious to what was about to happen. ′Overflooding! Run up! There comes a flood! ` I shouted. Shortly after, we saw a wave of dark water, rocks, and mud that came rumbling through the riverbed and rolled those who had not reached to save themselves in security, and we could only watch helplessly while ten to twelve of our comrades were led away by the flood. When the wave had passed, I shouted to the rest of the group, ′We must go out and see if we can help the others! Gili, stay with the girls` A few hundred meters further the riverbed, it struck a turn, and there, in a huge puddle of stone and mud, we found our comrades. We pulled the victims out of the mud and carried them to a dry place, where we began to check whether they were hurt seriously. Most had escaped with bruises and superficial injuries, but two had broken legs, one had a broken back, and two others were unconscious. There were only a few who wept while the others sat with shocked gaze and froze in their wet clothes. There were some who ran out to the highway, which was three kilometers away, to get medical help, while the leaders gathered their groups and told them to check whether somebody was missing. When they had calmed down, the leader of the expedition patted me on the shoulder and thanked me for my resourcefulness. I smiled shyly. Smadar came to me and saw long at me. ′Thank you for saving me! ` she said and gave me a little hug. I looked down, shook her hand, and whispered, ′It was nothing . . .` She still looked at me, but I could not look at her and walked over to the injured.

In the evening, we gathered all around a large bonfire to celebrate that the day which, after all, ended with a miracle. Each group performed a little sketch, some sang in the choir, and others played the flute and danced while they drank sweet chicory and ate baked potatoes from the fire. At one point, I was invited to talk about the day but I refused. Gili and I whispered together, and so the circle around the bonfire was turned into dance scene. Smadar tried to pull me into the dancing ring. ′You know that I cannot dance, ` I murmured. ′You can learn it if you try, ` she said quietly. ′No. It cannot do that!" I replied. She turned around and mingled with the dancers, while I was angry with myself over my reluctance and stupid stubbornness. I was aware by now that luck is a combination of charm, resolute action, and creative brain and a chance which appears, and she asked me to dance. Since many people, if not most, guarded their ′flanks` too much, being afraid to fail or become objects of sneer/shaming, they reduced their chances of luck, banging on their ports. And now I did the same as the other fools . . .

I saw a young guy with blond hair approaching Smadar and offer her to dance. He held her hand and put his arm around her while I looked into the darkness behind me. When the dancing stopped, Gili came sweating and sat beside me. ′What the hell's the matter with you?

This dancing is not a part of our oath to wait with the penetration. It is only a prelude` he said. ´You are sitting here all by yourself as if you carry the world's grief on your shoulders! ` ´I am just not in the mood! ` I said, distressed. ´ cannot dance` ´So learn it, dammit. You have learned many things by trial and error. You are not a chicken, so why do you do it against yourself? If you do not learn to dance,

how will you be able to score a girl, you fool? ` he lectured me. ´You're right! I should learn this . . .` I said resignedly. I looked over to Smadar, who sat with the blond guy, holding her hand, and they seemed to enjoy themselves. She whispered something to him, which made him smile. I got up abruptly and started walking away into the darkness. Gili jumped up and asked, ´Where are you going right now? ` I, close to tears, said, ´I need to be alone! ` Then I added brusquely, ´Just keep being seated, I. I don't need you as a nanny! ` I could see that Smadar sent me a long, searching look.

´Why do you make this scene? ` her eyes asked. My heart constricted. It was too much pain, and I could not bring myself to tell her. I was so upset and felt all alone in the world. approached a hill,

which I began to climb on in the darkness. When I came up, I pulled my dagger out of my pocket and was ready, but I could not find out whether I was ready to cry or ready to fight against anything that might emerge from the darkness.

Right there, the moon came up behind a cloud and cast its silver light on the hill. I turned around and saw a figure standing motionless a few hundred meters away. It must be Gili. He cannot let go, my annoying friend. Both defiant and sad I turned, and continued my silent hiking up toward the top of the hill and then down again while the night became cooler. I saw the little enticing stars on the horizon and thought that they could be my torches in the darkness that could show me the way, and then I went through a little goat track down another hill that was bathed in moonlight. Suddenly, I heard a sound that made me stop abruptly and listen, and in the silence, I heard something chuckled and whispered. The gurgling sound came from a rock nearby, and I decided to find out what it was that chuckled. I picked up a stone in my left hand and held the dagger ready in my right hand before creeping silently toward the source. When I reached the cliff, I could see a stream that flowed along the rock wall and went into a recess under it, and that rock was surrounded by desert flowers in full bloom and with a heady scent. I threw the stone against the stone recess to scare animals or perhaps a snake that could hide there, but nothing was moving over the water. Then I continued but made sure to pass the large rock where snakes and other vermin could hide. I collected water from the spring up in my hands and drank from them, and suddenly, it was as if a large gate opened inside me, and I drank and drank while tears welled out of my eyes. I sobbed aloud while I tried to be alert to possible dangers. ´How could you, ` I said to the little brook, ´find me here in my unhappiness? How did you find me all the way from the Bustan? Yes, I drank from your water then in my Bustan, I remember, and now you came here when I needed you most . . .`

The water chuckled and gurgled. The water chuckled again, and I felt as if my pain melted away, and I knew I found the right answer as the brook showed me the way. I knew that i, despite all the hardships that surely lay ahead, would again find the thread that was posted for my life journey, only I had to remember that it was there. I sat by the brook and drank his Bustan water and felt no more pain in my heart, not even the pain of unrequited love, death, or other sorrows.

´Where can I find you again? ` I asked the water. ´Your life journey will lead you to me and to your evolving Bustan…` I seemed to hear. The ear-piercing cries from the wild dogs nearby brought me back to reality, but I was not scared or sad any longer. A starry sky of infinite dimensions was unfolding around me, and a small spring in the desert had just told me that I would one day reach my Bustan and make it evolve further, whatever it meant... I knew I could look forward to a hard and challenging life but that I was prepared to take on, even if the price would be turning my back on love, for an evolving Bustan was the greatest I could achieve. The feeling was scary but also magnificent.

Suddenly, I realized that only people who managed to sacrifice much of their comfort and habits and were willing to wander through real and mental ´deserts` to pursue their calling, were able to rise above a life that is shackled by commonplaces, illusions, and often escapism from emptiness.

I knew that somehow that night, an invisible force had handed me a helping hand to find the secret of creating an evolving Bustan- metaphorically- in the desert.

I heard a shout that faded away in echoes through the hillside. I hurried to get up as I swore to myself that I would not reveal the location of the brook for my friends now, perhaps first many years from now. I left the rocky, dry, and fragrant desert behind and went in the direction of the shouts, which had called me back to the present moment, and when I was halfway down the hill, I saw a figure came up to meet him. ´It is me! ` Gili cried out in the darkness. ´What the hell are you doing here? ` I shouted back. ´What the are you doing here? ` he cried angrily. ´I've been looking for you for a few hours, man!'

´Few hours? ` I repeated uncomprehending. ´You can thank me for not telling the leader on your disappearance. He would have sent everyone out looking for you. It would not have been fun for you! ` ´Pardon, I am sorry for making this trouble. I must have lost track of time! `.

I gave him a hard hug and then looked into his eyes. Gili gave me a hug and muttered that he was alarmed but felt now relieved. ´So what have you been looking for? It can only be heartbreak or revelation! Is it right? ` I laughed through his tears. ´I think it were both at once! ` I said quietly. ´But now my heartache's evaporated and . . . regarding the revelation . . . Yeah, I cannot talk about it yet because I cannot distinguish between what I have seen and what was pure fantasy . . .`

We started to go back to the camp with Gili in front. ′What did you see up there? ` he asked casually.

′I met something that I cannot describe now. Maybe I can do it another day`. we kept descending.

When we reached the camp, I saw that Smadar was waiting for us down there. ′Why don't you sleep? ` I asked her, wondering. ′Ask yourself! I could not persuade myself not to be troubled by your behavior. ` She rose up and hugged me, and I was about to cry and mumbled an incoherent excuse since Smadar looked at me with tears in her eyes. ′What have you seen up there? ` she asked. ′I cannot talk about it now! ` I whispered hoarsely.

The next morning, we continued the journey, and Smadar came to me and asked shyly whether it was her fault that I had gone from the party. I looked at her, cleared my throat, and said in a hoarse voice, "I cannot talk about it now, but I hope that one day I can show you what I've seen. It was great, and I'm not sad anymore! `. ′I will be glad to see it with you`!` she said and gave me a hug.

It was summer 1964:

The Combines drove on the kibbutz wheat fields that stretched as far as the eye could see. They drove day and night, harvested the wheat, and spat straw in bundled straw bales. I and some of the other young people took turns to drive a big tractor with a pickup truck as they loaded the bales up.

Smadar and the other girls also joined the fieldwork, but since lifting bales on the cart was too demanding, she stood on the platform, along with two other girls, and stacked the bales. The sun was going down behind the dusty cypresses, and I was sweaty but happy, and the day's work was soon over. I thought that soon, all who had taken part in harvesting would surrender to a well- deserved rest after the day's work, but as soon as the evening breeze surged in from the sea and summer evening violet silk screen unfolded, I could feel that all my fatigue disappeared. There were some people who laughed and whistled in the gathering darkness, and I heard Smadar call my name in the darkening evening. ′I am coming! ` I cried as I went in the direction of her voice. It was an enchanted evening, and I was excited to tend a fire and cook the food that we had brought with us, and I looked forward to the cool, black, and sweet malt beer. Maybe I would also take courage and put my arm around Smadar's shoulder and look her in the eyes and finally tell her what I had felt for her in the last four years. She was just the most beautiful and loveliest girl I had ever seen, with her golden hair, her cute face with the most beautiful blue eyes, and her slim body and beautiful skin.

She was intelligent, attentive, knowledgeable, and lively. I was supposed to be soon enlisted into the army for two and a half years, so if I was to tell her, it had to be now, I thought. I knew I had to control myself and be open about my feelings. I should be both open and eager but also cautious.

Somebody had lit the bonfire, and she had to be there with the other girls. The fire blazed up, and the people who stood around the fire looked like shadows that danced in black and red movements. There were more and more people coming from the fields, and some of them began to sing, accompanied by a mouth harmonica. Now I could catch a glimpse of her. She turned and looked at me in the velvety darkness, and I went straight up to her and put my arms around her as if it was the most natural thing in the world to do, and she pressed her warm body against me. We kissed, and she pulled me into the circle of the young people who passed the time until the food was hot with three-voiced song. I sang without taking my eyes off her, completely intoxicated by her scent, the smell of new harvested grain and the cool, salty breeze from the sea. I thought that I had never sniffed somebody as pretty and that I wanted to prolong this moment into eternity, and here ended my restless quest. So began another girl to sing with crisp voice, and the mouth harmonica followed, and some of the people stood and started dancing. Smadar pulled me up and began to dance around the fire. I dance! I dance and sing for life! Smadar danced like a dream, and I was enchanted by her beautiful oval face, her elegant neck, and her supple body and beautiful legs. She had a short white dress, a white cotton shirt, and light sandals. She moved gracefully, aware of how beautifulshe was, and every movement pulled me further into a magical universe of love and total surrender.

The food was ready, and we sat on the ground and ate hungrily, holding hands. When we had finished, she jumped and pulled me gently but insistently in the shirt. I stood, and she took my hand and led me into the warm darkness with a dedication I had never seen in her before. ′Come! ` she whispered to me. ′Where to? ` I asked, taken aback. ′You will find out soon. ` She smiled with a cocky kid voice. I turned to her and hugged her, and she put her arms around me and kissed me, and then she freed herself and pulled me away from the noise of the company and to a dark spot in the field, where she again kissed me, lay down, and pulled me down on. All of a sudden, I knew what to do as she turned suddenly into a woman with a glowing sensuality. She moved under me in strong spurts. As I penetrated her, I felt on my back and the shoulder her sharp nails. I was seized by her desire, and we disappeared into a vortex that threw us toward the sky, tinkled and in a gentle motion and brought us slowly back to the present in total exhaustion. We lay side by side on the ground; I caressed her breasts, and she looked up at the moon, which rose against the sky, and whispered in my ear, ′Now you're mine!` ′Yes, I am yours!` I whispered back. ′And you will never leave me? ` ′No, never! ` I replied firmly. ′So it cannot be better! ` she whispered. ′I just have to believe in it! ` ′What do you mean by that?` I lifted myself on my elbows. ′It has nothing to do with you. It's me . . . There is a voice inside me that I need to calm down and get it to be quiet. Don't you have more than one voice in your head? ` she asked, and then she looked into my eyes. I thought about it. ′No, but I often talk to myself in a kind of dialogue, and then we agree I have only one voice, but it can become capricious and also melancholic. It's my voice, but it changes and surprises me all the time, and I do not know always how it will grow up to become more stable. ` ´It was a fine answer. Shall we sleep here tonight? ` ´It is too dangerous because of the wild dogs and tractors, which come when it gets light, but we can go back to the kibbutz and sleep there if you wish. ` ´So you take no chances? ` She laughed. ´Not when I'm with you and not without a submachine gun, but we can do it another time with submachine gun and mosquito net. ` I laughed. She kissed me, and then we hugged each other and did some more things as only young new lovers can do on the way through the fields.

In November,1964 I was enlisted to military service which lasted to the end of Six-day war in Juli,1967.

CHAPTER III

MILITARY SERVICE, MY WARS AND KIBBUTZ LIFE:10.1964-1972

Both humans and animals fight against each other and against other groups, for territories and resources gains, and for dominance.

Historical events: Global reality and my reality converge. The pendule of human conflicts-tensions and short- lived peace.

1965

1. Race Riots Break Out In Watts, California leaving large parts of the city burnt and looted and 34 dead.
2. The Voting Rights Act, guaranteeing African Americans the right to vote becomes law
3. The Gemini Space Program continues into 1965 and lay the groundwork for an eventual manned mission to the moon.
4. The Palm Sunday Tornado Outbreak on April 13th: An estimated fifty-one tornadoes (forty-seven confirmed) hit in six Midwestern states(the first signs of climate change)
5. Dr. Martin Luther King Jr. leads civil rights march in Alabama from Selma to Montgomery.
6. Lyndon B. Johnson announces his program to create Medicare and to expand his war on poverty.

1966:

1. Anti- Vietnam War Protests from 1963 to 1966.
2. NASA launches Lunar Orbiter 1, the first U.S. spacecraft to orbit the Moon.
3. Soviet Union Lands Luna 9 on the Moon in February and the US follows on June 2nd with the Surveyor 1 soft moon landing.
4. Ronald Reagan enters politics on June 7th becoming governor of California

1967:

1. Six Day War between the Arabs and Israel. Six Day War Redefines Middle East's Balance of Power

As a small country surrounded by hostile neighbors, Israel has worried about its security since its founding. By 1967, Israel had already fought two wars (over independence in 1948 and against Egypt in 1956), and Israelis feared that a third conflict was imminent. Egypt's then President Gamal Abdel Nasser repeatedly promised to avenge displaced Palestinians and was parading troops and tanks through the streets of Cairo. In response, Israel launched a preemptive attack against its Arab neighbors on June 5, 1967. These strikes destroyed the air forces of Egypt, Jordan, and Syria, paving the way for rapid Israeli ground advances. By June 10, the land Israel controlled had tripled in size, as it took over Egypt's Sinai Peninsula to the banks of the Suez Canal, Syria's Golan Heights, and the territories of East Jerusalem, the Gaza Strip, and the West Bank. Known as the Six Day War, this conflict redrew borders within the Middle East, established Israel as the region's dominant military power, dealt a devastating blow to Arab armies, and exacerbated the numbers and plight of Palestinian refugees.

2. Following the publication of Ralph Nader book puts pressure on the government and the automobile industry to improve safety in cars.
3. The first successful human to human heart transplant Dr. Christiaan Barnard performed the Operation.
4. The SS Torrey Canyon supertanker ran aground off the South of England causing a large oil spill and ecological disaster.
5. The Beatles release Sgt. Pepper's Lonely Hearts Club Band, one of rock's most acclaimed albums.

1968:

1. Prague Spring: The Soviet Union invades Czechoslovakia and arrests President Dubcek.
2. Assassination of Martin Luther King Jr. Leader of Negro Civil Rights Movement.
3. U.S. Senator Robert F. Kennedy, also known as Bobby Kennedy, was assassinated.
4. Anti-Vietnam war demonstrations turn violent during March in London, England
5. NASA's Apollo 8 space mission was launched on December 21st.
6. North Vietnam and Viet Cong troops launch the Tet offensive.
7. Dutch Elm Disease continues with tens of thousands of trees now destroyed.

1969

1. The first man is landed on the moon on the Apollo 11 mission by the United States, and Neil Armstrong and Edwin Aldrin became the first humans to set foot on the Moon.

and the famous words: 'That is one small step for man, one giant leap for mankind. ` will become part of our history.

2. Woodstock attracts more than 350,000 rock-n-roll fans.
3. The U.S. Air Force closed its Project (Blue Book) concluding there was no evidence of UFO.
4. Golda Meir becomes Prime Minister of Israel.
5. Cold War Sparks Birth of Internet in the USA.

1970

1. The Nuclear Non-Proliferation Treaty goes into effect after ratification by 43 nations.
2. Boeing 747 makes its first commercial passenger trip to London.
3. The Aswan High Dam is completed during July of 1970.
4. USA Invades Cambodia.
5. Cyclone in Bangladesh kills 500,000.
6. 100,000 people demonstrate in Washington DC against the Vietnam War

1971

1. Border battles between India and Pakistan erupt into full-scale war.
2. The Soviet Union launches the first space station, Salyut 1, into low Earth orbit.

1972:

Nixon's Visit to Beijing Restarts U.S.-China Relations.

Summing this period up: Both progress and regress for humanity, while human nature seems unchanged.

In my kibbutz: Pre golden calf period:

In these years, my kibbutz functions still with zeal and a notion of mission, but the cracks in solidarity and determination to continue in this direction starts to show up, as the growing material welfare and free choices of the populations in Israel` cities, attracts more and more many kibbutzniks, who lived under semi austerity for a long time. They want a better life, which later may turn into a greedy consumption, as the case has been in the rest of the world.

My history as a combat soldier and beyond:

On Oktober,1964 I was enrolled in the Israeli armed forces. I was destined to serve in it up to Maj, 1967, if nothing happened to me in the meantime and there was no way out, so I accepted it with very little enthusiasm, as it meant that I had to keep away from Smadar for long periods. It was a rainy winter when we came to the base and from the start of my recruit period, we suffered not just of lack of sleep-we often did not sleep more than 4-5 hours a night, partly due to mentally breaking down drills at night and partly due to guarding duties at night- but also of constant humiliations, no information at all and no right to speak up or complain.

With just two short duty-free leaves-from Friday late afternoon to Sunday morning- in these four months of military basic training- and with three hours′ transport for me to reach my kibbutz, these short leaves became more a stressor rather than a pleasure. The drills started at 5 in the morning and continued up to 22 at night, with surprise drills in the middle of the night. They were very strenuous and demanding and we were not allowed to walk, only to run all the time. It was a demanding period in my young life and it lasted 4 months. The rain kept pouring on our tents in a muddy field up in north Israel and we, being constantly wet and tired, hated this period, but did not protest or complain. I-due to my kibbutz background, being used to hardships, being mentally tough, and trained in social skills- could endure the hardships and got along with most of the youngsters in my unit. There were lots of youngsters from poor and criminal areas in Israel, some criminals and even psychopaths, but there were also some youngsters from other kibbutzim with whom I got befriended and we helped each other.

One of them had a brother who could get us some plastic sheets, so we could lay them over our tents, to prevent the rain from penetrating and overflooding us and our sleeping bags. Another one came from a rich kibbutz and got parcels with food and sweet much more often than I got, but shared willingly them with us, other kibbutzniks. So altogether, being solidarity minded, helping other recruits in difficulties, volunteering when needed, I was again liked and appreciated. They called me Soap, the one who glides over difficulties without frictions and does not complain. But this was what I learnt from my kibbutz life, so I just repeated it in this tough climate.

Looking back at this period from my new homeland (Denmark), I am certain that no current Danish or European youngsters would be able to come through such a period, maybe the American Marines would.

The idea of making us into tough combat soldiers was old British military thinking: Break-Make and Shake. In the recruit period, they break the new recruit as a civil person. They treat you as nothing.

They curse you, humiliate you, shove and push you and scream in your face, but are not allowed to beat you. If you refuse an order, you will be punished severely. Once you pass this period of recruitment, starts the second phase of making you into a combat soldier. There, they stop humiliating you, but the training is very demanding.

When the training period is over and done, they will shake your hand, as you became a combat soldier, a disciplined, killing semi machine. So much I have to say on this in retrospective, but the experience was valuable to me, as it extended the mental/physical boundaries of what I was used to.

I learnt how to be detached, when screamed at or humiliated and how to walk and walk all through the day and night, totally exhausted, and how to sleep very little and still keep functioning.

I remember the party which we held after finishing our recruit period in februray,1965. I remember it clearly because it was the first time where we could fully relax and enjoy a party after the break- make-shake bloody months. At last, the roads and paths in the military base were not ′electrified` any longer, so we did not need to run all the time as recruits. At last, the sergeants stopped cursing us and calling us idiots. Now I could sit peacefully occasionally.

I was assigned to decorate our military dining hall to the party, before I and some others were sent to corporal training period in the desert. My comrades came by and patted me on the shoulder and shared their delight of me being chosen as the excellent recruits in the unit.

As the party started, I looked at the girls who were invited and listened to the music, but I did not get up and offered to dance with any of them, because I had Smadar on my mind and could not dance with another woman. Some of my friends considered it to be puritan kibbutz′ Bullshit and went to the dancing floor with their invited girls. I kept sitting although I was also invited by the girls, but I refused again and again and explained that I could not dance. I thought about Smadar, whom I had not seen for two months, and it made me sad. I looked at some of my soldier` friends, who, as easily and elegantly, swung the pretty girls around, while with great aplomb and agility, pulled them closer and closer to them.

I must concentrate on my tongue's eloquence and on my brain's endowment, but it is perhaps not what the young women look for, I thought to myself. Somebody started singing, ′She loves you, ya, ya, ya,` while the dances became wilder, and then they continued with another song that overwhelmed me: ′If I fell in love with you, would you promise to be true . . .` and my comrades and the girls continued to dance, and a kibbutz friend of mine kissed a girl on the mouth and I did not know what to think about it.

Then he came up to me, dripping with sweat, and took me by the hand while he bawled, ′Do you always need to be such a sad and dried-boned saint? It is a celebration for us, and when do you think it will happen again? Come on, I'm tired of your solitude` Then he waved a girl to me and said, ′Dina! Here sits my best friend who graduated with honors yesterday, and now the corporal school is awaiting both of us . . . He is good as gold and even very clever, and he is popular and sporty, but he cannot dance!

He can dance a little chain dance and circle dance, but the Slow dance that is danced here, he does not know. I would be grateful if you would teach him that! ` he said and kissed her hand. She smiled at me, and I smiled at her. ′My naughty friend is right, although I find it hard to admit it, ` I said hoarsely. ′You are so cute! ` she said, taking my hand. She danced very close, and I tried to follow along and suddenly I realized that I danced and also was about to get an erection. She crept even closer to me under George Adamos's "Tombe La Neigh," and soon, I found myself in a dreamlike embrace with a warm and sensual body and arms that closed around me. And then it dawned on me that Dina, who, five minutes ago, had been a stranger, had broken through my armor, had awakened my libido, and had made me free in a new way. You do not always need to cultivate the solemn love that also can lead to anxiety and idealization of people, I thought. But I was doubtful whether it was this freedom I wished to attain.

Shortly before we should leave to our new training camp in Shivta in the desert, Smadar appeared up with my family in the base. She had succeeded to persuade my parents to make the trip, and we were all happy as it meant that with a little luck, we could see each other more often through the whole military service.

I was sent to the desert for 4 more months for corporal training. When I finished this course, which was physically demanding not the least due to high temperatures in the desert, I was sent to infantry officer course in the central part of Israel, and after finishing it, I participated in artillery officer course. All together it took me about 18 months to advance from recruit to artillery officer. I did not choose this course of events. The army made decisions for me, which I could not refuse.

As I proceeded in these courses, my life conditions improved significantly. In the officer courses, there was no more guard duties, and I got more off duty leaves. I advanced to become a lieutenant in the artillery unit, not of any personal wish but because the authorities decided so. In the end of my service, I in Maj, 1967 I was offered a professional contract but rejected it on the spot, disliking military life. I was in combat more than few times but was lucky not to be hit and injured. As my discharge period came closer, Smadar and I split up, as she came to suffer of some mental problems.

In the start I was unhappy about this turn, but again, I was good at adapting to changing reality, and now I knew I could handle love relations alright.

In Maj 1967 I was discharged from service and in June, the same year I was enrolled again to military service as Six-day war was to break out.

In May 1967, Egypt expelled the United Nations Emergency Force from the Sinai Peninsula and amassed 100,000 soldiers at the border with Israel. The Six Day War had its origins in disputes between Israel and Egypt over the rights of Israeli shipping to pass through the Suez Canal and the Red Sea.

The Six-Day War began on June 5, 1967, when the IDF, led by Chief of Staff Yitzhak Rabin, preemptively attacked Egypt's air force and Jordan attacked Israel. By the end of the war, Israel had gained control of the Old City of Jerusalem and the West Bank (which Jordan had occupied since 1948), the Gaza Strip (which Egypt had occupied since 1948), the strategic Golan Heights from Syria, and the Sinai Peninsula.

From 1948 to 1967, Jordan had controlled East Jerusalem and barred Jews from the Western Wall and the Jewish cemetery on the Mount of Olives. When Israel gained East Jerusalem in 1967, it gave each religious group control over its own holy sites. While the Six-Day War is seen historically, from an Israeli perspective, as a momentous event because of the recapturing of Jerusalem and the overcoming of great military odds, it is also the preamble for many of the conflicts and controversies that exist in the Middle East to this very day (2024. The questions of Palestinian refugees and statehood are directly linked to the events of June 1967. In retrospective cannot blame any side of this futile conflict as strong as I blame it on human treacherous and half dumb war monger nature.

When the war was over, we were in euphoria, believing that now, we would get peace from the Arabs in return for the occupied territories. This was the major hope among Israelis at that time. What did the Arabs do? They held the Arab League summit in 1967.

The 1967 Arab League summit was held on August 29 in Khartoum as the fourth Arab League Summit in the aftermath of the Arab defeat by Israel in the Six-Day War, and is famous for its Khartoum Resolution known as 'The Three No' No peace with Israel, no recognition of Israel, no negotiations with Israel. This was their immense contribution for the immense escalation of the conflict ever since. It was at this juncture of time, when I began to realize that not just people, but all nations and whole blocks can act against their best interests, of sheer stupidity. Ergo, I learn that human beings were not just sapiens. They suffered of spell of self- destructive stupidity.

I believed in peaceful solution many years afterwards, because I assumed that humans, basically, would choose the best solutions and compromises out of given other possibilities, but I was wrong. This was my big lesson on human nature and the divisions and conflicts it generates. I would not be fooled again to believe in the claim of us being only wise.

Slowly it occurred to me, that we-sapiens- are much more fools regarding conflicts and excesses. then we are willing to admit. We are rather often both self - destructive and destructive. Therefore, this conflict like other ones, kept bleeding all parts for no avail, as the favorable conditions in 1967- 1970 passed by the three rejections issued I Khartoum. As a result of this idiotic three NO by the Arabs, I had to take part in a second war, Attrition war against the Egyptians from 1969 to the end of 1971.

I saw people killed and injured, and at least three times I was lucky to escape direct hit, and I came out of my wars in one piece and with my souls intact. Strangely, I am much less afraid of bombs, wars, and catastrophes than most people around me in Denmark. I have not become a daredevil; I just learned to calculate risks and odds and take my precautions…and believing in luck.

In 1967 the world was not peaceful either. The continued presence of American troops increased further and a total of 475,000 were serving in Vietnam and the peace rallies were multiplying as the number of protesters against the war increased. The Boxer Muhammad Ali was stripped of his boxing world championship for refusing to be inducted into the US Army. Once again in this summer, cities throughout America exploded in rioting and looting, the worst being in Detroit on July,23, where 7000 national Guard were bought in to restore law and order on the streets. Around this time (1967-1970), I stopped believing in Utopias created by the fractured, contradictory Homo sapiens.

I became more attuned to the world outside my kibbutz, military and Israel. I started to watch the trends in the world with growing astonishment, as my teenager ideals, did not seem to suit the world around me.

Six days´ war and afterwards:

In early May 1967, I completed my military service as a lieutenant. After I flatly rejected an offer to sign up a professional officer contract, I returned to my kibbutz. I planned to go on a trip to Europe, which should start in Denmark, on which I heard good things from a young woman, a Danish volunteer named Margit. She promised me that I could stay with her and her family.

In a way, I was relieved to be free of the strict framework of military service, and was happy to have civilian routine life, while focusing on my plan and starting on my own initiative student examination studies. Yet often I felt a kind of melancholy. I had created in the military service many close ties, and the distance and my new life routine in the kibbutz made it hard to maintain them. The years where we had been challenged to our utmost and shaken together formed some very strong and close friendships, which only soldiers under difficult conditions can shape, but I also knew that these friendships were bound to die out when life pulled us apart. Like with me and Smadar. And then there was the matter of taking responsibility in the kibbutz working and administrative life. The thought scared me, but I had no doubt whether I should stay in the kibbutz. I was also a little afraid of becoming a hardened combatant and wrote as a reminder to myself, "Miserable is the man who has lost his child heart!" as Lao-tzu had written. I was asked by the kibbutz secretary to consider becoming a teacher. They wanted to make me into a teacher in high school of the local school. It did not appeal to me as I had my father as a live example being forced to become a teacher and dissatisfied with this work all these years. I wanted to travel a bit and then to study at university and I knew that I had both the brain and will accomplish it. I was afraid that without these challenges for me my life would become banal and routine prone without other challenges than those the kibbutz could offer me. I knew I was too restless to settle down in a kibbutz or a bourgeois life for the rest of my life with marriage and family right then. I began working in the kibbutz chicken house with some sixty thousand chicken for meat hens laying eggs, and after one year- in the end of the war- I was appointed to become responsible for the whole chicken business. I was to run this business until I could start in the teacher seminar, which the kibbutz had decided for me, ignoring my wish for a travel for the time being. In the kibbutz, a person could not say no to a job offer or even choose his career, but I was not ready to submit many years of my life to the Kibbutz priorities, and a journey to Europe could buy me time to find out what it was I would like to invest my energy in. So, I told the kibbutz's secretary and his friends that he was planning a Europe trip within two years period.

But then started six days war which changed my view about what I should use my life to. I got tired of people telling me all the time what to do, whether it was in the kibbutz, military and in the Israeli society.

There are no absolute justice and easy solutions for the animosity between people in this pained world as people and nations are infested by double moral, self- interest and short sight imbedded in human nature.

And then the war broke out. I was given a command of artillery unit with 4 mortars, 120 millimeters, and around 40 reservists. Hell broke loose. While I was training with his new unit, I was told to move quickly towards Jerusalem. Roads were blocked by military vehicles, tanks, and armored personnel carriers, all headed towards the same place. It was what they call I military jargon: The fog of the battlefield or Chaos. Night fell on the first day of the war, and I and my force had to stay overnight in a small valley twenty kilometers outside Jerusalem. The next day at dawn, we proceeded toward the city and stopped at the city's central bus station to await new orders. Shortly after, we drove in a long column of military vehicles up the mountains encircling the city and crossed the border with Jordan and down to the first Arab city, Ramallah, where we had our first fight with the Jordanian soldiers, and my crew driver was injured in the back, just 20 centimeters away from me. The rest of the war seemed as a surrealistic dream in which I for the first time in my life saw the bloated corpses of Jordanian soldiers on roadside, wounded soldiers on their stretchers, and plunder that both my own soldiers and soldiers from other units participated in. I wanted to stop it, but my sergeant advised me against it, saying that my soldiers would not listen to this command.

I realized very quickly that all agreed rules for war conduct were suspended and replaced by others and harsher. In Jericho, I tried to take five Jordanian soldiers as prisoner, but they were mowed down by my soldiers before I could force them to surrender. I saw all this and had to accept the grim reality of death, destruction, brutality, and mad euphoria, which bewitched some of my soldiers. I saw the rapidly growing war economy and the robbers that drove their trucks stuffed with looted goodies back to Israel proper. I saw how a distant family member, along with other reservists, break into the city bank and steal millions of dinars. Others got hold of trucks, all sorts of goods, automobiles, and machineries and drove them back to Israel all the while we were fighting. It was something I had never been able to imagine, but now I saw it with my own eyes.

Our unit continued to the Syrian Golan Heights. I was fed up with what I saw, but many of my soldiers were in the clutches of euphoria of the triumph and I had to shut up, as my task was to command them to victory, not being out of context moralist. In Syria, I saw something that I also had difficulty accepting. A Syrian soldier without a gun had strayed into our ranks and had been taken prisoner, and I and another soldier took him to the high commander of the column. When the officer saw the prisoner, he ordered me to shoot him on the spot. I refused, but my soldier was willing to carry out the order and gave the prisoner a moment to make one last prayer, and then he shot him in the neck. I was furious but could not raise objections as we were at war, and I could not defy a higher- ranking officer. I went furiously back to my unit, along with the soldier, but made clear to him that in the future, I would not have anything to do with him.

I met my distant relative after one battle, when my relative and his soldiers crossed my column with trucks with stolen property. This fellow stopped his convoy and came smiling up to me along with some of his men. ´Bravo! ` they cried.

´Well done, boys! We need some warriors like you`. My soldiers, who were tired and dirty, looked questioningly at me, and I had to explain that he was a relative.

My family´ relative asked on the battles our unit had been involved in and pulled me aside and asked me whether there was anything I wished to send to Israel, and I asked him to call my parents and tell them that everything was in good order. ´Was that all? ` he asked and patted me on the shoulder.

´What have you got on the trucks? ` I asked. ´The less you know, the better! ´ he said offhand. ´I know! ` I said. ´So close your mouth! The guys that you see here can be dangerous. Do you need some more trouble than this war? ` I had just heard one of the guys from the column boasting that he had raped a woman in her home and told laughingly that she had been like a rutting goat. ´ Is it a threat? ` ´No, a fact. They are not the best company to mingle around with! ` he said. Then he pulled a pile of crumpled banknotes out of his pocket as he tried to put them into my hands, but I refused.

´Yes, I'm speculator, war profiteer, and I need these guys. We do not live in a fantasy kibbutz. Here, we grab what we can get our hands on . . .` he admitted, gloating about my moral. He pushed back the crumpled banknotes into my hands and said, ´Stop acting like a saint. Saints do not belong in this world. Take what you can get, enjoy it, and enjoy your life` so he gave me a pat on the shoulder and went back to his column. This meeting with my unscrupulous family member and his gang disgusted me deeply, and I was furious.

On the other side, I saw on the battlefield some of my soldiers breaking down and crying because of the fatigue of battle, of overwhelmed by weariness, and because they could not make their mortars shoot when it was needed. For them, I felt compassion and tried to soothe them as much as a twenty-one-year-young officer could, yet I did not trust their capacity to maintain calm under battle after these episodes.

What is my point with these memories? Once you have a chance to see people under stress and strain behave unacceptably or are not able to manage the pressure, you see some of human nature reveals itself.

But my task now was to look after myself and my soldiers, and the other issues had to wait for another time. What the kind of world I've got into, I thought. I thought that we had to defend our country, not to behave callous and disgusting. The ideals of the socialist revolution are too far away here, too lofty here. In peacetime, we in the kibbutz allowed ourselves to be dreamers and fantasize about a better world and better people, but the meeting with the war hit me like a shell shock. At the same time, I had a sense of both responsibility for my soldiers and moral helplessness. This I had to learn to deal with after the war, but how does one come to terms with the boundless greed and evil, which apparently are hiding just under the surface of civility in these people while they harbored deep and close camaraderie with one another? This mixing of the vile with very close relation may be one of life's paradoxes. I shook my head.

I handed the crumpled banknotes out to my soldiers while I still felt sullied by my relative` farewell salute: ´And remember! One day, when you get tired of kibbutz monastery, I can help you with any business. I need an honest man like you. When this dirty war is finished, we will go out and eat at the best restaurant in Tel Aviv. Remember it now, Benjamin! `

The end of the war

We were many soldiers in the bus. We drove northward toward Israel proper. We were dirty and exhausted and lay wherever there was some room. I and a friend of mine were dozing in the back seat. We had planned to do a short stay at the military base, which was also the bus last station, so we could wash and change clothes, and then we would drive to the kibbutz and lay down to sleep in a clean bed. It was the only thing we wanted to do right now. I planned to visit some injured guys in the hospital in the next days. The bus growled, and I looked around me and saw my comrades sleeping in all impossible positions. I closed my eyes and thought about how we could go on after all the deaths We had witnessed to and how we could have confidence in life again and how I could sum up this chapter of his life. 'All right, we won a great victory . . . but we lost some good friends, some died in front of my eyes. Maybe we were not good enough at safeguarding them . . . and maybe I'll never get to feel my heart happy again because right now, it's like, it's completely numb!'

The thought of their death exhausted me furthermore, and I needed to sleep away from my memories, though they are hell vivid. Suddenly, I heard the tune from the bus radio. And through the engine humming, the snoring soldiers, the song spread beyond our tired and dirty bodies, floated through our wounded minds, and embraced me, tired young man, who now had seen and experienced life's brutal arbitrariness. It felt like a caress on my sweaty forehead and, for just a magic moment, wiped out all the dead corpses, the dying screams, and the horror that I had experienced. In a magic moment was darkness displaced while I listened with open eyes. 'Like a bridge over troubled water, I will lay me down ` sang Simon and Garfunkel with their silky voices as a cool breeze in the summer heat, caressing, consoling, and redeeming, and I was there again with them. I whispered to myself: 'It may well be that I am crazy, but I feel that life has been granted me. What do you think? ` I nodded to myself, and life seemed somehow a little easier to bear.

After the war:

The time after the war was strange and a bit confusing. As all my moral principles and values were shaken by the war, and I had to learn to accommodate this new, grim reality, there was something left of me, the old one. I still could function well under strain and proved myself to be a good, tough commander for my soldiers, without visible scratch on my soul, just one nightmare. I decided to live life as good as I could, watching it in the war to be almost worthless or worse, painful for those who lost their dear ones and for those who became handicapped by it. In my kibbutz, a fellow, a bit older than me, was hit by a bullet in his spine and became paralyzed from the arms all the way down. He was already married with two small kids. He was mentally kaput. I could see it. Later, he committed suicide after his wife found a lover. This was my second awakening to the cruelty of life.

So, I went on partying in the kibbutz and learnt to dance slow and enjoy the warmth and closeness for the girls who danced with me. I was not ready yet to commit myself after the break with Smadar.

I became glad for songs from this period, among which was Tombe La Neigh, sang by Adamo. Love was sweet, bitter, and regretful, I thought, a bit sentimental, and it was melancholic. At least I felt something, I praised myself. I did not become numb or hard as an old combatant.

So, I danced with Georgete or Anette while Adamo swayed me away from my reality and memories into a falling snow and yearnings after the great love and grotesque western desperado.

And at the same time, there was much frivolity in the air: In England a new type of model became a fashion sensation by the name of Twiggy and miniskirts continued to get shorter and even more popular with a short- lived fashion being paper clothing.

During these years new Discotheques and singles bars appeared across cities around the world and the Beatles continued to reign supreme with the release of ´Sgt. Pepper's Lonely Heart Club Band` album, and 1967 year was also coined the summer of love when young teenagers got friendly and smoked pot and grooved to the music of ´The Grateful Dead. Jefferson Airplane and The Byrd's`. The movie industry moved with the times and produced movies that would appeal to this younger audience including ´The Graduate` and ´ Bonnie and Clyde. ` Color television sets become popular as the price came down and more programs were made in color. I would not become outdated- I was also part time opportunist, as I had admitted before-so I followed this development of frivolity mentality/culture.

But as I mentioned before, in these years-from 1964 and up to 1972- I spent much of my time gaining invaluable experiences on the dark side of human nature and its immense futility, beside assuming responsibility in my kibbutz.

The wars in which I participated taught me a brutal lesson, yet they too contributed to my view of being lucky. I saw people killed and maimed beside me, but I did not get hit. There was no god in this but sheer luck. I Learnt in the battlefield that luck and coincidence in our lives play a tremendous role, not so much God, as religious people around me, close to me, were hit, maimed and killed.

I learnt that in a fraction of a second, you risk being a lifeless body or a mutilated human being. And if you survive these ordeals, you must be foolish or mentally disturbed not to learn to appreciate and nurture life as a gift. Wars teach you something very fundamental about what it is to be a human being beyond our polished civilized manner and humanistic life view. You come to understand that wars will not disappear from the face of the earth because of naïve, humanistic, wishful thinking or religious scripture or prayers. Only by fundamental change in our awareness (from local awareness toward global one), in our global priorities and long-term goals, we may one day reduce their role in our lives. Nothing less will make them disappear.

My wars had equipped me with the capacity to discern between what is essential and nonessential in our lives and in regard to our long survival as human beings.

I get quickly tired of repetitions and nonsense, which is very pervasive in the talkative culture of our modern times. It taught me also the lesson of ´if not now, when? ` Instead of endless talk, introspection, and reflection, come to the point and act sensibly and resolutely. My participation in wars and my study of the history of human violence and nature have taught me that if you wish to maintain peace, you´d better prepare for war as long as we keep being screwed up sapiens. And remember to build up defenses and deterrence. I came to view the fulfillment of people's lives from their willingness to challenge and fight against their mental and body and soul. Self- destructive people, abusing their bodies and mind, were at that time and enigma for me, as life based on frivolity, but I decided to learn the cause for these so-called aberrations.

My wars taught me yet another lesson: When I was about twenty years old, I met Zorba the Greek. I saw the film and I read the book and fell in love with this intense, dancing man who experienced both great happiness and deep sorrow. Zorba had a lot of chutzpa, a Yiddish expression that means gall, brazen, nerve, effrontery, incredible ´guts` blended with some charm and charisma. He knew how to flirt with life even though life was hard on him. He might have been defined today as slightly manic-depressive, but he had a great heart and brought color and engagements into other people's lives, not always by being very good at what he did, but often because he could shrug failure off and go on living without being broken.

Many people I have been socializing with were so bloody afraid of flirting with life and experimenting with this chutzpa, which is in its neat form a proactive taking chances attitude. When I look around me at the countless Israelis, Danish and other people whom I met and who had had lots of talents, virtues, and potentials and what happened to them throughout the years, I thought of the gift I was granted by adapting my Zorba life attitude. All these promising people, when they grew older, became bloody ordinary. How had they turned into good but ordinary citizens, conforming, self- focused, yet had resigned their dreams and visions? I wondered whether or not they knew why they had lost their sparkling potentials: their culture have not taught them what chutzpah was all about, so they came to use much of their creative energy on guessing what other people thought of them rather than what they burnet for and were willing to fight for. I realized later that it was a part of Groupthink that does this damage to the human soul and aspirations. What a shame!

I become the boss of a chicken farm in my kibbutz.

In the years 1969-1971 I was the head of my kibbutz chicken farm. I did not like this industrialized way of treating them, which became common in Israel at the time. Time became money, also for us, declared socialists. We put these small chickens in cages shortly after they were hatched, and they stayed there during their ten weeks of lifetime. In this period, they managed to gain at least 2 kilos and became thereby very fragile due to lack of movement and too fast growth. In their short lifespan, we had to treat them with antibiotics as they often suffered from all kinds of infectious diseases, due to extreme density. In the areas on the ground, we put so many of them, so they pecked each other to death. They made hellish noise, something that I considered was due to their stressed, abnormal social life and which remind me today-2024- of the noisy communication that we produce nowadays in the public space and in the mass media and our ego centered ′pecking`, which means literally that most people can′t `see the forest, but only the trees`. With the nonsense deluge of the mass media` news, I feel like the biblical Noah`, sending his doves to see whether the deluge is subsiding.

These nonsense` deluge combined wit the ego pecking is a one weighty reason for this ignorance. Unfortunately, when I write these lines (2024) I am certain that modern mass-produced people start to resemble my chicken. Back then I felt a strong distaste to the way we were treating these mass- produced chickens. I had a notion that one day, this degenerated way of treating animals would hit us in the neck in our big cities and mass societies, where people get access to lots of cheap food while being crammed together in a small area as big cities are. I predicted that modern humans would become obese and physically/mentally frail.

Unfortunately, this prophecy has - largely - came true. The chickens in my time lived a total of ten weeks (now adays in 2024, they live an average of 6-7 weeks before being slaughtered), so it was impossible to record their mental state during such a short and brutal existence, but they were stressed and so are we in our big cities.

Over half of the Danes are overweight and in Israel 46% of the population is overweight (2020). The same trend applies all over the world. in Denmark, 46% of 19-year-old girls need psychological help, 10% of all children have a psychiatric diagnosis and the numbers of mentally ill Danes is rising alarmingly and constantly. Mental disorders constitute the largest economic disease burden in society with 25% of the total disease picture, while cancer accounts for 17% and circulatory diseases account for 15.2%.

(The National Research Center for the Working Environment estimates that the total direct and indirect societal costs of mental health problems in Denmark amount to DKK 55 billion annually.

NOK (2017).

I met a Danish girl in my kibbutz. She came as a volunteer, and I fell in love with her. Being experienced in demanding hard life and war, I was inexperienced regarding mental problems, and she had some. I just did not know what it all meant and being rather loyal-I learnt by heart in the military service not to forsake an injured soldier or another human in the battlefield or outside it- I took responsibility for her and backed her up. The idea of visiting Denmark came up.

Yet, the other old voice, telling me to find my calling, kept nagging me. One day I heard the following od story.

It was a good story about the creation of the world. When God created the world, he created three types of people. He created one type, who worked hard, earned his bread in his face's sweat, and followed all the rules. He always went on the same track and was disciplined enough to never come out of its fixed route. This kind of people followed instructions as camels in a caravan, and therefore, man called them camel people. The second type which the almighty created were those who could rise above everyday banalities and hover over life pettiness and generate therefore higher perspectives of life. They observed the world from a bird's view, and therefore, they were called bird people. The third type was strong, enduring, and quickly running people with small wings, who could not lift themselves up because they were too heavy. When they felt in danger or face a challenge, they run away as fast as they could or stuck their heads in the sand. Those creatures, God called: Ostrich people.

Very fine story, I thought, but what then? I asked myself. `What type are you? You must soon decide` I inquired myself. ´ I do not know who I am right now. I do not know myself anymore. I only know that my life is fucked up and confusing right now, and how long it will keep being like this, I do not know. Basta! `.

My second voice asked insistently: ´But if you could choose to be one type, which one would you choose? `. ´In the old days, I would prefer to be alternately a bird and a camel, or both, with both their strengths so that I could adapt myself and switch strategy in line with changing contexts. Right now, I have come far away from these considerations. I just want to live without thinking deep`. But I knew that I have chosen. I did not though have the strength to focus on it right now. I needed peace! I thought to myself that this weariness would leave me soon. Right then I was looking at the clouds, and they sometimes to form as face of some who died in the war. I felt sort of self- pity but I knew it was momentary. ´The dead won´t come back, and I will have to say goodbye to them and move on. I must slowly move them away as the little marble stone I had on my table, further and further away from my focus so I´ll get my vision back! They -the dead- are going to approve of it because I allow myself to rediscover the meaning with my life, and I will not forget them either. ´Do you understand that now I nodded to myself.

´And if it's never going to happen? ` my first voiced whispered. ´It is going to happen. I can see it coming. I will slowly, almost without realizing it, find a small path which will lead me to a larger one that will lead me to my broad, big, sun lighted road. I can see it for myself. The road will come to me . . .`said the second voice.

´Does a road that come to one? ` my first voice said doubtfully. ´Yes, if I will help it actively . . . so my road will come to me! ` my second voice This dialogue in me reminded me of another story from Persia; There lived a time a man named Rumi, who said, 'I was first created as a stone, and it took some time before I turned myself into a plant and then went there again immensely long time before I turned myself into an animal, and then millions of years passed by before I turned myself into the person I am today. What can prevent me from turning myself one day into an angel?'

Rumi knew that our ultimate destination is to transform, further evolve, and improve ourselves incessantly. I felt vaguely that my destiny was to pursue this option, creating an evolving push, but how and what it should be. 'In due time I will find the purpose and the direction. Do you understand that now?'

Bridge over troubled water

It was the end of 1971, and I was granted four months` vacation with my Danish wife. It was agreed that after this period I would come back with her and resume my kibbutz life. I would be sent to a teacher seminar and was supposed to become a teacher, something I detested, as my father had been forced to become a teacher. I was also promised by the committee that they saw light in me and would 'advance me` further, later in the kibbutz, maybe becoming the kibbutz secretary or a political rising star. I said Yes to all their promises, just to get out of the chocking feeling of discussing my future many years ahead. I loved kibbutz life as a child, adolescent and up to the end of the 60eeth, but then I started to get bored as every step along my way was already planned for me by them.

I figured out that I deserved taking calculated risks in my life, throwing myself into some adventures and new circumstance and making some bold steps, as my mind was restless, exploring and knowledge seeking. The idea of having a fixed life on the kibbutz, which my kibbutz life could offer me did not appeal to me at all. Now, the 'ugly duckling` became a full born swan which would fly away from my bonds, attachment, shame, guilt and conditioning. I knew I wanted to learn human nature and history more than anything else, and to figure out where was humanity heading.

I knew I wanted to be Like a **Bridge over troubled water** for people, using my life experience as a combatant to help people. Do you become a better 'bridge over troubled water` experiencing war and expecting them to come again? Can they give place for love and compassion? I asked myself. On one hand I needed compassion to help people, I needed to understand their motives, desire, anxieties, shortly their mental makeup(habitus), but on the other hand, I knew that people needed guidelines as well and a sure hand to help them over what they considered as their crises and difficulties, and I was good at both. I helped my soldiers in hard times. I was both pragmatic, good listener with good overview and strategic view and a scent of idealism and solidarity with the weak ones.

Having this notion, I took in the years 1969-1971, between my work as chicken farm` foreman and my reserve military service with a war going on in Sinai, all by myself student examinations.

I did not understand why they in the Kibbutz gave such a young man as I was in these years, such a responsibility as the be the foreman of this big chicken business. But I was partly a dare devil and therefore, took it upon me. I was also used to act like this due to my kibbutz` attitude (We volunteered without doubts and worries, with determination to do our best).

One summer in 1971, when I was fighting the Egyptians along the Suez Canal as a reservist, a heat wave hit Israel and all the areas around including Sinai, where I fought. The temperature soared up to 50 grades where I was situated with my artillery unit. We could do nothing more than sitting motionless in the shade, but in my kibbutz, the chicken could not manage the heat and tens thousands of them perished in one day, regardless all the effort done as to save them. Lucky me, that I was not thereat to witness this catastrophic day. Could I manage the situation better? No way, but it would´ve hanged upon me as a personal failure, as I was a bloody achiever. So, with three- four time escaping death in my wars and one time evading an economic catastrophe, I figured out that I was lucky. It was the time for me to try my luck somewhere else…

In the beginning of 1972, my wife and I, left the kibbutz for what it meant to be four months` vacation. We travelled to Denmark by sea up to Genova, Italy and then trains all the way to Copenhagen, where I live this very day. So, this tour turned out to become my destiny, where I became a real BRIDGE OVER TROUBLE WATER more than in one sense.

CHAPTER IV

DENMARK: I STUDY PSYCHOLOGY. FIRST THOUGHTS ON HOW WE ARE BEING DUMBED DOWN THROUGH CONDITIONING 1972-1980

The collapse of the utopia of ever lasting peace and the noble man: 1972-1980.
Historical events: The human nature` pendule goes on and on…

1972:

- Arab terrorists murder 11 Israeli athlets at the Olympic games.
- President Richard Nixon visits China.
- SALT Agreement.
- Managua is leveled by an earthquake.

1973:

The 1973 war between the Arabs and Israelis was a watershed for U.S. foreign policy toward the Middle East. It forced the Nixon administration to realize that Arab frustration over Israel's unwillingness to withdraw from the territories it had occupied in 1967 could have major strategic consequences for the United States.

My uncle dies in the war. Oil Embargo by OPEC.

The United States ends its involvement in the Vietnam War after the signing of the Paris Peace Accords.

According to the Vietnamese government national survey and assessment of war casualties (March 2017), there were 849,018 PAVN military personnel dead, including combat death and non-combat death, from the period between 1960 and 1975. An additional 232,000 military personnel were still missing as of 2017, a total of 1,081,000 dead and missing for the American

War.[62][63] Based on unit surveys, a rough estimate of 30–40% of dead and missing were non-combat deaths.

1974

1. IRA begins bombing campaign on mainland Britain.
2. Richard Nixon becomes the first US president forced to resign after the Watergate Scandal.
3. Lucy an almost complete hominid skeleton over 3 million years old is discovered in Africa.
4. The Global Recession Deepens.

1975

1. The British Conservative Party chooses its first women leader, Margaret Thatcher.
2. The Vietnam War ends as Communist forces take Saigon and South Vietnam surrenders unconditionally.
3. The Suez Canal reopens for the first time since the Six-Day War.
4. The Unemployment Rate in the US reaches 9.2% and recession is recognized by President Ford.
5. Britain's inflation rate jump up to 25%.

1976

1. Apple Computer Company is formed by Steve Jobs and Steve Wozniak.
2. The first commercial Concorde flights take off during January of 1976.
3. Jimmy Carter wins Presidential Election.
4. NASA unveils the first space shuttle, the Enterprise.
5. Tidal Wave in Philippines kills 5,000.
6. First Legionnaires Disease affects 4,000 delegates in Pennsylvania

1977

1. First Apple II computers go on sale.
2. Elvis Presley Dies at the age of 42(Show business` exposure and deadly drug abuse seem tragically connected).
3. Alaska´ Oil Pipeline completet

1978

1. Egypt and Israel sign the Camp David Accords.

Following the 1973 Arab-Israeli War, Secretary of State Henry Kissinger brokered a series of agreements, laying the foundations to resolve the Arab- Israeli´ conflict and remove the schism between America's interests in Israel's survival and good relations with Arab oil producers (notably Saudi Arabia). In 1978, President Jimmy Carter built on these foundations to promote a breakthrough to peace between Egypt and Israel. While Egypt deeply distrusted Israel, it saw a peace deal as an opportunity to regain the territory it lost in the 1967 Six Day War, improve relations with the United States, and boost its struggling economy. President Carter invited both countries' leaders to the United States for two weeks of secret negotiations that culminated in the Camp David Accords—a landmark peace treaty between the two formerly bitter rivals. This agreement removed the largest and most militarily powerful Arab country from the conflict with Israel. For decades, U.S. administrations have sought to replicate the success at Camp David, and, today, five other Arab countries—Bahrain, Jordan, Morocco, Sudan, and the United Arab Emirates—have established formal diplomatic relations with Israel.

Camp David Accords Provided Glimmer of Peace Between Israel and Arab World. Will it work in the long run?

2. People Temple Jonestown´ Suicides.
3. United Kingdom - First Test Tube Baby Born.

1979

1. Three Mile Island Nuclear Accident.
2. China institutes the one child per family rule.
3. USSR Invades Afghanistan.
4. Margaret Thatcher is elected Prime minister in the UK.
5. Sony releases the Walkman.
6. Snowboard is invented in the USA.
7. 63 Americans are taken hostage in the American Embassy in Tehran. Iranian Revolution Leads to Severed Ties with United States and growing tension and polarization in the middle East.

My story:1972-1980

Coming to Denmark in the winter of the beginning of 1972 was the new challenge I needed, to shake up some of my habitual vies and convictions. It was cold and the snow was lying in the streets, not white but grey -brown due to the traffic. We got a 2 room´ flat, with a sink. No toilet- there was a common one in the back stairs- and no shower, which was a rather common then in Denmark and Copenhagen in the old flats from the 1930-40eeth. It was my first challenge as I was used to washing myself daily in Israel. Due to the Israeli climate, you had to wash yourself daily-not so in the military service and in wars-, if you did not wish to stink of sweat, but here in Copenhagen I could smell this old, sweaty stench of sweat in the buses, and it was often nauseating.

I could not discern the words in the Danish spoken language, as the sounds of it were far away from the syllables and consonants of Hebrew. When they talked it sounded for me as unarticulated flood of noise. Yet, I did not worry as I knew that I managed more demanding challenges than cleanliness, mentality and language in my life.

I had some difficulties finding myself in the new political and moral climate, which was partly pacifistic, without any understanding of the sacrifices we, young Israelis, had to bear and endure, giving our best years to military service and wars. The young Danish generation which I came to meet through my wife, hold to entirely different value and views than me. They built up in the Danish country a massive rejection or amnesia of their collaborative role with Nazi Germany under Second World War (Of course, I did not mention it to them). They were like most other Homo sapiens who are experts on whitewashing the dirty part of their history.

By now I knew that Sapiens had a very strong disposition to be morally righteous regardless our record, and it also included us, Israelis, who were prone to idealize our merits and high moral.

After the Six-day war, this moral justification became almost a parody, when some Israeli writers wrote that we- the combat soldiers shot at the enemy and sobbed at the same time. So much nonsense has been uttered by humans regarding this matter of beautifying their deeds and misdeeds I figured out that regarding the Danish position under Second World War it was partly alright of them to surrender but why they tried to glorify themselves with their dismal resistance?

Some Danes came to provoke me, asking why one had to fight, if the option of dialogues and compromises were a better alternative. Why should I waste my time in the army? were common questions I was asked by people in my first years in Denmark. Sometimes I could have screamed: ′Cabbage heads, do you know why you enjoy your freedom? You do it because other nations and soldiers liberated you. And the troops from the United States and England serve right now as deterrent against the Soviet Union, letting you live in peace and prosperity. We, in Israel had neighbors who had declared that they wished to throw us all into the sea, so how can you talk to them? Sometimes you have to fight because there is no other alternative` I said to them. ′When your survival is at stake because of beasts like Hitler or other terrible tyrants who slaughter people by the millions you must fight to remove the threat`. I did not scream, I said it politely, but I wondered how historically ignorant and politically naïve they were. Already there I realized how my unique life experience granted me some perspectives on the human condition, nature and...foolishness.

I tried to understand their lives and their grievances, but a lingering feeling of dismay kept surfacing up in my mind for years on. These three very essential human mental coping mechanisms—rejection, idealization, and denial—are essentially universal and help people, groups, and nations to keep and entertain a good self-image and they used it profusely if not excessively.

There is something good which can come out of denying: As Danish people denied their country's collaboration policy with Nazi Germany under the Second World, they magnified all the moral attributes of themselves: being boundlessly tolerant, amiable, and peace loving… which later, backfired in a form of disguised intolerance toward many immigrants and refugees, on top of being self-destructive through all kinds of drugs abuse and alcohol. It is very hard on ones′ psych, trying to play and angel on this blood-stained earth. In Denmark, I learned later that focusing too much on one's own navel and problems is very seductive, and you are inclined to do just that, when you do not have a mortal enemy or great visions to follow. Some people may consider this to be a refinement of the human needs. I would consider it, in their excess, to be a mental trap, which makes people petty, focusing and zooming only on their private sphere and transitory satisfactions.

I could easily become a hateful man with this kind of futile self- introspection. I could hate Germans, Arabs and even all the people who committed pogroms against the Jews in modern history. I could hate the British for what they did to us under their mandate. They say: Hatred and rage against suppressors may lift one into war stage... or into a bitterness cage and always makes one quickly age! But I did neither become hateful nor bitter, because I realized that it won′t be wise and healthy for me. It is enough to be vigilant and avoid being a Love/ compassion idealist.

I was proud because I did not come up with empty words. What I promised to do I did. I was proud because we were in the kibbutz at that time an avant-garde for the working people, because I belonged to the first Israeli generations of Children of the Sun; Free of diaspora` mentality, live of my labor, worked with my hands, and fought in wars.

I gained a life experience which made me realize that I should be thankful for my life, health, clear mind. Life appetite and wish to become wiser.

I read this story of alexander the great which reaffirmed my life view regarding being thankful:

A wise man said to Alexander, ′You have made such a great empire, but it is nothing. I consider it worthless.'

Alexander became very angry. He told the fakir: ′You have to answer well for this or I will have your throat cut. You have insulted me. My lifelong effort and you say it is nothing, worthless`

The man said: 'Imagine that you have become lost in a desert. You have strong thirst. You are dying.I appear. I have a pot filled with fresh water. I say I will give you a glass of water, but for a price. If I ask for half your Empire, will you give it?'

Alexander said, 'If I am dying of thirst in the desert then not just half, I'll give the whole thing. ` Then the man said, ' The matter is closed, the price of one glass... the price of your empire is one glass of water. It's not worth even two cents, because water is free.'

To save his life Alexander was ready to give his whole kingdom. But you have life: have you given thanks for it? You have received free that which you can give an empire of the entire earth for – and you haven't even What man receives for free has no value for him. Existence has given much to me that is invaluable, and I learnt to consider it as invaluable.

In Israel we were taught to bear both an olive branch in one hand and a sword- in the other hand. By the time I landed in Denmark, I knew for sure that I stopped being a pleaser. I was fair, decent, respectful and could accommodate other people` shortcoming as long as they did not bother me with their particularities, especially by being Nudnik (one who nags all the time). I was a warrior, who would turn into a rebel, and one day along the road, he would follow a new course and road, and would develop the chin and the heart to take the beatings which are the inevitable menu for the ones who work on a new road. I found it necessary to turns away from the well-trodden humans ideological Highways, as they did not bring any enduring solace, peace and wisdom to the pained sapiens. I had the guts to envision that one day I would pursue this untrodden road.

I had a vague notion that being a mental warrior-not a jihadist- is the best investment in attaining and obtaining enduring life meaning.

In a series of studies later, researchers have discovered that viewing one's life through the lens of the Hero's Journey – a narrative framework where a protagonist overcomes challenges and undergoes transformation – can significantly enhance the sense of meaning in life. The findings, published in the Journal of Personality and Social Psychology(2023), provided evidence that reshaping personal narratives to align with this archetypal story can lead to increased well-being and resilience.

But as I already demonstrated an independent mind and combinatoric- analytic and visionary tendencies, I started expressing some of them, as a young bird, trying its wings. Some of these attempts ended up in some verbal dog fights with consensus/humanistic loving people, who considered my ideas to be mesotrophic, because all went so well and the future seemed so bright. But knowing by now my history lessons combined with my experience with human nature, sobered me as to believe in our capacity- in our current developmental stage- to bring force a fanciful utopia on earth.

I was proud of us in my kibbutz and in Israel achieving so much by working together and not complaining. I was proud that I learnt to think beyond my naval, nurtured great aspiration and believed in life affirming vision and mission, but I saw clearly the shadows and the beast in humans.

Most of these Danish youth I met were also proud of their country, its inheritance, tolerance, human rights, freedom, but they achieved nothing spectacular in their lives and they were spared of the confrontation with the human beast. They were just ordinary youth which the West mass produced, yet they thought they were special, even superior to some of us, foreigners, still fighting each other in `the jungle`.

The human environment plays most significant role in molding us as both individuals and group members believing in the same convictions and behaving as a swarm, no doubt. The environment constitutes the whole fabric of human society, self -deluded, superstitious, and often sick and irrational, clinging to the collective fantasies of the world. How can you change such a rigid construction to the better, I thought for myself.

By then, knowing much on human nature, it was self- evident that we have a disposition for pretending to be better than we are. There was a disturbing gap between our Talk and our Walk.

When it comes to it, we are partly animals, partly humans and shifting circumstances, bring force, alternately or together, these two parts.

The four months of my vacation passed away and I asked my kibbutz to prolong it. It turned out that my wife had to use four years to get her student examinations and I didn't know what to do. What was I supposed to do? The conflict with my kibbutz became inevitable. They rejected my request, and I informed them that I decided to stay for the meantime. Making this decision I started to learn some elementary Danish and looked for an interesting study in the University, while waiting for my wife to finish her studies. I considered English literature, Anthropology, and sociology but all of these disciplines demanded extra courses which would take time for me to accomplish, so I chose as the fourth option, psychology. In September, 1973, after 20 months stay in the country, I started studying psychology in the university of Copenhagen without knowing much Danish. I was promised that in the first two years I could write my works in English and that was good enough for me. After my wars, nothing really frightened me much.

In March, 1973, working in the Israeli Ambassy as a student, I met a young Danish girl who wished to visit Israel, and working in the consulate, I informed her on the possibilities. At the time my relations with my wife got sore, so I invited this new girl out. This was the beginning of a new and long relation, which eventually resulted in me departing from my wife after much drama. It was not an elegant chapter in my life, but I honestly did not regret it, knowing that being a bit dare devil I could end up sometimes in tumbling, falling down but coming up again.

As I in my relations with my wife and my new girlfriend I played for a while double standard, probably for the first time in my life-it was not just a white lie or a common lie, which all humans use once in a while- it was me cheating for some time-I wondered where I learnt to be cunny and partly opportunistic and scruples. Maybe it was a lesson which the wars handed me without me being aware of it. But what the hac. I had to live with my deeds, trying to learn something out of it but without guilt. I knew for a long time that I was not made of saints′ stuff, and it was alright with me.

Escapism as camouflaged cultural trends/brands:

I read the observation in one of Maxim Gorky` books (My Universities): ′People seek forgetfulness and comfort in their lives, not knowledge! `. The Russians at his time were straight forward people, and expressed this kind of human escapism clearly. The Americans of modern time, so heavily dependent 1) on self- growth and 2) Disney foolish optimism- ′If you wish it, you will get it! `, which is bound to success and wealth- and 3) overflowing positive psychology as the bearing meaning of their lives, were not fully aware that all three attitudes reflected massive escapism. This American over optimism was but a brain washing, mass produced attitude, stinking of superiority of finding the right way to live, but basically it was an escape from both life boredom, suffering and meaninglessness.

I wrote then:

The human Maj flies, shout ′foul` when the others they decry, while both lies and contradiction in their brains programming lie.

There was no Paradise in sight, and there would not be one, being what I knew we were. The human world was crooked!

I reminded myself the story I lately read about an Arabic child and an apple tree:

′A young child who had climbed up on an apple tree noticed that one branch was crooked. He crawled towards it, his mind set on straightening it out. Suddenly, he lost his grip and fell down, sobbing violently. His father heard him and came running. He lifted him from the ground and soothed him. The child, who wasn't hurt badly, stopped crying. Then the father asked him how he, who was such a good climber, had fallen from the tree. The child pointed at the crooked branch and told his father that he had tried to straighten it out, had lost his grip, and had fallen down. ′Silly boy! ` exclaimed his father. ′You try to straighten a crooked branch out, while the whole world is crooked?'

Yes, our human world was crooked, arbitrary, and unfair. I knew it for sure by now.

Part of the blame for the world's state had to do with the way Mother Nature always functions. (It is basically based on a principal of a brutal/parasitic food chain in sharp contrast with our noble moral codes.). The other part of the blame had to do with the developmental stage that we-humans- were in, which was also the outcome of the evolutionary groundwork of Mother Nature. We have become sophisticated social animals who can form and construct our reality, and in this process, we create both progress but also a lot of shit. This is both our blessing/curse, and like Sisyphus, we can't escape this trap as long as we in this developmental stage, and therefore, this human world is crooked.

We dream of creating paradise but can't escape the negative fallout of our actions. Yet most of us firmly believe that we can escape this trap by improving ourselves personally and in groups, or by "second to God," by being innovative.

I just wanted at that time to live in my skin, accept my human faults, avoid harming others on purpose, and find a way to help this pained humanity with some solid and enduring contribution.

But what it should be, was still a mystery for me.

I knew also that most of my life in Israel I was a dedicated Group thinker. I did not try to evade the conventions, which I was taught from childhood. I followed and pursued them. Now, in Denmark, for the first time of my life I was literally free of group pressure and did not wish to replicate automatically what I was taught to think and mean. Now I could think whatever I wished to, still being under the influence of my childhood/adolescence/military conditioning. I read a Sufi tale, which made me wish to break away from my groupthink` mode.

'A man who interpreted a message from the Teacher of Moses as to mean that on a certain date, the water in the world would disappear. It would then be renewed with different water, which would drive all men who drank of it crazy. This man collected the old water and stored it.

When the day came, the event took place as anticipated. The old water dried out, and after some time, new water started flowing. The man walked among the people he had known and realized that they thought and talked in an entirely different way than before. When he tried to talk to them, he realized that they considered him to be crazy. For a while, he drank his own stored water, but since he could not bear his loneliness, behaving and thinking in a different way from everyone else, he started drinking their water. And he forgot all about his own storage of special water, and his fellowmen looked at him as a madman who had been restored to sanity`.

I knew by now that humanity is basically a meme-prone herd. Here we are, potentially unique, and yet we easily conform and become uniform—in the basic things, a herd. Once we concede to the herd mentality, we can be controlled and directed by a tiny few. And we are being controlled.

We are terrified of being ignored, stigmatized, and excluded, which makes it easy to form us into such a conforming herd (we are being conditioned to believe that it is not so by promoting ourselves as unique individuals). This fear of being excluded is wired into our brains for a good reason; our survival, physical as well as mental, was dependent, for most of our history, on us being together with others and getting their protection, help, and support.

I studied Groupthink mechanism in the University. Groupthink, it was written, describes a psychological phenomenon where peer pressure, prevents critical thought. Eight symptoms characterize groupthink: (1) the illusion of invincibility, (2) stereotypes ("us and them"), (3) rationalization ("we can always explain our failings and shortcomings"), (4) the belief in moral superiority, (5) censoring thought, (6) the illusion of unanimity, (7) pressure on deviants, and (8) the fear of exclusion keeping disruptive ideas out and cementing the cohesion of the group.

Once people identify themselves with a reference group (it often happens in childhood), they acquire its shadowy side: semi-omnipotent or vainglorious attitudes sometimes combined with prejudice toward inferior outsiders. This emotional and unreflective reflex is the essence of groupthink.

Group think can also manifest itself positively, as in the Egyptian Exodus, Gandhi in India, the peace march for ending the Vietnam War, etc. As in all human phenomena, it can manifest itself in many variations and directions, depending on the shifting contexts, but its best outcome depends—as ever—on shifting contexts as Time, Place and People.

Now it was time for me to operate both conform in my social and professional relations and try to find an independent voice when it has to do with my thoughts on our current humanity, the human condition/nature and where are we heading as intelligent beings.

In October 1973, in Yom Kippur, invaded Egyptian and Syrian troops both Sinai and The Golan heights, both were areas, where I fought before. I was torn apart regarding my duty to go back and fight, but I had some security duties in the ambassy, and they asked me to stay, so I was glad to use their decision and stayed.

In the very early phase of the war my uncle, aged 33 years old, a father of four girls, was killed by a missile, hitting him in his tank. I was sad to hear it and I was worried because my young brother was fighting down in Sinai. He survived alright. I felt sad for my uncle, who I was attached to, and for his family, but I realized that in the age of 28 years old, I was granted a shield, a kind of mental Teflon shield. I could feel sorrow and even sadness but did not miss my drive and pro-active energy. Where did I get it from, I wondered. It was probably the best gift I have been granted due to my tough background and the much death and destruction I experienced. It protected me against resignation, depression and anxiety. It seemed as I became partly immune to them!

As I pointed out before, I was caught up in a drama with two women which ended with my wife giving birth to my first son on the 15.11.1975, and half a year departure from my girlfriend. This departure did not hold, and we met again and I moved away at last in1977 from my wife, though I kept close contact with my son. It was a painful compromise for my girlfriend, but she chose it. I did not force it and could not do so. My wife and I divorced, and she obtained the flat which I paid for with my saved money. On top of it, she got three times more a month of the child allowance a divorced person pays for the mother. This was my way of settling this matter and it did work right with my ex -wife up to her death on the 25.12.1983.

In these years I felt great- almost without remorse- regardless some deaths and some mess in my private life. I progressed well with my studies. As for my case was with two women, maybe there was some weakness of my character as two women fought to get me. Yes, there must have been some vanity involved in this unfair affair. Did I feel for a short while that I deserved such extra attention? Not at all. I just got into it with no experience at all.

Yet, many of us believe in young age that we are the crown of creation, that we are unique, each of us, and endowed by great tributes. The core problem of human beings is that their folly is not only invisible for them but makes them think that they are special. I probably lost mental balance and fairness by this sudden infatuation.

Serving in the army and thereafter in the Ambassy in the most secretive office there, I knew the Name of the cheating Game, but it was confined to protecting my country and to this affair I just referred to. With the love affair I got it complicated, because I could not make up my mind for a while. I looked at myself with amazement, realizing that I, like most people, could cheat and get entangled in emotional traps.

Cheating and deceiving are not strangers in nature and among other animals, but they have evolved much further with us as to become more than survival strategies.

We can cheat one another and ourselves as well to avoid facing off difficult life situations, to keep up positive self- image and to inflame hope in critical situations. They help to feel good about us and our causes and convictions and, therefore, we use them so profusely. But the risk of them backfiring in miscalculated, vainglorious, and foolish acts are overhanging.

When I was assigned as a psychology student in 1976, to work in a psychiatric department in Israel- my own choice- as a part of my studies for four months period, at the age of almost 30 years, I felt like `coming back home`. It was an open psychiatric department in Ashkelon, Israel, and the clients were all with psychiatric diagnosis and often medicated.

I did experience in this period, many episodes which could have made me think that I was special, but I did not as cow/chicken shit-I worked with cows and chicken in my kibbutz life-made me immunized to omnipotent fantasies. I experienced a psychotic man in the ward which saw me- the newcomer- as a kind of Messiah with the right formula to open Heaven and release him from his sufferings. Of all the staff, he chose me to deliver him. In another occasion as one patient became extremely violent in a group session, and banged down two nurses and one psychiatrist, and broke the nose of another psychiatrist I took part in trying to subdue him… I tried with the other staff members to put him down on the floor, but he did not hit me. When we overpowered him and he got his injection and shortly afterwards fell asleep, I realized that I was the only one from the staff, whom he I did not hit. I assumed it was sheer luck or he did not have enough time to put me in his paranoid human gallery. When he woke up the other day from his slumber, I went to him and asked him for the reason he did not hit me. He told me that I was protected by glowing green aura. Something similar happened with another extremely paranoid man, who tried to strangulate my friend in the ward, assuming that he was a Nazi collaborator. I talked him away from harming my poor friend, who was in a state of chock.

So, what really happened there and in other occasions of similar character? The suffering people just felt that I was on their side, and even in their psychotic state, they did not attack me, but others. This was the point, and had nothing to do with grandiose or omnipotent ideas on myself as a savior of humanity.

Now adays, in the social media as Facebook, I identify not so few people who truly believe that by working on themselves, they can change our world. Their attitude reminds me of the psychiatric departments I had been through, where everything from miracles to great change of humans` mind sets could be achieved by heavenly formula.

Mundus Vult Discipi (The world wishes to be cheated) is the weightiest mental mechanism we possess in distorting reality/our self -view. It manifests itself on both individual and collective levels.

Arthur Schopenhauer, a German philosopher, stated that we will fight to be right also at the expense of the truth or, in his words, "the basic lowness engraved in human nature." Schopenhauer said that if the truth and the desire to reach it were really the most important thing for us, then in any discussion or debate, the only purpose was to discover the truth without any connection to our early opinions.

We would not care if the proven truth supported our opinions or that of the opponent. But in the human reality, what really matters for us is to be right. Our natural bend to be presumptuous does not allow us to admit that our original position is wrong while that of our adversary is right. For most of us, our inherent vanity is associated with lack of fairness. In many cases, speech precedes thought, and even after people understand that they were wrong and that they talked before they thought, their pride does not allow them to admit their mistakes. They will rather distort reality than admit that they were wrong. The truth becomes a lie, and the lie becomes, to them, the truth. For this observation, there are, of course, also exceptions.

From my life on the kibbutz and in my military service and wars I learnt to value simplicity and modesty in behavior and lifestyle. While living in Israel it was easy to follow this approach as Israelis were at that time, if not poor, so very modest materially, so there was no place for Show off and indulging in the god life.

In Denmark the reality was different as both welfare and growing affluence in society broke the backbone of the old moral puritanic life attitude which most of the Danish people were accustomed to, and due to the new bobbling affluence, more and more people became incarnated consumers of goods, experiences, and services (traveling, indulging themselves in all kinds of activities, gourmet etc.). It was the time for the GOOD LIFE, with less God and much more Greed.

I watched this rend with growing suspicion as it was followed with growing individuality and self- focus on account of the solidarity which created this welfare society. I dubbed this trend as: **The corruption of modern man soul ´by compulsive focus on uninhibited greed /efficiency.**

The modern person cannot feel when ′enough is enough`, as he is both addicted to pleasure and obsessed by blowing up his self-image and reckless efficiency. Efficiency was not a life approach I advocated for it was it that destroyed my Arabic Bustan and poisoned the fields of my kibbutz and orchards with chemicals penetrating the groundwater and infested the air with cancerous agents. It was it that made us treat our chicken the way we did, and now I could see it infecting humans` life. I did not like it when I had to slaughter the chicken we grew after 1o weeks. From my point of view, it was a curse which one day would harm us, greedy humans.

Many years later, this efficient lifestyle- Time is money- hit my kibbutz members with much higher frequency of neuro degenerative and cancer ailments compared with other populations which did not have fields to be sprayed with Parathion.

I started talking about **sustainable efficiency**. It was the first time I got outside of mainstream line.

Sustainable efficiency was for me the efficiency in work and living together that did not generate waste, pollution, deforestation, adverse climate change, human drug abuse, mental misery and loneliness in big cities, which worsen the life conditions for both us and all living things.

At the time I was fond of The Wu Wei attitude as illustrated in the following story: ′When Tsekung passed through Hanyin, he met an old man who was about to dig a trench between his fruit garden and the well. Then he filled water over in the ditch with a bowl he held in his hand, but the results were very small in comparison to his effort. Tsekung suggested that he used a trench cleanser that could contain one hundred times the amount of water. This amused the gardener and he said, ′My teacher has taught me that those who have efficient tools also are efficient in their actions, and when they are efficient in their actions, they are also efficient in their hearts. Therefore, they cannot be honest and pure. And those who are not honest and pure in their hearts are without rest and not fit for Tao.

It is not that I don't know of these things, but I am ashamed to use them! ` Tsekung's face darkened, and he walked for a long time before his good mood returned. ′Who was that man? ` a disciple asked him. ′I was told by the master [Confutes] that the proof of an object's worth is its practical application and that the goal to any work is for it to succeed and that one should always attempt to reach the biggest result with the smallest amount of work possible. It is not like that with this man.

He lives his life amongst people without knowing the boundaries of life and is self-content. The demands for success, usefulness, and knowledge of skills will probably have the effect that people lose their feelings. But this man goes nowhere against his will and does nothing that conflicts with himself. He is above praise and blame` (Chuang-Tso, Chinese tale) The words on the gardener summed up for me the problem of our time's efficiency and greed: We have partly lost our souls, minds, mental health, and overview. Money and profit became our subtle yet strongest motivators`.

Equipped with my new designed Sustainable efficiency, I was ready to pursue this new path of rebellion against what I considered **humanity dumb down course**.

So, what could be the next building stone for a man like me, who was thrilled thinking in a new, different way than mainstream people? What about dropping altogether the security garments of conformism and go for a while half dressed?

The chance was granted to me as I was fascinated by old tales, be them Chinese, Japanese, Zen, Buddhist, Taoism Suffi and Jewish. Many of them could turn upside down my views of life, by challenging my convictions.

There was a beautiful, Chinese story about a stonemason.

When he observes a rich merchant coming into his village with his procession, he considers this man to be the mightiest man in the world and wishes to become this powerful man instead of being a stonemason.

A miracle occurs, and he becomes a rich merchant. But he soon realizes that the province administrator is mightier than him, and so he wishes to become such a mighty administrator. Soon he realizes that the emperor is stronger than him and wishes to become the emperor. In this succession of events he wishes to become the sun, which is stronger than the emperor; the clouds, which the sun's rays cannot penetrate; and thus, be stronger than the sun and the wind, which can play with the clouds as it wishes.

He becomes all these things, and he is now sure that he is the mightiest force in the world. Then he—as a windy storm—blows and blows, but a cliff stands in his way and won't yield. Therefore, he concludes that the cliff is the strongest of all forces. He becomes a cliff, and in the morning, being a cliff, he heard a stone cutter bangs and breaks pieces of him…

This was a metaphoric tale for people who were traveling all around the world in search of their true destiny, only to find out that it was, all that time, right there where they lived. It tells the meaningless aim of striving for more/different power because all the while, human power is relative. They can get both power and meaning, if they look closely, at what may lie in front of them, right where they had started their journey. Yet the journey—as this metaphor indicates—is necessary to make them realize this.

It transforms their minds with different experiences and insights but not their basic life situation. Its point is seeking humbleness/humility and the meaning derived by small acts that they attain.

I did not like the lesson. Becoming humble is the result of either fighting ones ego or being subjected to brain washing or/and subjection.

I observe it mostly in the latter situation. We are born selfish, and that takes different forms as we mature. Sometimes humility also has a strong component of selfishness- in disguise.

In some situations, fighting one's ego may lead to humility. Such as a monastic order of monks/ nuns. But I have heard egos are alive and well in there, too!

I did not like that being humble is a goal, maybe for the ordinary, earth-bound multitude of people inhabiting this earth, but the price for sufficing with such a solution, for such one as me would be too high; to stop challenging my own mental prison by accepting that my destiny lied within the confines of humility and resignation? Never!

Leaving the little prison of one's own life to end up in a bit bigger one—granted by altered awareness but with the same settings—is what lots of Homo sapiens soothe themselves with and consider as a great achievement. It is not. It is accepting the confines of one's own life! Becoming rebel who challenges all confines in a life affirming manner and become far sighted wise, moving the boundaries of both human life and our common comprehension is what I thirsted for even if it would cost me the Icarus's destiny in my attempt. I did not give a damn about fear of Hubris after the bullets in the wars left me alive and intact.

The Hallmark of the Enslaved Human Mind

We have just enough religion to make us hate, but not enough to make us love one another.

—Jonathan Swift

I did not have problems with God` existence at all. I could easily accommodate God and all His kingdom of angels and Arche angels and even Satan in my mind, knowing pretty well that they were creations of the human mind. For my mind, God was a good friend as long as He pursued the noble goals of helping humans out of their stupidity, cruelty and other less charming attributes and convictions.

To refer to God the ideas of Jihad or `You chose us of all nations` were again the creation of human minds, splitting humanity into warring groups so the so-called right believers could despise, hate and prosecute the others. This was not the God in my mind that advocated such futile, blood thirsty and self- defeating ideas. It was the Satan in our minds that nurture them. It was obvious to me that we projected out our split-up minds of being both beasts and humans aspiring to become better and wiser, on our gods.

But what to do about such schism which often ends up in blood bath in human history?

Most people are mind slaves of some religion, ideology, doctrine, or their own idiosyncratic systems due to their habitual mind-sets.

Most people seek in their life forgetfulness, reality denial and comfort, not knowledge/ far sighted wisdom.

Yet, Humans are meaning, striving creatures, and the meaning they can extract out of their short lives is mostly bound to some heavenly authority with limitless power, compassion, love, and wisdom or having faith in their own virtues and causes.

People with such mind-sets cannot imagine a meaningful existence without this form for dependence/escapade. They don't know how to generate this life meaning beyond external God and/ or their bloated, unrealistic self-image ('I am superior to others`).

Being servants of God, capitalism, liberalism, communism, or other Isms, enslave our minds as we stop thinking out 'of the box` of rigid constructs and convictions. This state of mind becomes most visible when our convictions fail to serve us as a guiding star for our further progress and further evolvement, and when we wade from failure to failure, into decline, pain, and sufferings, a process I saw clearly in the Arabic world. In this part of the world, they blamed everybody but themselves for their failure. This must be a problems projecting mentality underlying their religion.

It is obvious that most people need such absolute mental constructs that can function as guidelines for their half- automatic actions, free of self- reflections, but at what staggering price?!

I read some papers of Dietrich Bonhoeffer.

Dietrich Bonhoeffer recorded- while awaiting execution under Second World War- a number of his thoughts in a work we now know as Letters and Papers from Prison. One of these essays, titled 'On Stupidity, ` records some of the problems that Bonhoeffer saw at work in Hitler's rise to power. He wrote that upon closer observation, it became apparent that every strong upsurge of power in the public sphere—be it of a political or a religious nature—infected a large part of humankind with stupidity. It seemed to him that under the overwhelming impact of rising power, humans were deprived of their inner independence and gave up establishing an autonomous position toward the emerging circumstances.

The sobering fact is that mentally blinded people—holding to their faulted convictions and faith, thus are prone to repeat their failures—are also often stubborn. They come easily under a spell, blinded, misused, and abused by a religious/ideological /political powerful entity. Being unaccustomed to exert free/critical thinking they become mindless tools, capable of any evil and, at the same time, incapable of seeing that it is evil.

I was brought up to think, but very much from the point of view of ideals and convictions. At least, I was granted some freedom to explore other ways of relating to humans and their reality than pure indoctrination. Most children who attended from childhood religious schools, are not trained to think as to come up with critical questions. They lose the spark of defiance, rebellion and challenge, so essential for a thinking human, that they end up in being half automated beings.

I learnt to think contextually, that changing circumstances, humans, places and time must come forcefully into the equation of the proper thinking and conclusions, instead of innate, rigid thinking and response. I learnt to accept complementary thinking, where difference, nuances and even opposites complement each other instead of the common dichotomic thinking of black- white, right-wrong superior- inferior, bad- good, which is not only primitive but very harmful. Both nations and people excel in this mode of thinking!

Most religious and ideological believing folk feel - even without admitting it openly- that they are better and more right than those who don′t share their convictions and this is the main cause for division and conflicts among people. Of this reason I detest this Biblical sentence on the Jews:′ I have chosen you of all people `

For example, we wasted much time in Copenhagen university discussing the matter of what is more important Nature or Nurture, a futile pass time. People still ask, ′Is it nature or nurture? `. Of course, the answer is ′both.'

Genes have much to do with it. Genes determine potentials and vulnerabilities, but the environment determines to varying degree, what, when, and how our genes are expressed. The environment includes not only our parents but also our families, neighborhood, school, community, and culture. The environment includes the womb we developed in, with variables like the nutritional quality of our mother's diet, any substances she ingested or toxins she was exposed to, and the hormones that flowed through her system.

Yes, it's hellishly complicated.

I became painfully aware of the human forces pacifying people and using them as instrument to their ambitions and goals, by teaching them convictions, not thinking.

I said to myself: Beware of the moralistic people who claim to be paragons of both conduct, ideals and meanings in this muddy human area. They are fake and sometimes even dangerous!

One lesson which I carried out with me all the way to peaceful, tranquil and affluent Denmark and it is still with me in my search for l solutions for the human nature` conundrum: NEVER AGAIN. This lesson from the Jewish long history, culminating in the Holocaust and in my wars, made me militant in mind and warrior in action. I found it as a sign of feeble mind, when some naïve Danes told me that the ERA of wars was over. How could it be over, when we did not put to overhaul our minds, which are partly beastly...but as the Jewish insight goes: If God will, even a broom can shoot, and if people believe, even the gutter is Heaven.

I fortified my resolution with both metaphoric and real stories, proving my unwillingness to compromise on this point.

`On a cold winter day, a little bird sat on a branch on the top of a tree, singing her lovely songs with great dedication. The blowing icy wind and the falling snow made it numb, and eventually it fell from the branch. The numb bird was fortunate to fall down into a warm shit cake,which a cow just left behind. The warmth from the shit cake brought life back to the little bird, and being so joyful for being saved, it started to sing again. A cat passed by, heard the beautiful song, and rushed to the site. He ate the bird and the songs as well! ` (Russian allegory) **and then I read at the same time a real life story told by Elie Wiesel.**

Elie Wiesel, the Nobel Peace Prize laureate, wrote in his book All Rivers Run to the Sea a question that had haunted him as Holocaust survivor—whether the people who were sent to the gas chambers by the Nazis knew what destiny awaited them.

Again and again, he argued that they—including him—didn't know. Yet there were plenty of signs. Fleeing refugees passing the towns and cities where Jews dwelled, BBC and Radio Moscow reporting on atrocities against Jews in their news. Many Jewish towns got the message from other Jews who had escaped from the transportations. But as in Wiesel's town, so as in other towns, these people were considered unreliable, and the events they described were considered improbable. Therefore, Wiesel's family continued, as did many other families, their lives up to the Jewish Passover in 1944, denying the knowledge that they had been offered.

Shortly after the holiday, the German soldiers established a ghetto for Jews in Wiesel's town. Even then, when people still could escape and hide in the mountains, Wiesel's family, among others, did nothing. The family's faithful servant, Maria, begged them time and again to hide in a hut that she had provided, but they wouldn't listen. The first shipment of Jews was sent, and Wiesel's family still waited for their turn to be sent away.

When he began writing about the Holocaust in the fifties, he kept saying, ʹMaria knew, but we didn't.'

He didn't see the oncoming danger because he and his brothers and sisters—with long-suffering history—didn't wish to see that humans have a very sinister core, which can, under certain circumstances, become beastly and murderous.

Therefore, they and he had chosen the world of delusion, which is very common among human beings. This form of stupidity—denial of reality and facts— plays a huge role in human history and in clouding the human mind. It demonstrates how fear/anxiety can easily turn people into blind and stupid beings: what I fear seeing does not exist!

I would never choose this faith in delusion, knowing what humans have done all through the human history. Struggling for change- Yes, but not on the wigs of mass delusion, as humans are both beasts and humans!

I decided that I would fight hard to break this spell put on many people, them being hardwired to groupthink and gullible (and thereby, easy prey for brainwashing propaganda that can mislead us). I knew that choosing soothing delusions was meant to minimize people` anxiety, but when the price was included also stop for thinking critically and hoping that the danger will go over by magic, I consider the mechanism to be dumbing down rather than of granting survival benefit.

Some Danish friends asked me for the reason I went to war twice. I explained them that I had no real choice, as with my and the Jewish folk history, not fighting back and winning means ultimately our annihilation. There was no excuse or dispensation for this observation, and not refusing to do so, was not even an option as it was betrayal of what I stood for both as Jew and a human being. I would probably refuse to go to unprovoked war, but when it was a matter of survival, my options were just null. Therefore I went to wars hoping that I would survive them in one piece and thereafter enjoy the fruit of enduring peace. This was my motto.

It never occurred to me to hate the Arabs so intensely as to wish to rape their women, kill their children, elders and civilians. The focus was on fighting their armed forces and defeat them. I was strongly against killing enemy soldiers who capitulated. They were prisoners of war and should be treated as such. As I told before, not all my soldiers shared this view, but they did not kill civilians, children and women. We did not touch the fleeing Palestinians or those we found in the occupied areas. There was a basic moral code, then.

The war with the Palestinians since I left Israel has become much more brutal with indiscriminate killings of Israelis by them and targeted killings by the Israelis. The beast in men came into the open in this bitter conflict.

Then I was confronted by the idea of jihadists, who were willing to sacrifice their lives to kill Jews/Israelis without any tactical or strategic gains, inflamed by bondless hatred and thus inflaming even more hatred between the two sides.

It was a psychological riddle at beginning: Those people who buy the idea of being Jihadists and thus becoming martyrs, ending in Paradise by killing Israelis, were not the humans I knew, who could think over their actions in terms of gain or loss. These jihadists were not thinking folk. They were rather brainwashed to the level of dumb, emotionally raging/hateful beings! They were creatures of the worst past, and yet they went on the scene in this very present, demonstrating for me, that we can easily be manipulated to become the beasts from the past.

And they had their absolute truth and would not accommodate nuances, differences, and other views. They did not know that there was a Macro dimension for our life, free of vandalism, tribalism, and other human destructive ISM, in which we can transcend and merge one day as one humanity. They knew just Islam, jihadist ideology and that was all. They knew nothing what soever on our defect, contradictory nature, or the fact that human truth was both divergent, relative and absolute, and religions and ideologies did bring most often to divisions and hatred than to unity of this truth.

Many of these people or with extreme Islam as their mental luggage were invited or came to Europe in the years where I studied psychology (1973-1980). You did not need to be very knowledgeable regarding human nature and different groups` incapacity to become compatible, to realize that this experiment motivated partly by economics-need for working power- and partly by naïve humanism which bloomed in Europe as counter reaction to their shadowy collaboration with Nazi Germany (Both Sweden and Denmark) would end up stirring social tensions and conflicts.

At that time, anticipating this unavoidable clash of two different mindsets, religions and culture, I tried to warn the readers of one big newspaper on the danger of importing Middle East problems into Europe. My article was rejected (1980) on the ground that I was fabulating on danger which was not there.

It was an impossible struggle against both hyper-false- moralistic politicians and public opinion which would white wash the collaboration policies by becoming super tolerant and accommodating.

A representative for this `When the saints go marching` Prime minister Oluf Palma from Sweden.

He was both moralist and a fake. This combination is in fact common among people and politicians.

Olof Palme was basically a reformer, but he was also one of Sweden's great speakers and agitators. His passionate commitment and challenging terminology aroused strong feelings both inside and outside Sweden. Some individuals disliked him to the point of hatred and pursued a virtual persecution of his person. I disliked this man, too, for pretending to be what he was not; a man with dignity and moral integrity. I could smell his falsehood.

So here we were in Europe with a social experiments of importing the radical Islam to Europe, and the Europeans letting them come by the drove. A feast of idiots, who would suffer greatly because of this silly utopia. Now (2024), the Islamists talk openly on making Europe into Islamic continent.

I wanted to shout out loud to these 'Feel good` Europeans already in 1978: Read Rabbi Nachman story about the Bird of wisdom and you will know what is awaiting you.

Rabbi Nachman from Breslow described the acquired human stupidity, nature, and magnitude by telling the following story about the bird of wisdom: There was once a king who had dreamt that somewhere in the thickest of the forest dwelled a most exceptional bird that had the wisdom which human beings were in great need of. By attaining this wisdom, they would become peace lovers and fill their lives with meaning, cheerfulness, and humane devotion. The king consulted his wizards and wise counselors, and they all suggested him to send an expedition composed of the wisest people in his kingdom to look for the bird. Once they found it, they should bring it to the palace. After some wrangling, the expedition was prepared and started its way into the forest, where the bird was hiding. After a long travel in the woods, they arrived to a tree, on top of which the bird nested. It was an astounding, beautiful bird. None alike they had ever seen. Now, as the bird was standing on a high branch, they had to figure out how to reach it. They started to discuss this subject very seriously since everybody in this expedition was wise and thus had its weighty meaning. And since they haven't yet come with the bird or the bird's wisdom, they must be discussing this matter to this very day.

Self-knowledge implies constant vigilance against the sneaky onslaught of human institutional stupidity and often it comes nowadays in hyper humanism package. Stupidity is not a new phenomenon, but its impact has grown due to our sheer numbers, our unsustainable and polluting lifestyle, and our self-exposing, pornographic culture, and it was clear that collective stupidity was on the march in these affluence years in Europe in the 1970eeth.

Aldous Huxley said, 'At least two-thirds of our miseries spring from human stupidity, human malice, and those great motivators and justifiers of malice and stupidity, idealism, dogmatism, and proselytizing zeal on behalf of religious or political idols. `

Erasmus from Rotterdam described in his famous book from 1511, The Praise of Folly, the intricate aspects and manifestations of human folly. He reached the conclusion that folly is essential for humanity since humans, at their very core, prefer to daydream, to live in self-deception and pretension vis-à-vis their role and importance. Perceived from this angle, folly seems not just comforting, but necessary for us to bear and come to terms with our lives.

I remember once reading about a Chinese wise man who took a disciple with him, trying to show him the best conduct of life. They came to a place where a tree was standing with its entangled branches in disarray. The wise man pointed at the tree and said, "Here you see how the meek survive longer and better than the others. All the great beautiful trees were cut down, but this one, which does not call for attention, is still here. They went farther and came to a farm where the owner knew the wise man, so he decided to slaughter a duck. His son went outside with his knife, then came shortly back and asked his father which of them he should slaughter, the one which makes much noise or the silent one. ′The silent one! ` said his father, ′because it is good for nothing` ′What is this? ` asked the disciple to the wise man. ′It is opposite of what you taught me. ` ′Yes, it is true, because in life it goes both ways and many other ways,` replied the wise man.

I would not recommend anybody to be meek and self-effacing as a full-time job. This attitude results in becoming both awfully dull and ordinary. You cannot build on this foundation any real creativity, innovation, and wisdom. All these three attributes need courage and some devil daring. What do I mean by that? I was once to a seminar where we were asked the question: What do you like in your life? The question was meant as a guide for telling who we were and how to help us engage, on a personal level, with what we really liked. The other professionals named lots of things like sports, nature, social contacts, traveling, etc. I was the only one who said that I liked to excel and engage in projects that demand hard work, ′sweat and tears` for the benefit of others. I explained to them that by engaging in it, like writing this book and involving many people in the process, I attained the by-product of true engagement—delightful flow. It did not matter if I came to defy some mainstream conventions or break out of conformity and consensus as long as my life was not endangered; on the contrary, the pleasure could be even greater by exploring new vistas of the human existence as long as I did not harm other people. Yet I will go to war if it is justified from my point of view, as I had done it twice before.

When I was a child, I once saw in the children magazine, a sketch of an old Chinese man watching soldiers pass by holding their spears and swords on the way to a war. The old man, tearful, asked the soldiers and the world, ′Why? Why do you have to go to war? ` My father explained to me the reasons for his tears and anguish. The old man asked the question that many people before him had asked and many people after him will wonder over: why do we go to war time and again? Is there no better ways to settle conflicts? Probably, but not under all circumstances! We go to wars because we find them necessary and the alternative as worse. We go to war because war making is an integrated part of our repertoire of solving problems and conflicts as rather primitive Homo sapiens. If we were completely free of this aggressive urge, we would probably pay a price by being without any zeal, passion, and even self-determination. Maybe one day, when we depart ourselves from the gross/beastly Homo sapiens' essence, we will be able to reduce also our warmongering nature.

Attaining great feats:

Seneca wrote once, 'There has not been any great talent without an element of madness`. Madness can be understood also as a behavior characterized by lack of intimidating inhibition, doubt, and ruminations. This so-called madness is spiced with courage, resolve, determination, and even some portions of brutality to reach your goals. Madness involves one's willpower to follow one's own path, to take on a confrontation with mainstream thinking and behavior, and to rebuff sometimes the dominating consensus and accepted norms. This streak of madness does not live in peace with the ideals of easy, leisure-prone, and convenient life, which is the underlying characteristic of most people in Denmark and probably in the West. Materially/ impulse satiated lifestyle, devoid of hardships and struggle for greatness, kills systematically this drive, imbedded in many people, I must admit. I saw many foreigners and Danes being promising/revolting young people, but ended up being conformists. I try hard not to succumb to sirens of this state. Step by step I extend the perimeter of my mental courage and defiance, looking for something new and promising. The modern capitalistic/democratic order, so solidly founded on prosperity, individualism and consumption, will eventually crack slowly due to its visible contradictions, and also because it lacks high motive spurring us to evolve further and it is plainly unsustainable. Too many people, too much consumption and production will generate both pollution, mental and physical problems among us.

I detest too, the big bluff being sold to the masses, telling the ordinary people that they are unique.

The Western societies claim that all people are unique deprives many of them from the drive to become unique, making them complacent/self-sufficient. You need a mental suspension/ exertion of enduring effort for the long-term common well, bound to social rewards/prestige to become a unique by becoming through your deeds a better, and wiser human being. Our individual so-called uniqueness has become, through the commercialization of our minds, our collective trap as it is bound basically to overconsuming and seductive lifestyle.

We were taught that the Jews who served as the founders of Israel and my kibbutz were mental giants. This was part of the ideological narrative but of course it was not based on facts. They had a chance to change history, and they rose up to the challenge, still being faulty human beings. In the neighboring village, people and their children believed in God, while we believed in socialism. Our different faiths were, of course, self-confirming and promoted in both groups a sense of identity through their religious and ideological narratives. It took me time-it happened in my first years in Denmark which gave me the sense of comparison between culture- though, to realize that humans' constructs of reality and human aspirations do shape reality in both constructive and destructive manners. The Jews in East Europe under

Second World War waited for God to save them from the Nazis or… as we, humans practice right now an unwavering faith in our capacity to resolve our growing global problems, all the while, we- in the West- are living more and more unsustainable. When you live in a world with finite resources, you can't live the way we currently live in the West with greedy and relentless consumption, without destroying our life conditions on the same time. This self-destructive behavior is promoted by the narrative of liberal capitalism with its proponents claiming that Malthus would always be irrelevant regarding his dark prophecies on resources qua the growing population, because we are so innovative. Soon according to their hyper optimistic narrative, there would be no hunger, epidemics, and wars. Again, a stupid prediction due to our ideological blindness and lack of knowledge of human nature. When the defining narrative was based on prudence and impulse control in my childhood, moderate progress was achieved with less global self-destructive outcome as the underlying idea was partly sustainability. We control our whims to a certain degree in times of hardships and shortage, but abundance destroys it all as the narrative of cognitive capitalism has proven so vividly, giving free run for our greed.

As long as people have a progressive/evolving vision/mission to fight for, backed up by impending, visible necessity, I believe that we may be able to keep these shortcomings under control, but if we won´t, we will be out fighting for our survival.

I figured out a fascinating way of learning about the human condition and nature by combining my life experience with my knowledge of history and big politics (A must for interested soul in politics is Machiavelli 'book ;The Prince) and then cementing them with tales and stories summing up in metaphorical manner the gist of these insights. These tales must highlight both the experience and its essence and add it as a building block to my understanding of humans and their constraints and lives. This was the process I went through after reading the following story, as I had experienced beforehand the experience of Groupthink from my kibbutz life and the observations of what it implied for us to be rejected by our reference group.

I read about A man who interpreted a message from the Teacher of Moses as to mean that on a certain date, the water in the world would disappear. It would then be renewed with different water, which would drive all men who drank of it crazy. This man collected the old water and stored it. When the day came, the event took place as anticipated. The old water dried out, and after some time, new water started flowing. The man walked among the people he had known and realized that they thought and talked in an entirely different way than before. When he tried to talk to them, he realized that they considered him to be crazy. For a while, he drank his own stored water, but since he could not bear his loneliness, behaving and thinking in a different way from everyone else, he started drinking their water. And he thereafter forgot all about his own storage of special water, and his fellowmen looked at him as a madman who had been restored to sanity.

Yes, most of us are terrified of being ignored, stigmatized, and excluded. We cannot thrive and feel good about ourselves unless we nurture emotionally nourishing relations with other people. This fear of being excluded is wired into our brains for a good reason; our survival, physical as well as mental, depends on being together with others and getting their protection and support. We are willing to pay a heavy prize for being socially accepted and valued, often even to the point of suppressing essential aspects of our individuality or acting like flock of sheep. Due to this mechanism, most humans can easily be manipulated and brainwashed to cling to false and misleading dogmas, be them social, religious, or ideological.

Any attempt to challenge the premises of the group would most likely be regarded as heresy, and the critic risks being shunned or dismissed as a threat to the group's integrity. In fact, the only thing more aggravating to a group than a critic is an idealist who lives up to its stated creed. People use their group′ values to judge their world. If anything, they are black -white judges. Thus, the groupthink brainwashing starts from childhood and its prime motivator is the archaic, universal fear of being excluded from the protection of the ′group`. I decided to break through this invisible′force fence` around us, which incapacitate our potential virtues and capacity to think clearly- beyond or conditioning and convictions, thereby flattens us down to becoming a ′swarm` of ordinary passerby May Flies.

In the 1970eeth I felt a bit alienated from some of the changes taking place in the Israeli society. While I stayed there up to 1972, the aspiration of seeking peace with its neighbors was shared by lots of people. Solidarity and the old spirit of sacrifice for the young country were self- evident. But in my last visits there, I could sense some changes. Israelis in the big cities began to imitate USA′ values and lifestyle. The material good life and show off became also more pronounced, and the right winged and religious parties electoral power grew considerably. They claimed openly that there was no partner for peace on the other side of the border, which was also partly true, when I think of the three ′NO` to peace, negotiations, and recognition of the Israeli state, formulated by the Arabic top meeting in Kart hum, Sudan in 1968. One thing was that the Arabs acted stupidly and delusional in this conflict, but while waiting for some signs from them, the political picture in Israel changed and the settlements in the West Bank, in the Golan heights and Gaza strip got started.

I felt in a way that I become sort of a encapsuled in a time bubble of ideals, values and aspirations which slowly became redundant in Israel proper. young Israelis as well as my own generation became ego fixated and entitlement oriented and mentally softies. They followed the social experiment from the west, where men became feminized by talking about their feelings profusely and weeping in emotional conflict situations.

Some of my friends′ children did not serve in the armed forces, were not willing to contribute for their society, and thought only on their own petty lives, like youngsters in the West.

There were also youngsters who deserted our secular, cooperative, solidarity-oriented ideals and came back to religion. Often these people enjoyed before converting into the Jewish religion the good life in the cities, becoming pleasure seekers, exchanging occasional partners, easy come -easy go, consumed drugs-all these things which we kept away from- and one day they probably felt emptiness in their lives, which they had self- created, as unbearable. Their seduction prone new path turned out to be a mental blind alley for most of them. It brought up pain and doubt, soul-searching and constant self-examination, which I was free for, as I had both a sustaining vision in the making and a concrete mission to pursue (I wanted to help people qua my profession and ideas). My parents` generation, which was consumed by creation zeal, started to die out or was worn down, so their words and experiences did not count any longer. What did I learnt of it? In lack-or in denial- of collective impending necessity and a vision aiming to counter it and overcome it, people are prone to be self- preoccupied to the point of decadence and pleasure seeking as their meaning of life, thus they risk ending up in existential void and therefore seeking back to religion or another transcendence promising ideology, as a baby to its sucker.

31.12.1977: My father death and its lessons

I came back with my girlfriend from a New Year party in the city. It was after midnight. In the corridor leading to my room, I saw a common friend of my wife and me.

She informed me that they received a telephone call informing on my father death the same day. He got a stroke on his way back from the dinning hall, fell on the pavement, unconscious. Then he woke up for a short while and tried to fix his artificial teeth in his mouth, while people were getting him into the car. On the way to the hospital, he passed away, 66 years old. I got sort of numb, as I was in the wars. I thought the situation over. I could not get a flight before four days later-at that time the flights were not so frequent, and it was also New Year- so I thanked the woman for bringing me the message, talked with my girlfriend and we went to sleep.

When my father died suddenly, I was engaged in a training program in the clinical department of the University of Copenhagen. We had gotten our first clients and worked with them under the supervision of a trained psychologist. At the time of his death, I had had two clients, and the work went well with both.

I left for Israel to participate in my father's funeral and then i spent two weeks helping my mother, talking with my brother and sister, and throwing away most of the trash my father had collected in his last years. After this stay, I went back to Denmark and continued my studies. Upon coming back to the training group, the students and the psychologist expressed their condolences and asked me whether I wished to talk about my father's death. I replied politely that I was thankful for their interests and sympathy, but I had some good friends with whom I could talk about such matters. The psychologist was sort of annoyed by my rejection of her ´generous offer` and tried again to press me to ´open up. ` Faced with insistence for ´sharing tears, ` I made it now very clear to her that I chose whom I wished to talk about personal matters. She retreated and I hoped, although annoyed by her, that this matter was settled.

But it was not because I broke an implicit code of psychological truism: ´Let us talk about things that burden you. It helps`. The psychologist could not accept my refusal and became sullen and condemning. Since she could not attack me for my decision, she tried to criticize my work with the clients. But knowing that it went very well with both my clients and being an uneasy target to intimidate (if she pointed a gun at me, it would have been another matter), I refused to give in to her critical comments. I confronted her by saying something to this effect: Well, for me it seemed that both clients have made progress in the areas that troubled them, so what was the problem?

One day I met her in the parking lot, went toward her, and asked her directly, ´Have you got some grudge against me? `. She replied to a bit startled, ´Do you think I have some grudge against you?'

I boiled inside listening to this imbecile psychoanalytic defense, but uttered, ´I am happy to be mistaken` and turned around and went away.

I took on the fight against her implicit intimidation and won it by confronting her on two fronts: (1) by presenting concrete results regarding my clients (you cannot discuss against success, as you know!) and (2) by ´asking` her if she did what she would not admit she did. She had to back out of this ´simmering` conflict or risk me bringing it into the open in the group, something that would have embarrassed her tremendously.

And afterward, she really behaved much better. Years later, she referred clients to me, so the ´undeclared war` was ultimately over.

What was my point in ´caving in` regarding my father's death? Why did I go into this conflict head on?

It was for me a simple matter: I would not accept anybody dictating me on what I should share with them if I did not wish to. I would not accept pseudo intimacy from well-wishing psychologists, from other people, or from mass media show makers who manipulate people to believe that they really care for them. This form for intimacy disgusts me.

This was a matter of personal integrity, and therefore, I went into my Casus belli mode. In our modern societies, in pop psychology and in the mass media, more and more people become infamous in their way of exposing themselves and their person. It is very revealing indeed, and hopefully many of them are not aware of the impression or lack of one, they leave behind them.

In times of mourning and difficulties, although we may be much more sensitive than in ordinary times, we must remind ourselves who we are and wish to be. We have to insist that our personal integrity is much more important to our lives in the long run than accepting ′soft‵ group pressure and coercion or intimidation from authorities. It is clear, though, that if the consequences of my attitude were extremely severe—like being thrown out of the university—I would reconsider my attitude because what really matters is the price, we pay for being who we like to be. If the price is too heavy, it may look heroic to take on the fight, but it is stupid; and unless you are born stupid, you should think of other options.

I just don′t understand why people are mean:

I kept warm and close relations with 4-6 old friends from our kibbutz. One of them, a woman, with same social, educational background as mine, surprised me one day by sending me a letter on how difficult it was for her to comprehend that people could be so mean to each other.

What seemed to be self- evident for me due to my life experience -she had the same kibbutz war trauma in 1947-8, but did not participate in wars as a grownup, as I did, as girls were exempt from combat duties- was unexplainable for her. It was of course a mental blockade, denying what she had experienced on human nature as a child and holocaust survivor.

My friend wanted very much to take a course in criminology dealing with human evil and cruelty. The reason for her choice, was that she would not accept, emotionally at least, that human beings were both ′good and bad‵ and that they could become, due to their brain wiring combined with certain circumstances, devilish. She did not accept that a lot of human cruelty and malice were in fact the outcome of emotional, mental, and institutional, shortsighted stupidity; that cruelty and malice were both inherent in and acquired by us. We just needed to have real or self- created enemies to detest and hate them, viewing them savages, inferior, sub humans and a threat for our way of living.

This episode brought me back to the time with the flower power hippies who came to our kibbutz in the late 1960eeth. They were borne by this old utopia, that we could nurture love and compassion and harmony among us on the account of our negativity, potential hatred and paranoia. They had to drug themselves these ideas surge up occasionally, mostly among young people as a sort of winter influenza, though hard one, as many of them destroy themselves by getting depressed and by drug abuse.

Upon finishing my studies:

In June 1980, when I finished my studies in the University of Copenhagen, my wife and I went to Greece on a summer vacation. I was proud of my accomplishment but kept it to myself.

One day on top of a mountain where our town was situated, we saw a man cycling up toward the top. It was a very demanding ascent, but he did it at last. We stood there and watched him working his way up the mountain and when he reached the top, I complimented him for this and came to talk with him. He came from a rural part of Spain. He asked me what I did, and I explained him. He was still polite when he expressed his reservations regarding my new occupation, telling me that all these problems modern people are burdened by are the results of thinking too much. The best medicine for these problems was albeit him, hard work. I told him that I partly agreed with him, since I came from a similar background where we had worked hard since childhood, but I could not agree that everything could be solved alone by hard work. I tried to explain him the principle of ′everything with moderation and with some sense of complementation. 'That too much hard work may lead to too much repression or lack of any reflection and the breakdown of ones` body. That work can help as long as it bears meaning and does not break us down as well as understanding of core problems can help in finding ways of solving them. That too much thinking is as bad as too much labor without thinking and reflecting`.

I do not think my argument made a great impression on him this very day . . . but we never know, when we don′t meet the person again! Working as a psychologist, I realized time and again, that insights which I uttered in a session and were not accepted on the spot, where used by the clients and upon meeting them, they stated them as their own invention.

Later in my life, I came to think of this Spanish man riding up the mountain and his simple life view. At the time, I talked with a Danish star in the entertainment business, who had suffered from compulsory thoughts ever since he was a child. He earned good money and could allow himself to get out of bed whenever it suited him. Fighting his compulsory thoughts and rigid mental system became our focus in the therapy. We came to identify, divert, and undermine them, while agreeing that some physical work would be a good counterbalance for his circulating thoughts. And he did it: He found a two-day job in a carpenter workshop, and truly enough, not having the luxury of time to think too much, since he was preoccupied by his new job, his obsessive thoughts became much weaker.

So, in the summer of 1980 I was a graduate psychologist with a yearlong internship′ contract with Rigs Hospital, psychiatric department, the flag ship of Danish psychiatry. A better start for myself, who was under tipped, due to the fact that I was a foreigner without a language fluency, I could not wish. My formula of both working hard and focused and learn well in an innovative manner proved to be holding.

CHAPTER V

FUNCTIONING AS A PSYCHOLOGIST: 1980-2000

The human condition/nature.

Historic events:

1980-1989:

Important historical/psychological observation in these years:

1. The Soviet Invasion of Afghanistan in 1980.
2. On June 5, 1981, AIDS Struck the United States of America.
3. A Regional Debt Crisis Was Started by Mexico in 1982.
4. The Internet Was Created In 1983.
5. In 1983 Over 241 Marines Died in A Terrorist Attack in Beirut.
6. In 1984 thousands of Chemical Deaths Occurred in India.
7. Indian Prime Minister Indira Gandhi Was Assassinated in New Delhi in 1984.
8. The Terrorist Attack on Air India Flight 182 in 1985.All 329 passengers were killed.
9. The 1986 INF Treaty Marked the Start of The Cold War's End.
10. The Lockerbie Bombing of a Pan Am Flight In 1988. 269 passengers and staff were killed.
11. The Fall of the Berlin Wall in November 9th, 1989.Euphoria and hopes for a better world.

1980s: As the Soviet Union Falls, Liberal Democracy Rises: The West is in Euphoria of a new utopia` world and The end of history.

In the late 1980s, the Soviet Union was on the brink of collapse. The country's economy was creaking under the strain of a costly military intervention in Afghanistan initiated in December 1979. Meanwhile, domestic problems—including the Chernobyl nuclear meltdown—led to outrage among Soviet citizens, who felt empowered to voice frustrations thanks to political reforms by Soviet Premier Mikhail Gorbachev. These factors, among many others, led to the fall of the Berlin Wall in 1989 and the breakup of the Soviet Union in 1991. After nearly half a century, the Cold War ended in a triumphant moment for the U.S.-led Western alliance. From the ashes of the Soviet Union arose more than a dozen new democracies; indeed, the world appeared to be on the cusp of a new era in which peace, liberal democracy, and free trade would prevail. But since 2005, the world has become less free and democratic every year in a concerning trend known as democratic backsliding.

1989: Tiananmen Square Massacre Demonstrates China's Intolerance of Dissent

Important international events in the world in the years 1990-1999:

1991: United States Leads International Coalition to Liberate Kuwait.

Yet, the 1990s is often remembered as a decade of relative peace and prosperity: The Soviet Union fell, ending the decades-long Cold War, and the rise of the Internet ushered in a radical new era of communication, business and entertainment. However, the decade was not without violence and tragedy, including the Bosnian genocide, the Rodney King beating and subsequent L.A. Riots, and the bombing of the World Trade Center. The Columbine High School shooting marked a solemn chapter in gun violence, and the devastatingly deadly Oklahoma City bombing by a domestic terrorist followed lethal standoffs between federal agents and armed civilians at Ruby Ridge, Idaho and Waco, Texas.

The emergence of Google and Amazon fueled the growing popularity of the Internet and forever changed everyday life.

A combination of factors led to a realignment and consolidation of economic and political power across the world, such as the continued mass-mobilization of capital markets through the wave of neoliberalism, globalization, and the end of the Cold War caused by the dissolution of the Soviet Union.

1992: Will the world become a cooperative global village?

Maastricht Treaty Lays Foundation for European Union.

1992 - 1997

Countries Promote Global Cooperation on Climate Change.

Climate change is a growing global concern, but its deniers are countless and sabotage real progress. Human denial of growing body of irrefutable facts, indicates that human nature has not changed.

1993: a new beginning or another self`- deceptive trap?

The Palestine Liberation Organization Chairman Yasser Arafat (R) shook hands with Israeli Prime Minister Yitzhak Rabin (L), as U.S. President Bill Clinton stood between them, after signing the Oslo Accord, in Washington, D.C., on September 13, 1993.

Oslo Accords Offered Chance for Arab-Israeli peace, or did it?

This intractable conflict seemed to demonstrate some mental defect in Hom sapiens, wishing to reach peace, yet sabotaging it all the time.

1994: Global humanism is but a wishful thinking?

World Fails to Respond to Rwandan Genocide.

In 1994, UN peacekeepers monitoring local elections in Rwanda stood on the sidelines as simmering ethnic tensions erupted into genocide—more than eight hundred thousand Rwandans were killed in just three months. The failure to stop this violence—in addition to further atrocities unfolding in the former Yugoslavia—led, in 2005, to UN members endorsing the responsibility to protect (R2P) doctrine, which states that countries have a responsibility to protect their citizens and, if they fail to do so, that responsibility falls instead on the rest of the world. In other words, countries can use all means necessary—including military intervention—to prevent large-scale loss of life. The R2P doctrine represented a potentially meaningful shift from previous decades in which unilateral humanitarian intervention was considered an unlawful violation of a country's sovereignty. However, the doctrine would lose international consensus in 2011 after a once-narrow humanitarian intervention in Libya quickly evolved into a destabilizing regime-change operation.

How was life in the 90s?

The 1990s was a decade of extremes and contradictions. Americans built bigger and more elaborate homes and drove more expensive automobiles, then worked longer hours to pay for them. Americans spent more, borrowed more, and went more deeply into debt.

Persian Gulf War. Eastern European Communist Regimes Fall. ...
South Africa Repeals Apartheid. USSR Breaks Up. ...
William Bil Clinton Elected President. ...
North American Free Trade Agreement (NAFTA) ...
Nelson Mandela Elected South Africa President. ...
Taliban Seize Kabul. ...
Hong Kong Returned to China.

Summing this period up: Regardless our educational/spiritual efforts and self- realizing projects, **HUMAN NATURE** did not change. It kept being partly deranged. Being unaware of our conditioning due to our nature, nurture, narratives and life experiences, most people kept being faulty thinking replicators!

My story as a psychologist, starting by learning the human nature /condition.

'The graveyards of the world are filled up by people who believed that they were indispensable.'

And if you wish to know, how important you are, without being useful/constructive for your surrounding and civilization, put your finger into a glass full with water, and then draw it out. The hole you left in the water tells how important you are.

These two insights became cornerstones in my view of both the human condition and in our aspirations to break away from this unacceptable destiny of pretending to be what one can only be by his proactive contribution to humanity long term survival /evolvement.

By practicing Psychology, I came to know myself, my reality, human nature and the world much better than before, as they are as-contradictory as they seem to be- are deeply interconnected.

I did not follow the popular preoccupation most people in my environment pursued, self-realization and growth. What is the enduring value of personal growth, I asked myself, ending in imminent death, if humanity does not change to the better? Nothing, as a man and his actions end up in oblivion.

I did not find my essence being so exciting as to track all the time my thoughts and feeling as to reflect over them. I did not buy Dalai lama` misleading quote of us-each of us- is the universe. I was a fraction of society, where I could contribute my share, without any influence on the universe…

I found the self- realization focus a rather phony project of two reasons: 1) When your whole focus is on pecking on your own little piece of ground, you know nothing of the world beyond it. If you don't know the history of man (including its infested illusions, delusions, and blood-stained journey), the history of human nature (and how conflict filled we are), the dynamic of politic (self- interest precedes often moral), you will never know yourself. 2)Self – knowledge means engagement in the huge project of bettering humans and humanity, not just you, which implies collective energizing vision/mission to follow. Otherwise, your self- knowledge and -growth is a mere private matter.

Therefore, I concluded that the project of knowing yourself is a farce if it is not connected with knowing the world/reality and human nature.

´If by the time we're sixty we haven't learned what a knot of paradox and contradiction life is, and how exquisitely the good and the bad are mingled in every action we take, and what a compromising hostess Our Lady of Truth is, we haven't grown old to much purpose. `--John Cowper Powys

´I am quite sure now that often, very often, in matters concerning religion and politics a man's reasoning powers are not above the monkeys. `-Mark Twain

As a psychologist, trying to teach people to resolve their problems, to improve their emotional balance and to think more clearly, attaining some overview over their lives and humanity´ zig zagging course, I realized to what an extent we are being brain washed by outer forces assisted by our own mental deficiencies.

1. We've been dumbed down by the Public Education system.
2. We've been indoctrinated by the corporate-owned mass media.
3. We've been socially engineered by Hollywood movies, pop culture music and TV programming.
4. We have supported this dumb down process by being enslaved by our dichotomic thinking and acting and...
5. By being enslaved to Mundus Vult Decipi (The world wishes to cheated, and therefore it is cheated)

I identified Sapiens` Achilles hales:
Sapiens is a cheater and a self- deceiver.
He is absurdity/miracles` blind believer.
He is also a failed past lessons retriever,
and facts/overview/far sight´ receiver.

Saving the escapists, semi beasts?

Humankind is a patchwork of escapists:
Narcissists, hedonists, nihilists, masochists,
sadists, idealists, realists, exhibitionists,
self- focused propogandists and utopists,
being kept together by the grand spirit
of the pragmatists/evolutionists,
who add stardust in this pack of semi beasts.

Realizing this state of man, which means that many of us are kind of mere blind replicators, I had to identify a comforting aspiration:

Therefore, I had a dream serving me as a light beam:

That one day humans will stop their self lies and vice
And will become benevolent, far- sighted and wise!

On September 1980, I started working in the psychiatric department of Rigs hospital under the wings of both psychiatrists and clinical psychologists in the department. I, being ambitious, wanted to prove that I was a promising young psychologist, and was eager to get in touch with some psychiatric patients believing that I could help them with my knowledge, enthusiasm and skills. I was, of course, without experience regarding this category of patients, who were often swing door patients. I did my best and probably for the first time in my life, put so much of my ambition into curing some of them, that I started to feel exhaustion trying to help them. It took a month or two for me to adjust my expectations to the real world, yet it taught me also another lesson: That my enthusiasm and courage could inspire these suffering people, but not at any price. I would not burn myself down due to my ambitions.

One assignment which I got by my supervisor- a drunkard psychologist- and a young psychiatrist, was to help a woman in her late forties out of her anxiety regarding a lung ailment she was suffering of(cystic fibrosis) . Both my supervisors told me, that she pretended to be sicker than she really was, and could live very long time with this ailment. My task was to get her out of bed, train her to walk again and motivate her to engage in physical exercise that would made her fit for fight. I accepted the task by these authorities and pursued it. I got in touch with the woman, and we both liked each other. I also talked with her husband, and he was very much supportive regarding my help. I visited her twice a week and she did great progress. She got out of bed and walked with me longer and longer distances. She was very happy to see me, talked with me and did much to please me by walking longer and longer with me. But then I realized that she got blue lips and fingers walking like that, and I became alarmed and asked my supervisors, if they were sure that she did not suffer of this progressive ailment. They admitted reluctantly that it was a serious lung cystic fibrosis, but she could live with this at least ten years more. Ups, I thought to myself, how come they made on the first place such misjudgment. I went back to her and upon observing her having breathing problems under our exercises, I decided to stop them and told my supervisors that I found these exercises counterproductive. I talked with a doctor in her department, and he conceded that she had maximum 2-4 years back. I became angry at my supervisors but as it was teaching job, so I had to keep my temper down. How could they bring me into this bloody situation with a woman who believed in me and in my competence and I was bringing her to total exhaustion?

Then there was a big teaching conference about a week after I stopped motivating her and I was supposed to present this case with this woman, who believed in me helping her so much, and how I was misinformed about both her diagnosis and prognosis. I was to present how I came to motivate her and how she did fine progress until I saw her blue lips.

I did my part, stood on the podium and told the audience my version of the story, without, though blaming anybody for the bad judgement or supervision. When I finished, the psychiatrist who instructed me, went on the podium and told the audience, that she just died two days ago. I sat there in a strange state of mind, digesting this news and just did not believe my own ears. How could they misinform me so badly on this woman, and then again did not inform me before the conference on her death? I went back to my office and said nothing, but it was obvious for me, that my respect for them was gone.

In the psychiatric department, they started the first course for training psychologists and social workers to deal with sexual problems of clients. I was invited and learnt what we called at the time; sex therapy. Very quickly I figured out that most of the sexual problems people suffered of, were of psychological origin, yet we learnt to focus on the symptoms. Nevertheless, it was a good experience, as I was not familiar with talking with strangers and clients about their sexual problems and less so, by assisting them to resolve them.

Coming from a puritan kibbutz education, this seminar made me overall more competent to deal with the multitudes of psychological/sexual and social problems countless humans suffer of.

In this period, I met Ruth, a clinical psychologist from the team in the Hospital, who became my good friend.

Ruth suffered from the age of 17 of degenerative muscle atrophy and when I met her, she moved around in motorized wheelchair and had an assistant on her side. She could not do practical work, but she was an imminent psychologist and a great diagnostic expert. Due to her state, she suffered a great deal and had to sleep in her last ten years connected to a lung machine which kept her breathing. I visited her often and fed her two dogs. She was a person I really respected both for her endurance and for her sharp mind. She was both tough and wise, and she in fact encouraged me to start writing, and came to read my first works. She was also a medical miracle, living with her condition to the age of 70.

There was also another psychologist, a woman in the team who taught me to test and score the tests. One day she became angry at me, as I wanted to go back to the test` scoring and told me out of the blue that I would never be a real psychologist. I did not understand where this vicious comment came from. I just looked at her and said: ´We will see!'

Later, I figured out that she was diagnosed with breast cancer and was probably uptight. She lived long enough to realize that her prophecy on me did not come true. On the contrary, people who had tried to intimidate me, were both rebuffed and proved wrong in their negative predictions.

Working as a clinical psychologist with my background, it became my motto to build for my client's sustainable bridges between the ′mud of their lives and the twinkling stars, we strive to attain/nurture. I had learned a lot from my clients, sometimes through their own ways of dealing with difficulties and crisis, sometimes through their ways of relating to the world and the human existence as a meaningful journey. I was more than once been asked by my clients: ′Have you got a mission, Benjamin? ` ′Why do you ask? ` I retorted. ′It looks as though you have one! ` I heard some of them say. Once a very special client asked me, smiling: ′ Have you got a mission, or are you just a transitory wanderer here?` He cancelled the next appointment and just disappeared, so I did not get to answer him. I do not know what he had gained by our talks, but his question rotated in my mind ever since. Have you got a mission in life? What a question to ask. Yet all of us have a ′mission` even though we tend to ignore it due to life's hardships and temptations and our survival struggle.

I got my mission presented for me as so often, through a tale of wisdom. I read a book: The Way of Man, by Martin Buber, where he tells on a Chassidic rabbi, who was imprisoned for suspicion of conspiracy against the regime. The commander of the prison visits him and wishes to catch him in religious contradictions. He asks the old saga: ′How come God asked Adam: where he hid himself after eating from the Tree of Knowledge 'Where are you, Adam? If this God knows all, as you Jews present Him, why does God ask this question? `

The rabbi changes not only the context of this discussion but also its focus by telling the commander that God is all-knowing, but the question should be understood as God's inquiry to all Adams who have existed since the first Adam: ′Where are you in your life? Are you hiding from yourself and me? How are you shouldering your responsibility to find the way of meaning within your life? ` And the rabbi ends the discussion, telling the commander: ′And you are forty-six years old. Where are you, Adam?'

Adam tells God, ′I am hiding! ` so, he knows he is hiding, escaping his responsibility. Acknowledging this, he has made the first step toward an awareness of finding his way— his responsibility to repair the human world by bettering and developing the human soul and mind.

I did not need God or religious tale to confirm, what I grew up to believe in. I just needed the nod of this wise tale to remind me, in the bustling life of material adulation and individualism worship, to wake me up to my forming mission!

The generation of Bon vivant people: The times are certainly changing

In human behavior, I observed, repeated exaggerations are often signs of mental strain, indications of compulsive personality and lack of emotional balance.

At that time, I came to know both Danish and Israelis living in Copenhagen, who I would characterize as Bon Vivant folk. They lived for the sake of their own pleasures, and lacked other external goals with their lives. Many of them were total failure in nurturing long term relations or committing themselves to family and children. They seemed to love only themselves, their freedom and pleasure beyond everything else.

The transient nature of our existence can affect us in various ways. Caring more, or caring less - living for sake of pleasure, escapism, blind faith, or living with purpose to repair the human′ world and the human mind. It is a tug-of-war at times.

Knowing these Bon Vivant people, lacking higher motives than pleasure, I figured out that they were possessed by lust monomania like excessive sex, travels, drugs, booze and other self- destructive habits. They were in this sense compulsory, and their driving force was, mental strain and anxiety from the void, thus they were driven by their demons, writing their lives on the water.

To me, it seemed as an exaggeration of our idea of individualism which can generate diffuse anxiety, which can also be disguised as narcissism, and the idea that we are very important without any credit. We are mainly important for our usefulness, which can encompass many things.

When I started to practice as clinical psychologist, society became richer, and psychotherapy became more legitimate in the eyes of the public. As years went by and more and more people asked for our services, I realized that my occupation is based on a paradox, as most of human existence is. On the one hand, we attempted to bring well-being into the life of tormented people (and often succeed), but on the other hand, the human mental misery seemed to swell and grow throughout this period due to growing estranged, isolating, and stressful big city life and the lack of close contact with both other people and nature. There had been a sharp increase in the last sixty years in the prevalence of mental problems like chronic stress, sleeplessness, depression, and anxiety in the world population all due to modern lifestyles in mass societies. The litany of human misery kept growing dramatically ever since I went into this business, even though the numbers of professionals in the area have soared also dramatically in the last forty years+. This paradox made me realize that although we helped people on individual and social level, we basically mended and patched them up, without addressing other human aggravations affecting us both physically and mentally, like our modern lifestyle, economic priorities, ruthless competition, societal and traditional dissolving trends, and, not the least, our lack of unifying and elevating common values and vision. Two aspects attracted my attention: the state of human beings adjusting to modern life or rejecting it, and the state of the planet that started to go from bad to worse.

I slowly began to realize that most people are conditioned to become loyal to their religions, ideologies, nations, sects and current life style and the values they are embedded with …and above all, they are addicted to their short -term self- interest. This is what happened in West Europe in these years. From the 1980eeth on, they opened for big- scaled immigration/ refugees coming from incompatible religious/cultural backgrounds, as Muslims from the Middle East, Africa and Pakistan, most badly educated and ill prepared to think free and critically. The Europeans political leaders let these people in, being steered by their hyper humanistic declarations on tolerance and multicultural and pluralistic societies. They could see what happened in USA or Israel with their suspected declarations on the positive impact of melting pot process, but the fact remains that, when different groups of people not compatible in culture and religion, are pressed together, ghettoes will rise up and they will have conflicts with each other in hard times. Yet, Europeans being renown for their appeasing and conflict avoiding behavior after World War II, have chosen to bring this future calamity upon their populations… and it will surely come within 50 years from now (1980-1), if this source of immigration will continue. In this respect both the economic growth proponents and left winged idealists played masterfully the role of useful idiots for future religious/cultural flare ups in Europe.

How can they be so foolish, I thought. It could be partly because Mundus Vult Decipi, steers us so often. People, regardless how well educated they are, can believe in ideals and utopias, not learning human history and about human nature and its pitfalls. In my class in my Kibbutz, I read on the multitudes of false saviors and messiahs the Jews had in their time in the diaspora. They were fooled time and again. Multi-cultural society, without common values-religious faith makes this impossible- is in crisis time a ticking bomb.

The way most people think:

'Human beings have a strong dramatic instinct toward binary thinking, a basic urge to divide things into two distinct groups, with nothing but an empty gap in between. We love to dichotomize. Good versus bad. Heroes versus villains. My country versus the rest. Dividing the world into two distinct sides is simple and intuitive, and also dramatic because it implies conflict, and we do it without thinking, all the time`-Hans Rosling

I became aware of the drawback of our dichotomic thinking, when I observed people suffering of it.

It is not just beneficial in making you right, good and wise and therefore superior to the others, while you opponent contains all the negative aspects, which can make both reality check problem solving into a nightmare, but it can hit you within.

Lots of Danish people with whom I worked suffered of trying to be perfect- good, just, wise etc. suffering thus of two mental afflictions: worries and bad conscience. Many of them felt bad conscience because of a little conflict they were involved in or by some "forbidden" thoughts they cannot accept. Their thinking was dichotomous thinking prone. I had to remind them that in the world of reason and wisdom, we were judged only by our actions and verbal expressions, not by our private feelings and thoughts. In the world of the shadowy Lutheran church or other strict moral and religious institutions, you were judged also by your own private thoughts. This idea of fighting "bad and forbidden" thoughts, which did not damage anyone, was psychologically completely foolish yet in line with our dichotomous thinking mode. It is crazy to demand from our minds to think only right thoughts, because our minds would always come back to these ′forbidden` thoughts if we were not allowed to think them.

The way societies` function and make priorities: The fools` invisible game.

In all political systems, people are brainwashed to follow/adhere to a common narrative for the group to promote cohesion and unity. It glues people together in destiny and often also in purpose/aspirations. What makes a difference regarding the impact of this brainwashing, is the level of the force, duration, submission, persuasion, and seduction which are applied. I was as a child/young adolescent exposed to socialism/communism` supposed bliss and superiority over other political systems. It turned out that I was not so gullible as most people are when it comes to accepting religious or ideological so-called truths. This fact that most people become uncritically hooked on some ideologies and religious thinking to the point of blindness, is why we-humans- must sober up and drop the futile fantasies regarding our chances to win globally over autocrats, tyrants, plutocrats and religious Ayatollahs. They all appeal to a part of humans′ primitive minds. It is a bit easier to fight against Unsustainable, short-sighted, hateful prejudiced and warmongers among us and for global cooperation than to subdue the fools among us. The light of our further evolution is turned on, but nobody seems right now to be at home...

Our short sight or rather foolishness manifests itself beyond political systems or religious affiliation. It is a part of who we are and drives most of our unsustainable and destructive economy, demography, and ecology.

Mogens Kischi

I came to think the other day, noting the huge profit Novo Nordic, a pharmaceutics concern in Denmark had earned in the last years. It is so profitable because there are many sick people in the world (Diabetes, obesity and other ailments). Most of ´these ailments in the West are caused by unhealthy life style like fast food (resulting in obesity and often diabetes), sedentary life style, massive abuse of drugs and alcohol and massive air pollution, cosmetics, plastic made various products, and contaminated water, roads and soil. On this self -produced misery a huge medical industry has evolved and flourished, making huge profits; The driving force: stupidity of the masses and unscrupulous greed exercised by the Concerns! The same mechanism I observed with military arms industry. The Concerns producing these weapons gain huge profits. The only thing they need are some wars and meat grinders and young soldiers who serve as Cannon feed. to do such a business, they need ceaseless tensions, conflicts and wars in the world. USA has shown to be an expert in this area. Once again people are being brainwashed that wars are a necessity. In both cases ordinary humans have been manipulated to become USEFUL IDIOTS for both old, ingrained narratives and those who profit by them. These are the forces behind our civilized facade.

Three types of harmful, useful idiots clot the human landscape: the manipulated ones(parrots),the manipulating ones of reality(often politicians), and the ones who know what is going on and are still accomplices to this absurd, self- destructive theater.

My question is:

Can critical thinking be taught to people who are brainwashed by ideologies/religions and lack life experience out of their mental environments and their groupthink? I doubt it.

Claiming mainly in the West, that we can teach critical thinking to anybody is humbug, as it demands varied life experience, good mental capacity, independent and proactive mind and understanding both complicated human nature/condition and life and human history from the recipient, and how to alternate between shifting contexts, complementation of contradictions and avoid fanatism.

My relationship with God is simple: He dwells in my mind and He wants me to evolve further as to defy sapiens mental/cognitive constraints

Abundance of hope and expectations from Human` dolls theater-kings queens and other saviors, show men and influencers, and waiting for the coming of the Messiah, are the comforts granted by the deceiving Satan...

We all know the mental benefits of believing in something, be it God, great ideas, medicine, New Age holism, or placebos. But we also know its downsides. People can be so damn convinced in their belief as to become stupid, dumb, and forget that in the human reality, belief in itself is not enough at all. Eleven members of my family in Poland believed in God and ended in the German gas chambers. Placebo is fine with me, religious belief is also fine with me, but there is no substitute for our capacity to correctly read shifting contexts, in our ever-changing mudded reality and act on them also in a preemptive manner. With only belief and without these skills to understand, and manage our antagonistic and complex reality, your faith will often shove you into conflicts, bloodshed and hubris. Compulsory Behavior and religious faith often hang together. In one of Luis Bunuel's movies, an agitated young man, who is married to a beautiful young woman, becomes suspicious of her loyalty to him and torments her. He believes that she has a love affair with another man and becomes totally obsessed by this misconception. When his jealousy peaks, he plans to murder her and burn down the house where they live. With what is left of his sanity and willpower, he realizes that the devil has taken control of him, and he leaves her and the house. Walking down the stairs on his way out, the camera follows him and his bizarre compulsory walk. Years pass, and the obsessed young man has become a monk in a monastery. He asks his former wife to visit him to apologize for his erratic behavior. She comes with her new husband, and the monk asks for forgiveness, explaining that at the time he suspected her for being unfaithful, he indeed was possessed by the devil and therefore he could not see clearly. But now, dedicating his life to God's work, in God's house, he has saved his soul and won both peace and clarity of mind. The woman accepts his apology, and she and her new husband drive away. The redeemed monk, relieved, walks up the stairs in the same bizarre and queer manner as when he left her.

God and the Devil May Complement Each Other if They Do Not Keep Fighting Each Other.

The following little story illustrates our essential dilemma regarding finding the appropriate balance in complementation: When God created the earth, he was delighted and pleased by his masterpiece. He looked at the beautiful earth, the green grass and trees, the colorful flowers, the roaming animals, the blue sky, and the white clouds and was proud of his feat. Then the devil stealthily arrived and stopped beside the Almighty. The devil clapped his hands with great enthusiasm and exclaimed, ′This is incredible, fantastic, amazing. Only you, the Almighty, could create such a thing. ` He paused, looked at the Almighty, and whispered, ′Wouldn't it be a brilliant idea to regulate this?'

The cunning devil within us, takes our godlike, beautiful fresh creations and turn them into something black-and-white systems, rigid patterns, and repetitive rites, debasing, burdensome, and boring, by seducing us to institutionalize our creations and creativity. I contend that life's complexity is present not just in antagonisms but also in the fascinating interplay between them. I do believe that through this interplay, we can create new properties and possibilities, which black and-white thinking are not capable of. The devil is in our minds as well as God—if they interplay in a balanced manner—support and supplement each other in our minds. If God creativity gets the upper hand without too many regulations, the devil power may be -in the long run- weakened. But if the devil gets the upper hand in our minds, people become detached from their creativity because of fear of failure and resign into ordinary, replicating, ritualistic lives.

God and science project human nature:

It happened in the waiting period in the summer of 1967. We were waiting there in the military camp. Would it be an all-out warrior will a solution be found in the last moment. Lots of religious people, including rabbis, came by, telling us that we would win since God was on our side. In the same time, they pressed skeptics like me to open our minds to God and accept the Jewish faith. One evening, we had a lecture on nuclear power; and after it, an argument ensued in my unit. A rabbi told us that the way atoms relate to one another, shows again the omnipresence of God, because this plan is so intricate and complex that only such Almighty could both design it and make it operate so smoothly. Already in some religious scripture, the idea of the atoms was extensively discussed, he told us. I said something to the extent that as long as natural forces can be attributed to an omnipotent designer, we could call him God, if he wished. For me, I told him this was not an issue. 'Where we look differently at things is that you attribute God a moral stance with a moral authority, a God that can punish and reward. You pray to Him and live according to your faith. I do not find the effect of such godly morality in our lives. ` He said that that the moral aspect is integrated in nature and natural laws. The lecture on atomic bomb illustrated that if we do not follow God's ways and try to change God's creation, we are being punished as the case was with atomic bombs. When we let the 'daemon comes out of the bottle` against God's wish, we are punished for it, he insisted. 'And how would you consider atomic power, where we 'restrain the demon' and which we use to produce electricity and energy for development and improvement of life conditions for lots of people? ` I asked him. Well, he said, this is an act of 'correction. ` As you know, we have 'correction of sins.'

Sensing that the discussion turned into Pilpul-arguments and counter arguments- I left the discussion there, as the war started and both religious and nonreligious soldiers died in it on both sides. The rabbi was convinced in his arguments, but I kept wondering over how he could identify—in the face of impending war—any godly morality in nature and in the natural laws guiding our lives and making us kill each other time and again. Where was the evidence for it? No wonder that when religion and science collide, it is like watching two combatants from different planets.

In my work as a clinical psychologist and by reading research conclusions on the mental state of the Western populations, I started to realize, that `something was rotten in the Kingdom of the West/world'(that regardless our efforts, people get more mentally disturbed).

Are people in our time more mentally disturbed than before? Yes, due to extreme individualism in a complex, mass society devoid of collective purpose and great mission for them, lack of nature and social skills (many are addicts to electronic devices), density, illusive possibilities, environmental pollution and noise, they become more disturbed! Are they become also dumber? I started to wonder.

Individualism is highly extolled in our modern society. Carried to an extreme, the self becomes the main object of love/caring. Family life and monogamy require sacrifices that can be enhancing - and sometimes - detrimental to self-development. But self- love alone also hampers a person's mental/spiritual growth. The line in Brave New World comes to mind: You buys your ticket; you pay the price.

The plague of perfectionism -1982

One Saturday when my son and I—he was seven years old at that time —went on a morning walk, we saw a child playing with the sand, his bag lying beside him. I asked him who he was waiting for, and he said he was waiting for his father. His mother who divorced the father did not wish to see her ex-man and sent the boy down to wait for the father. ′How does your father look like? ` I asked. ′He is very big and very strong. The strongest man in the world, ` the boy said. ′Well, is he bigger than me, ` I mocked him. ′Sure, ` he said, ′he is as big as this building` (which was thirteen stories high). My boy began laughing silently, pretty much aware of the fact that the boy was fantasizing. ′Are there people who are as big as this house? ` I asked. ′Yes, my father, ` the boy said. We wished him a good day and walked away. ′He is not really wise, ` my child said. ′There is no human being who is even as big as a one-story building, ` he said. ′Yes, ` I said, ′you know it, Daniel, because you know the facts. He has no facts in his mind, only fantasies.'

12.1983: Determination for fighting for a good cause

I remember the time after the funeral of my former wife. She died at the age of thirty-four and left me with our son, who was eight years at the time (1983).

He had seen her collapse all of sudden on the floor and sink into deep coma from which she never recovered.

Shortly after the funeral, people came to express their condolences. My son stood beside me, and three of her girlfriends came by and talked to us.

Anybody who had been through it knows how hard it is to say something sensible in this situation. They were tearful and emotionally shaken, but what one or two of them said to me just did not please me at all. They said to me in lowered voice, ′Poor child. It will affect him for the rest of his life, ` or something to that extent that he would not get over it.

I looked at them, feeling my glowing white anger rising in me, and said coldly, ′He will! Be sure of this! ` and I probably sent them one of my less-gentle expressions.

I reacted instinctively yet in accordance with my life view. Life may sometimes be hard on us, but if we are determined, get support and encouragement from other people in the right manner, and take on the protracted fight to come up again, we will prevail. And guess who was right?

He grew up with this fighting spirit, and he had done very well although life was not always gentle toward him.

This, fighting to prevail and find new meanings, is in my view the best way to build up good self-esteem, especially if you learn to appreciate your victories and accomplishments.

I remember another significant fight I had with my mother-in-law, a goodhearted woman whom I have loved very much. But she tended to worry too much, and I found it very tiring and life inhibiting.

When our children were small, there was no limit for all the bad things that could happen to them. They could get sick and hurt themselves; and, therefore, we, the parents, were reminded time and again to take them to the doctor or the hospital. And how dare we take them on a vacation to Turkey, etc.?

I asked my wife to tell her mother to stop this worrying chatter because I did not wish to let her infect our children with her worries. I said to my wife, ´It is better you do it because it will be gentler than if I do it. You know me, once it comes to showdowns that I find essential; I can be a bit brutal if people keep annoying me too long.`

My wife did not do it, and then came a day when there was no way out of this showdown. My little child had some fever, and on the same evening, my parents-in-law were invited to eat supper with us, and I came home late after a long workday. When I came in, my mother-in-law made me aware on the spot that our little son had a high fever and a stiff neck.

I checked with my wife about this matter of ´high fever, ` and it was not alarming (37.8°C). I asked my son to move his neck backward and forward, and he did it without difficulties. ´Are not you going to call a doctor or take him to the emergency? ` my mother-in-law asked me. ´No! ` I said. ´We wait and see.'

We all went into the dining corner and sat down, and she looked at me with this reproaching glance and asked me if I was not worried about how my child had it.

´No, ` I said, becoming really irritated.

Then she started telling me that we were not responsible, etc., which was my Casus belli. I told her—while her husband, my wife, and our two children were seated around the table—what I thought about her worries and spells of panic, and I told her furthermore that she would not be allowed from now on to influence our children with her worries.

We were the parents, and we were the only ones to decide what to do, and nobody was going to interfere in our upbringing unless asked.

My children and wife sat and watched the fight. They were all prepared because I made my children aware of her excessive worries and told them not to listen to them, telling them that too many worries affect not only our possibilities in life but our self-esteem as well. My wife sat silently because she knew I had to take on this fight with her mother. She tried to reply, but I did not let her ′off the hook` (I was angry as hell but kept to my point on her worries and unacceptable meddling in the upbringing of our children), and then she started to cry. I told her that I did not have anything against her; on the contrary, I loved her, but these interventions in our upbringing and all these worries were not acceptable to us anymore. I gave her a hug, and they went home. From this moment on, she did not intervene any longer.

1989: The stupid naiveite of western intellectuals: The pendula of utopian/dystopian stupidity.

Mogens Kischi

If you wish to identify instantly a stupid person, watch him/ her talk. Their binary black – white declarations and moral judgement regarding complex human phenomena's expose them.

As time went by, I become more and more convinced that human stupidity is the major reason for humanity` failings and intractable problems. The most crucial struggle we must wage is against this growing mental degradation of human thinking, as we destroy our life conditions on earth.

The writing of the book on The end of history(by Fukuyama) convinced me that stupidity dwelled everywhere and infected all sorts of people, regardless their social/political standing and educational background and achievements

What did Francis Fukuyama write about?

Fukuyama is best known as the author of The End of History and the Last Man, in which he argued that the progression of human history as a struggle between ideologies was largely at an end, with the world settling on liberal democracy after the end of the Cold War and the fall of the Berlin Wall in 1989.

What we did we get instead: Neo liberalism& liberal-American- hegemony and heedless consumption and greedy, self- focused, narrow- minded citizens in the West.

How could we keep recreating fantasies on human utopia on earth, without focusing on the most crucial element to attain something like this, our nature?

I thought at the time: If it is so good, why is it so bad?

A well-functioning democracy is based on imparting its citizens with human rights/ obligations and enlightenment/ free of brainwashing commercial/consuming thinking. Do we practice imparting enlightenment and demanding obligations in return for rights from our citizens? As I see it, we dumb people down by consumerism and infotainment, and lots of citizens are being put aside as useless, human trash.

How neoliberalism affects the poor right now in 1989?

Higher rates of poverty; less protection against poverty, unemployment, and healthcare risks; social exclusion.

1990: Casus Belli. If you avoid crucial conflicts in your life and try to contain them as the only solution, you invite both anxiety and resignation into you mind as consistent bedfellows.

The idealists among us-and they are many- believe that humans can contain pure love and compassion regardless of circumstances. Of course, reality tells a different story... Basically, as they are lots of bad people in the world, there are also many useful idiots and idealists. but as we say about the uncompromising, dim-witted believers: if God will, even a broom can shoot…

The medicine against anxiety and mental paralysis: Learn to fight well-1990-2.

Twice in my working career, I was on a collision course with people with whom I had been working for years. This is something rather likely for anybody who dares take on a well-justified fight in the workplace where he spent twenty-four working years, as the case was with me. In the first collision, I chose to fight 'dirty` to the end, and in the second collision, I decided to fight in an 'accommodating manner, ` using my opponent's mistakes without smirking them for this. The outcome in both was the same. I name these episodes because I consider both to be relevant to my emphasis on the 'art of skillful war` once imposed upon you. If you have forgotten the gains from a good fight, I wish to remind you of it: it builds up your mental backbone and self-esteem as well. In my case, I used these experiences to grant myself the courage to follow my 'maverick's instincts,` taking risks in thinking differently and following premises that do not always conform to mainstream thinking, which this book expresses clearly. The first episode involved an article I sent to the psychological magazine in my home country. In this article, I cited in two lines some statistic from my own workplace. This citation evoked anger among my partners with whom I worked for years, and the subject was taken up in our weekly meeting. The arguments I was confronted with were the following: 1. Who gave you the 'green light` to present statistics from the workplace? 2. 'Your figures were wrong, and you with this article may destroy our business. ` 3. 'How come you draw your conclusions in this article? `

It was very clear to me that they did not want me to write anything that implicated our workplace. I was angry at what I considered to be hysterical outburst, considering the scope of this matter, yet I decided to be wise in this conflict. I said to them in our first meeting that it was fine with me not to write anymore about anything concerning our workplace. It was also fine with me to send a written denial to the magazine concerning the statistical fault. And then I said bluntly that what I wrote about, did not implicate our workplace and how I came forth to my conclusions was none of their business, and I had no intention of discussing this with them. All that I wrote about was conveyed by me, and I took the responsibility for my thoughts. You can agree or disagree, but I did not owe them any explanation on how I drew my conclusions in our free country. There was no objection from their side because they could not refute such argument. So the 'battlefield` premises were defined by now, and we concentrated on drafting a written denial to the magazine. Knowing them well, I suggested that some of them would write the denial and I would sign it up and send it, to which they consented. A week was gone and we met again to see the draft. It was three pages long (my statistic figure constituted of two lines). I saw it and asked them 'innocently` if they wished to send such a lengthy response, especially because no one, so far, reacted negatively to my article. They discussed the matter and decided to shorten it. Next time, a week afterward, the draft was shortened to half a page. I repeated my willingness to sign it up and send it. By now, three weeks after the first encounter, some of them noted that nobody had commented on the article and asked whether it would be wise to send a refutation to something nobody noticed and thereby create a problem that was nonexistent before. They agreed and decided to wait. More than two years have passed since this encounter, and we 'kept waiting. ` How did the battlefield of this encounter looked like to start with, and how was it transformed by them and me? To start with, they got panicked and reacted too strongly, which is understandable if people were not aware of, that most of what we write and talk about is not remembered the day after, including what newspapers write and mass media people utter. I knew for the very start that their reaction was not well proportioned. I knew that two lines would not destroy our reputation and economy. I accepted the ′blame` for the citation and the statistic faulty quotation and accepted the consequence—a refutation with my name. No big deal for me because I accept mistakes when I commit them. I stabilized my ′front` by refusing to talk with them on other matters such as my motives in writing what I wrote. I waited patiently to see them ′land down on earth` and let them realize that they were overreacting without humiliating them. So, everybody came out of this encounter with feelings of ′saving face, ` which is the best when the cause of the row was not very crucial, yet the psychological stakes were high. I remembered and followed the truism: Let your woes have an honorable exit way from the battlefield.

The second incident where I decided to fight ′dirty" involved a person from our working group who was a psychopath. You know probably something about the psychopathic personality, which lacks empathy and sensitivity to what others feel and can be both pretty charming and ruthless. It is a known truth that many psychopaths serve in many high-profile positions in the business world, including big corporations, since they can act resolute and think more on profit than on the cost of human well-being. A part of the management ideology—emphasizing efficiency, growing productivity, competition, and self-empowerment—is clearly in line with psychopathic thinking once you look closely at the human costs of it. The different batteries of psychological tests designed for business life would not identify these people, but a good clinical psychologist would be able to identify them, though it may take some time. It seems that their affliction must do much more with their brain functioning than by their psychological background. The strongest clue for this is that they simply do not learn from their experiences although it is paved with conflicts, bashing, and discrediting of them. If you are engaged in volunteer relations with a psychopath, you do best by getting out of it because in the long run, the relations will become very burdensome for you due to the psychopath's lack of empathy. If you work with a psychopath, the case is different: you must consider a fight, and if you cannot win, a flight.

I met lots of people who were put down by psychopaths. Personally, I met few psychopaths, and if there was much at stake, I encountered them. One of them was a professional psychologist (yes, they are everywhere, also among politicians, doctors, lawyers, and psychologists) with whom I worked. This person played by her own rules without taking notes of the rules that bind people together as a team. As time went by, it became apparent to all that she did not care much about us, about our common solidarity, and about sharing the common burden. She was confronted by the team several times, but nothing came out of it. The situation got worse, and we had to act. Lots of people shy away from an open confrontation with normal people, but when it concerns psychopaths, they will do all to avoid this war of attrition because they know that you cannot talk sensibly with them. You must be blunt and have a punching credibility behind your words; otherwise, you're just wasting your time. They will both exhaust and frustrate you. When I realized that there was no partner to talk to and with, I made a statement in one of our countless meetings dealing with her breach of our moral codex and financial integrity, telling her right in the face that I did not believe in her capacity to understand how people cooperate in a team. I told her that I could see only two viable solutions for the stalemate that we had experienced the last year: either she would voluntarily leave the team and the workplace, or she would be excluded by force. These were the possibilities I saw. At that time, I secured the support of all members for this confronting line (they were so fed up with her that they just looked for an ′executioner`). Now with a solid ′coalition` behind me, we could start the real fight. We appointed a committee that would suggest the revision of certain paragraphs in our reciprocal contracts. I was one of the two who were elected, and we presented new rules to make it impossible for her to keep manipulating with us. The rules were accepted by the coalition, ` and the last phase of the fight against the psychopath ensued. She tried to blackmail us for money and other things and threatened never to leave the workplace. We proceeded to design a rule of exclusion and a rule ′of reciprocity, ` which prevented her from getting new clients from the common reference list of the workplace without honoring first her commitments and obligations. Now it was her who was pressed into ′the corner. ` As a result of being ′outflanked` and brought closer to a defeat, she tried to discredit me and some people from the workplace by filing accusations against us to some authorities. She sued me and tried to smear my professional integrity. She claimed in a letter to our professional organization that I had threatened her, so she was afraid I would harm her (which was a pure fantasy). The struggle ended of me being totally acquitted and in her leaving the clinic for good. It was a fight that sometimes was hard because she had neither decency nor a fair way of fighting, but I knew all along that she would lose. It was a question of keeping on the pressure and ′grinding her down. ` It was not a decent or a beautiful affair, but it was necessary and efficient. What helped us win the fight was the realization by all of us that there was no other way than the building up a solid coalition to carry on the fight to ′the bitter end` and the acceptance that some of us were mentally strong enough to serve as the ′executioners` When I tried to help some people in the workplace to outsmart a psychopath, I always told them to build first up a solid coalition, to ′close the ranks` and to stick to certain strategy and tactic if they wished to win. They should prepare themselves for a war of attrition if there was not a boss in the workplace who could fire the person.

The suppressive core of envy in our lives:

Envy and the exposure of a tormented soul:

When I visited my kibbutz after publishing two books, I met an old man whom I had very rewarding and inspiring contacts with before I left the kibbutz and years after. He was sort of a self-taught intellectual, very interested in literature, writing, history, and philosophy; and like many of these intellectuals, he was not good at expressing his private thoughts or engaging personally with other people. He was around eighty-two years old when I last met him, clearly frail yet clear in his mind. We talked about my life, never about his, and about the books I wrote, and he had some reservations. Asking him more about his reservations, I figured out that he misunderstood some of the passages, but I let it lie. Then he all of a sudden looked up into the blue summer sky and muttered, "All my grown-up life I wanted to write a book. It is too late now!" I listened and said nothing because there was nothing to say. It was a sacred moment, where he opened his whole soul to me, with its pain, with its silly envy of me, with its human deep, deep resignation and sorrow over opportunities, which he did not grabbed due to lack of courage and determination. This was his naked soul he showed me before he died shortly afterward, and I appreciated it in due silence.

Envy is one of the ugliest and most denied emotions in humans` repertoire, often being hidden under the argument of ′pursuing justice/fairness`. There is no doubt in my mind, that essential part of the conflict between the Arabs and Israelis and general antisemitism in the world is fueled by such envy from their side, camouflaged by their arguments on justice and prejudice.

It can also be clothed in laissez faire - letting the status quo continue to support the few, wary that expanded freedom/opportunity might unleash potentials in others.

Groupthink enhances it as it preaches for both consensus/cohesion in the group and coercion of those-individuals and other groups- who don′t comply with these rules.

Envy, like stupidity are seldom addressed as both human and humanity` mental cancerous tumors, wreaking havoc in relations between people, nations, and blocks.

In my childhood, we, the children sat often in a sandbox out in the yard and played with the wet sand, moving around small metal toy cars and tractors. We built castles, tunnels, and protective walls. Occasionally, as one may expect, a conflict would ensue and escalate. It went almost as follows: ′This is my car. Move away! ` ′This is my tunnel! You move away! ` ′You are a bloody ass (or worse).` ′You are a dirty pig (or worse).` ′My father will beat you!` ′My father will beat your father. He is much stronger than your father! ` ′My father and my big brother will beat your father and your mother . . .` Sometimes we threw some sand on each other, maybe we shoved and pushed each other a bit, and so one would start crying, and the fight was stopped for this time. I have been talking with many grown-ups who were sure that only children behave in such manner because they believe that grown-ups can reason. They were mistaken, I had told them: grown-ups do the same, but it seems as if they are not aware of it because it is a part of politics, religion and vain pride and they can roll their tongues trying to give suspicious sound arguments for their bad behavior But when you look at the outcome of most of the conflicts and wars in this world, what do you see? Information and enlightenment are poorly represented in them compared with all the hidden emotions that lead them often to conflicts and bloodshed, but the dynamics of the grown ups` conflicts are basically fed by the above-mentioned emotions and stupidity.

Psychohistory: a capacity I believe I slowly acquire.

The combination of my good brain, my knowledge of human history and nature/condition, politic, military and psychological warfare and propaganda, my thinking based on shifting contexts, complementation of contrasts, my combining skill and far- sighted perspective on top of my extensive life experience, helped me develop my knowledge of psychohistory as both a predictive tool and a vision bearing method.

Psychohistory was a term Asimov had coined, but I found it as potential predictive measure, and using it in analyzing different situations and contingencies, helped me avoid falling in the mental trap sapiens suffer of; repeating their divisive actions by not learning from their history.

Being able to use psycho history as a predictive tool for human/nations` tensions and conflicts, means that cognitively/ emotionally you can learn how to avoid these conflict prone situations in the future by training people to think of the long term consequences of their deeds and their often invisibly expressed emotions and latent stupidity, and instead learn to cooperate and find comprises which hold on all levels of the human existence. This purpose implies attaining a higher awareness than most sapiens can achieve right now, but it may become one day an attainable goal. Maybe, one day we will be able to mutate/upgrade ourselves away from our mental and self- destructive limitations. Psychohistory will then could gain the respect it deserves as a predictive method.

Humans as rats in rats Paradise?

Can we act like John B Calhoun rats in Utopia?

Humans start with gratifying their basic needs, and if they get a chance, then growing numbers of us want more and at last may lose their proportions and become aggressively greedy hoarders, without the sense of humanness and cooperation.

In the 1960eeth, John B Calhoun set about creating a series of experiments that would essentially cater to every need of rodents, and then track the effect on the population over time. The most infamous of the experiments was named, quite dramatically: Universe 25.

In this study, published in the Proceedings of the Royal Society of Medicine, he took four breeding pairs of mice and placed them inside a 'utopia`. The environment was designed to eliminate problems that would lead to mortality in the wild.

They could obtain limitless food via 16 food hoppers, accessed via tunnels, which would feed up to 25 mice at a time, as well as water bottles just above. Nesting material was provided. The weather was kept at 20°C (68°F), which was the perfect mouse temperature. The mice were chosen for their health, obtained from the National Institutes of Health breeding colony. Extreme precautions were taken to stop any disease from entering the universe.

As well as this, no predators were present in the utopia.

The experiment began, and as you'd expect, the mice used the time that would usually be wasted in foraging for food and shelter for having excessive amounts of sexual intercourse. About every 55 days, the population doubled as the mice filled the most desirable space within the pen, where access to the food tunnels was of ease.

When the population hit 620, that slowed to doubling around every 145 days, as the mouse society began to hit problems. The mice split off into groups, and those that could not find a role in these groups found themselves with nowhere to go.

Here, the 'excess' could not emigrate, for there was nowhere else to go. The mice that found themselves with no social role to fill — there are only so many head mouse roles, became isolated.

Males who failed withdrew physically and psychologically; they became very inactive and aggregated in large pools near the center of the floor of the universe. From this point on they no longer initiated interaction with their established associates, nor did their behavior elicit attack by territorial males. Even so, they became characterized by many wounds and much scar tissue as a result of attacks by other withdrawn males.

The withdrawn males would not respond during attacks, lying there immobile. Later, they would attack others in the same pattern. The female counterparts of these isolated males withdrew as well. Some mice spent their days preening themselves, shunning mating, and never engaging in fighting. Due to this they had excellent fur coats, and were dubbed, somewhat disconcertingly, the 'beautiful ones'.

The breakdown of usual mouse behavior wasn't just limited to the outsiders. The Alfa males mice became extremely aggressive, attacking others with no motivation or gain for themselves, and regularly raped both males and females. Violent encounters sometimes ended in mouse-on-mouse cannibalism.

Despite – or perhaps because of – the fact their every need was being catered for, mothers would abandon their young or merely just forget about them entirely, leaving them to fend for themselves. The mother mice also became aggressive towards trespassers to their nests, with males that would normally fill this role banished to other parts of the utopia. This aggression spilled over, and the mothers would regularly kill their young. Infant mortality in some territories of the utopia reached 90 percent.

This was all during the first phase of the downfall of the 'utopia'. In the phase Calhoun termed the 'second death', whichever young mice survived the attacks from their mothers and others would grow up around these unusual mouse behaviors. As a result, they never learned usual mouse behaviors and many showed little or no interest in mating, preferring to eat and preen themselves, alone.

The population peaked at 2,200 — short of the actual 3,000-mouse capacity of the 'univers` — and from there came the decline. Many of the mice weren't interested in breeding and retired to the upper decks of the enclosure, while the others formed into violent gangs below, which would regularly attack and cannibalize other groups as well as their own. The low birth rate and high infant mortality combined with the violence, and soon the entire colony was extinct. During the mouse apocalypse, food remained ample, and their every need completely met.

Calhoun termed what he saw as the cause of **the collapse 'behavioral sink`.**

'For an animal so simple as a mouse, the most complex behavior involve the interrelated set of courtship, maternal care, territorial defense and hierarchical intragroup and intergroup social organization, ` he concluded in his study.

'When behavior related to these functions fail to mature, there is no development of social organization and no reproduction. As in the case of my study reported above, all members of the population will age and eventually die. The species will die out."

He believed that the mouse experiment may also apply to humans and warned of a day when – god forbid – all our needs are met.

In recent times, people have questioned whether the experiment could really be applied so simply to humans – and whether it really showed what we believed it did in the first place.

The end of the mouse utopia could have arisen 'not from density, but from excessive social interaction, ` medical historian Edmund Ramsden told the NIH Record.

As well as this, the experiment design has been criticized for creating not an overpopulation problem, but rather a scenario where the more aggressive mice were able to control the territory and isolate everyone else. Much like with food production in the real world, it's possible that the problem wasn't of adequate resources, but how those resources are controlled.

I thought about the interactions for humans between density, overpopulation, and abundance of food.

Did we make some similar experiments with humans? Sure. That is what the world-through UNRWA- did in Gaza. They supplied their needs in their little maze, and the people multiplied there as to become 2.3 million on this little stretch of land, with immense anger, hatred and with immense social suppression being re directed by Hamas towards Israel.

In my view, it is the rat Paradise sinister experiment with humans.

Another drawback of this combination right now is growing obesity and its associated ailments and growing psychological distress among children, including isolation, fragmentation of social contacts, drug abuse and clear rise of aggressive/ violent gangs in the cities and societies. So, the results from the mice experiment cannot be completely identical with current human behavior, but there are serious ill effects for humans living under the Rat paradise Utopia.

Much of human history- also our current- revolves around our stupidity repeating itself in different variants, but with growing self -destruction.

The poverty of the 20st century is unlike that of previous generations.

In the past, poverty was the result of natural scarcity, bad trade routes, feudalism, and lack of social infrastructure. Today these factors have been effectively eliminated, making the modern state of poverty one that is entirely artificial; something that has been deliberately designed and then imposed upon the world by the immensely wealthy.

Consequently, the modern poor are not given sympathy, but viewed as lazy. In an odd way it is similar to the Hindu caste system (which mind you, doesn't actually exist in the Hindu scriptures). The impoverished are viewed as being responsible for their own suffering, while the well-off are viewed as being responsible, and therefore completely deserving, of their own luxury.

Meanwhile, everyone else seems to be completely oblivious to the role that luck plays in financial success, as well as the element of privilege (ethnic background, family/social status and connections, upbringing etc...).

This causes the masses to think that they too can become wealthy if they just work harder, save better, and study more, failing to take the time to look around and realize that they are no better off than they used to be. Nothing changed despite their best efforts.

Why? Because America has become a plutocracy, and it's not in the self-interest of the wealthy to allow you to also become wealthy. They don't want to share their power.

The sooner this harsh reality is accepted is the sooner that we can take action to address the problem.

I perform so called ´magic`:

My first experience with magic started as I studied psychology. I, as a student, was sent to work with psychiatric patients. One day I heard from one room wild screaming and sobbing. I went in, and there stood on her bed, pressed against the wall, a young woman, totally terrified. There was nobody in the room besides her and me. I asked her, what had terrified her, and she pointed on the floor, under her bed, and shrieked, ´A lion! A lion! ` ´Have you got a lion under your bed, ` I asked. She affirmed it, sobbing violently. 'All right, ` I said, 'stand where you are and let me deal with the lion. I know how to deal with lions. ` I crawled under the bed, 'caught` the 'lion` in his neck and tail, and came up with 'it. ` 'Now, ` I said, 'just watch what you do with lions creeping into your bedroom. ` I carried the lion to the washing tab, turned on the water, and washed the lion away. She watched me unbelieving and then started to laugh and laugh. She found it to be so amusing, to wash a lion away. This was magic! Often when parents send their children who feel alone and deserted into my consultation, the children take their animal toy—be it a bear, a dog, or a cat—and tell me that the animal toy is the only one who can understand them. I talk with these animals and express my respect for their wisdom and fine feelings. We talk a bit with the child, a bit with the animal, and at last, I come to my point, where I say to the child, 'Well, your bunny is a very nice and a wise friend, but there is something he cannot teach you: how to deal with people, conflicts, and problems without isolating yourself. True? ` They must admit it. 'Therefore, we must find some good people with which you can talk to, about how to deal with all these things. Your bunny will be there all the time as your very good friend, but there will also be your parents or others so you will have many good friends and advisers…`

And the magic encounters can be also applied to grown-ups, who need some new direction in their lives and are burdened by life's sorrows. Once, I talked with a woman in her sixties, whose man died suddenly. Now, because of their complicated and difficult relations, some unresolved emotional issues kept coming up in a particular way. Her deceased husband kept coming to their apartment, sitting on his chair, watching her eat, following her in the streets of Copenhagen, and insisting on sleeping together with her. She became very disturbed and annoyed by his 'refusal` to die properly and got very angry with him. One morning, she told me she kicked him out of the bed. I said to her, 'Well, it seems that you and your husband have some unresolved issues. Can you discuss it over with him, become good friends, and let him get peace? ` She bought the idea, and the next time I saw her, she told me with glowing eyes that he had left her for good and she was happy now. 'What did you do? ` I asked her. Well, she went to his grave and, knowing how much he appreciated good wine, emptied a bottle of good wine on his grave and talked to him in loving manner. And so. he let her live her life.

The mighty enslavers of the human mind.

As life lacks meaningful resolution, we invented gods to avoid despair/confusion, thus we added to life plenty illusions/delusions. This enslaver is called Escapism.

Another enslaver of the human mind is the Dichotomous thinking mode. It makes them believe that they are better, more just and humane than others. This is also relevant for Muslims, who often pretend to be victims.

More than 12.5 million Muslims were killed in wars in the last 25 years,(see Google), mostly by Muslims. Who is, then, the culprit committing genocide?

Another enslaver is Talk- Walk syndrome. Most humans suffer of unbridgeable gap, between their talk and their walk. They talk on justice, love and compassion, but not on human nature, which detract us from reaching these goals and are not willing to sacrifice something concrete for these lofty goals.

Selv knowledge-realization and pretending to obtain them:

There is a huge and profitable industry of attaining self- knowledge and realization. Much of it sells mental humbug, something I realized of very early in my psychology` carrier.

I talked once with a young man-who was a psychologist - who just lost his father. Shortly before dying, his father had conducted seminar about Indian spirituality, and while sitting in deep meditation on the floor, he passed away. His father was a known gestalt therapist, which kept developing himself and his spiritual capacities. Many people were afraid of him, including his son, who now in the middle of his thirties, longed for a father who was never there when he needed him. His father was, in my view, a neurotic par excellence who tried to gain self-insight by helping people in seminars and involving himself in the pursuit of ′eternal` insights but neglected the most essential: being close and intimate with those who were his family members and friends. You cannot be self-knowledgeable if you start with ′transcendence` and fame and neglect your obligations to your children and the people you bind yourself to as a friend. For them, he had no time because he had to impress the rest of the world. People showing such emotional discrepancy on top of the urge for fame and recognition demonstrate implicitly neurotic conflict and deficient self-knowledge.

You cannot become real self-knowledgeable unless you get some notion of how pervasive and intrusive human institutional stupidity and craving for attention and recognition are and how they affect our judgment and mental horizons in many situations. Human stupidity exerts great power on our minds and actions.

Self-knowledge implies constant vigilance against the sneaky onslaught of human institutional stupidity. Stupidity is not a new phenomenon, but its impact has manifested itself in our time due to the complex life we got created with our unsustainable and polluting lifestyle and our self-exposing, pornographic culture.

Aga lasts among us:

Agelast, as Milan Kundera once described him, is a man who cannot hear God's laughter. God laughs at us, according to a Jewish expression, because we stumble on our own feet looking for the truth and the mission in our lives in the wrong place/direction. Agelasts have a very clear idea that they have patent regarding both the truth and the mission and are so bloody solemn that they just cannot accept other views. It is here they become dangerous for others. They are devoid of any capacity to laugh at themselves and life. In this relation, I wish to let you know, my reader, that although I consider my ideas as very good ones, I can laugh at myself and at the world; otherwise, I would have become intolerable to my surroundings. I am also too dependent on other people's opinions. Many people were involved in advising me regarding my books, reduce the risk of me becoming such an ego-tripper agelast. I say loudly when I lecture that I talk, and write in, three different languages, but none of them I master eloquently. Talking about my mother language, Hebrew, I have become a bit outdated and 'rusty` and talk it in 'archaic` manner without much slang. Danish, I have learned when I was twenty-seven. This is not a language I will recommend to my best friends. Its grammar, sounds, and vocals are a bit intimidating, and yet I practice it in my life, write articles, and use it all the time in my clinical work and in lectures. I have learned to compensate for lack of fluency by intensity, content, and the 'magic presence. ` English I have, so to say, learned by myself. OK, we have learned some of it in school for some five years, but the rest, 'I did it my way. ` When I finish this manuscript, somebody with linguistic capacity and fluency will work on the language. This is my weakness and my fortune at the same time. My fortune was to be dependent on other people's feedback, so I was granted both good friends and many inspiring acquaintances. But as important is that due to my background, I did not become vain and stupid as to think that my truth is the only relevant one on earth! My friends and acquaintances and my 'peasant background, ` believe it or not, keep me down-to-earth. Admitting my linguistic limitations, I identify myself in what Nasrudin, the famous Sufi figure, said to a very learned man while ferrying him on the river. The scholar commented on Nasrudin's language, telling him that by not learning to talk correctly, Nasrudin had already lost half of his life. Nasrudin kept silent, but when they came halfway in the river, he asked the man whether he could swim. The man said, 'No, why do you ask? ` 'Because the boat is sinking, ` replied Nasrudin, 'and you are going to lose your whole life. ` To laugh at yourself is very important if you wish to avoid becoming a little Hitler or Don Quixote. I like to do it when I hold speeches, especially to round birthdays and lectures, in interacting with people, etc. I laugh at my Danish, on my 'metaphysical ideas. ` I laugh at my background, of me creating a new Danish accent, etc. It is not that easy to learn to laugh at yourself. It demands that you have been through lots of tribulations and won some unwavering self-confidence, which brings you out of these trials. When I came to Denmark, all my credentials, skills, charm, and history did not help me a bit. Communicating with Danish people was not the same as with Israelis, Arabs, French, or Americans. It was much harder because they were basically on guard for a long time in their relations to strangers and newcomers. In the beginning, I was angry and frustrated. I became conscious of how I talked and how people received my Danish messages. But then one day, I decided enough is enough. They were going to take me as I am. Black is beautiful. And this was the turning point. From this moment on, where I became beautiful in my own eyes, the gates of communication with them became open; and I entered in, and all my old, dusted social capabilities were greeting me again. What happened in my mind? I came back to the point of who I was and accepted the time it took me to decode the Danish psyche and communication modes and to make the adjustments and, therefore, I could stop being so touchy. I could make mistakes and laugh at myself. And at the same time, I did not let Danish people become my superiors or judges. I helped many of them to be less inhibited, how to open them up so they would not turn into reserved people or angry agelasts.

We cannot become self- knowledgeable if we follow our **Time is Money and Faster- Faster and ignore our ultimate mission:**

Possessing oversight in our time means being aware of our all-dominating motto and mantra: Faster, faster, until the thrill of speed overcomes the fear of death. (Hunter Thompson, American writer.) Do you remember the rabbit in the classical novel of Lewis Carroll, Alice's Adventures in Wonderland? This very flighty rabbit is in frenzy, all the time in a hurry for no clear reason or sense. Pulling his gold watch out of his waist pocket and looking at it, he finds, startled, that it is late and so he must leave in a rush. He rushes, so to speak, from nowhere to nowhere, keeping an air of urgency and importance. Combine the rabbit's pathetic show-off attitude with the four stooges of our time: faster-faster, over stimulation, hyper greed, and a kind of institutionalized, perfumed stupidity. Blend these four with the aura of technological progress and all of a sudden you come up with respectability and semi theological cover for a self-destructive and harmful lifestyle.

Acquiring self-knowledge, as you may realize, is a lifelong process, and yet a very rewarding one since you may be lucky as to experience yourself and life with all their varied glowing and murky rainbow colors and hues, and eventually you may get a sense of what is the essential purpose of our journey as a species. It is evolving further to become wiser, better and master our expanding lives/horizons far sightedly. This is our ultimate meaning beyond all theories, dogmas, convictions and faiths, which we alone can grant ourselves as intelligent beings. But to be focused on such journey, we should shed the crouching grip of greed, power lust and short sight which plague us.

As a child, adolescent and grown up, I was influenced to believe that achieving greatness through service to man and humanity was and ideal to aspire for. From childhood on I learnt on the lives of exceptional people who dedicated their lives and efforts to humanity progress and further evolvement with their deeds and ideas, which inspired to collective projects benefiting us.

On the other hand, I knew well that most people cling to a faith which is ritualistic, replicating and demand subordination, lacking new challenges and free thoughts. There are clearly some psychological and sometimes material benefits in accepting uniformity such faiths demand, but it blocks for the creative greatness of most believers and the clear vision /mission awaiting us beyond the clouds of collective conditioning.

I know for sure that the religious/ideological and the self- realizing approaches won't lift us up and out of our human conditions and self-destructiveness. I believe in projects of collective character forced upon humans by sheer necessity, like a comprehensive policy forcing us to live up to -on personal level- an ecological footprint quota. Without such a compulsory policy, all our talk and chatter — being religious, political, or self- focused - to stop climate change and unsustainable humanity, is but useless noise.

The value of a man from such point of view will be related to the efforts or lack of them He/ she has contributed in promoting a sustainable, evolving, just and far- sighted intelligent humans on earth.

′Every miserable fool who has nothing at all of which he can be proud of, adopts as a last resource pride in the nation to which he belongs; he is ready and happy to defend all its faults and follies tooth and nail, thus reimbursing himself for his own inferiority. `—Arthur Schopenhauer I am not sure when I felt it so vividly. It came probably slowly from the beginning of my fifties. I felt as if time became more and more precious, and I was not willing to waste it on lots of banalities, trivialities, and repetitions and on information that I knew was useless for me. But then one Christmas, I got a present, an autobiography of a known Danish journalist who I once respected. Yet I did not hesitate for a moment. I went to the shop and exchanged it for a map of Denmark and five packages of printing papers. I thought I made a good deal. I made a good deal because I did not get anything out of reading about self-promoting people, who might be clever or even insightful but who had not thought of some original ideas or done something worth writing in an autobiography. In my view, this kind of literature, which attracted so many people out of curiosity, was a waste of time. Show me a book with great endeavors, with determination to fight against odds to prevail, which shows insights, wisdom and velour beyond our current self-preoccupied politicians and showmen and I will be sold. And I can assure you that I have read some wonderful biographies of great statesmen in historical perilous times. I am not satiated by political or celebrity gossip or lives if it does not present the grand lines of our existence, the ongoing struggle, impending necessities, and our bearing meaning, which we must face our lives. When I have spare time, besides living, I would rather use it creatively and constructively for the benefit of others. I will not accept just a comfortable and ordinary life and be content with my material privileges. It is a waste of my precious time to be content with so little of what life can grant me, becoming an ordinary person pacified by comfort and NBB(Nonsense baffles brains) . I have this falcon sight for locating people who have potentials but just live a resigned, ordinary life. I identify them already when they are young. They are not doomed, but unless some good mental shake-up will turn their lives upside down, they will lose their potential velour and creativity.

In May 2000, I visited my childhood friends in Israel after a long time of not meeting one another. We were all around 55 years old by now, and the ′get together` was nice yet also ′spiced` by the recognition that the passing time had left its unmistakable marks on our bodies, faces, and souls. This aging brought certain moods up in me. I tried to keep this mood at bay by reminding myself of all that life had granted me, emphasizing the fact that I was mentally alert and hungry this very day, that my legs, lungs, and heart could, without great exertion of will power, managed half a marathon, and of the challenges which I would take on in the future would keep me fighting, challenging, and defying the urge to resign and surrender to the murmuring voice of 'closing time`. I decided to double down on my efforts as a kind of a warrior for the sake of civilization, as it granted me both the best spirit and peace. In such moments, I came to repeat to myself my 'battle cry, ` which is taken from the poem of Alfred Tennyson about the legendary Odysseus. ` How dull it is to pause, to make an end. To rust unburnished, not to shine in use! As tho' to breathe were life! Life piled on life Were all too little, and of one to me Little remains; but every hour is saved from that eternal silence, something more, A bringer of new things; To follow knowledge like a sinking star, Beyond the utmost bound of human thought. Death closes all; but something ere the end, some work of noble note, may yet be done, not unbecoming men that strove with Gods. The lights begin to twinkle from the rocks; The long day wanes; the slow moon climbs; the deep Moans round with many voices. Come, my friends. 'Tis not too late to seek a newer world. Push off and sitting well in order smite the sounding furrows; for my purpose holds to sail beyond the sunset, and the baths of all the western stars, until I die. We are not now that strength which in old days Moved earth and heaven, that which we are, we are, — One equal temper of heroic hearts, made weak by time and fate, but strong in will to strive, to seek, to find, and not to yield.'

We were not doomed to become mentally meek, rigid, and resigned as we got older, but we were very much prone to this process due to the way our minds work as we grew older. The mind seek often security and certainty in the known rather than challenge and struggle in new territories. It becomes comfort seeking and safeguarded us against 'taking risks, ` which slowly made us favor rigid patterns. Instead of assessing the risk's magnitude and what is at stake, it send us warning signals: 'Do not do this. What if you fail, or what if people will find you silly, or what if you die somewhere else than in your bed? ` This trickle of doubt and anxiety is our mortal woe because we become intimidated by its projective voice of all possible murky outcome connected with daring. Listening to this voice we become old in mind. And I could tell that after observing so many people, I knew that this danger was very real. The young curious and exploring Homo sapiens tends to become, as he grows older, tame, a shadow of himself, as he has lost his very living core: explorative, creative, defying, and challenging mind. If we did not explore and 'conquer` new "territories and vistas, becoming older, we would become resigned, suffering of silent existential despair, simply because only by the struggle for new horizons, wiser beings creating a better future for themselves and defying our mental /physical constraints as sapiens, we kept the battle for our 'ever young` souls.

Casus Belli or detachment:

In the middle of the '80s, people who left Israel and settled down in other places in the world were considered traitors by many Israeli citizens and even the political establishment, and the mass media, although it was legal to immigrate. We were considered as those who had sold our souls to the easy-going and rich 'golden calf `of the West and turned our backs on the nation struggling for its survival. I, who served in the military and took part in two wars, knew that the state of Israel was not, ever since the victory of Six-Day War (1967) in mortal danger due to its superior military power, technological edge over the Arabs, defendable territory, U.S. support and much-spoken secret weapon systems. But one thing is to know; another thing is to deal with people and a nation traumatized by their historical pogroms and current holocaust. One day—I was living in Denmark with my family—my parents sent me a magazine, in which I found an abusing and vicious article on people who, like me, left Israel for personal reasons. The writer was a history professor at Jerusalem University, and he compared us, to start with, to hookers. Later in the article, he revised his view of us, claiming that we were worse than hookers because we have sold our soul for good life's sake. This article, the incitement against us in the Israeli mass media, including what Israel's state minister Yitzhak Rabin had said about us (something to the extent of us being the leftover sediment of Israel's society) made me angry. I wrote a little column to the magazine, commenting on the tone of the article and pointing out that they should practice some more stringent ethical lines in their publishing of articles. Few weeks passed by and another article on the same topic appeared from the same professor in the same magazine. This article started with the same frontal attack on our integrity, but now I became the main goal of his attacks because of my comment: I, Benjamin from Copenhagen, whom he did not know, but nonetheless loathed and despised. Upon reading this, I decided to write an article to the same magazine. In this article, I commented shortly that it was not my errand to comment on the mental state of the professor, but I wondered why the magazine gave room to this mean incitement. And the rest of the article dealt with the actual challenges and priorities of the Israeli society, like peacemaking, ecology, integration of immigrants, poverty, and social discrimination, which I suggested the readers to focus on, instead of engaging themselves in this witch hunt. When my article was published, it was attacked by lots of angry readers, not for its content, but for me breaking the 'rules of the game. ` I was not supposed to tell them how to manage their affairs, as I was not one of them, living abroad. This absurd drama continued when I visited in the summer my parents and family. Lots of people in my kibbutz would not talk to me, and some of them compared me to a known atom spy. I tried to explain to them the context in which I wrote the article. It did not help. Then I became really furious and passed my judgment on them. Screw them and their views! I was done with their bullshit. I decided on the way back to Denmark that from now on, I did not care about what they said or wrote. I did not care about their meanings or views about my life or me. This very anger propelled me out of my dependency on their acceptance, out of my indoctrinating social background, to become eventually free. As time went by, my anger subsided, and when I came to my kibbutz a few years later, people who had not greeted me then did it cordially now and many were friendly as if nothing happened between us. But one thing did happen: I kept being free of their spin and of their old power. I was not any longer suppressed by their ideas or other better known peacock humans and their ideas or people who claimed that the absolute truths came right out of their mouths. I became free only through my struggle. I had to take on this battle because it was my inevitable Casus Belli (a reason for war), and I survived it and prevailed, and as an unintended reward, I became transformed out of it.

Many ego′ overblown people feel falsely that they are significant:

I like the story of a Jewish man in the old Eastern Europe who comes to visit an old friend who lives in a godforsaken and poverty-stricken little town. Upon arriving to the station, he asks a passerby if he knows where his friend Moyshe lives. The passerby spits on the ground and says, ′Oh, this Moyshe, this good-for-nothing idiot, lives in the next street close to the synagogue. ` The guest continues his search and finds another Jew and asks again for the whereabouts of his friend Moyshe: ′Oh, this intolerable creature! This terrible being lives just across the next street. ` The guest cannot orient himself in the small Jewish ghetto and asks another Jew the whereabouts of his friend. The third man looks at him and asks, ′Are you friends with this overblown, pretentious, good-for-nothing being? He lives just across the corner in his little room. ` At last the guest finds his Moyshe, and they are very happy to see each other after many years. When they sit down, the guest asks Moyshe, ′Say, my good friend, what do you do for your living? ` ′I have a very important job in the synagogue. I am responsible for the prayers, ` Moyshe says. ′Do you earn much money doing this? ` his guest asks. ′No, ` says Moyshe. ′I barely make a living out of it. ` ′Do the Jews here who come to the synagogue like you very much? ` ′Not a bit, they hate my guts, ` mutters Moyshe. ′So why do you do this job, my friend? ` ′And honor and respect does not count any longer? ` Moyshe asks his guest.

People have their own, often obscure, reasons for behaving in an excessive manner, as Moyshe did; often because they derive out of this a sense of worth, regardless the verdict of their environment.

`These were all commonplace persons. I would never have let them think so, but it is time to admit that I looked down on them. They were lacking in higher motives. They were run-of-the-mill products of our mass democracy, with no distinctive contribution to make to the history of the species, satisfied to pile up money or seduce women, to copulate, thrive in the sack as the degenerate children of Eros, male but not manly, and living, the men and women alike, on threadbare ideas, without beauty, without virtue, without the slightest independence of spirit - privileged in the way of money and goods, beneficiaries of man's conquest of nature as the Enlightenment foresaw it and the high-tech achievements that have transformed the material world` (Saul Below: The Actual : A Novella).

In this novel, a fictional person expresses some of these ideas, which are both derogatory and infamous, yet expressive of a real problem of modern man; his real insignificance beyond his own private life compared to what he is made to believe he is or can become. He is seduced to believe that he can become unique, but most often he has to accept much lower goals. There has always been a tacit agreement among the powerful, still in place in our societies: to cultivate the masses mediocrity and self-deception on the same time.

Mediocrity and stupidity are two very infectious mental viruses, but not so- wisdom.

In my practice I have interviewed thousands of people expressing the wish to become significant, special, unique. But they haven't a clear idea of how to go about achieving this goal because the landmarks of illusions are always hazy. It is illustrative to 'lock on` to the false uniqueness presented in the movies. Time and again we are served this idea of our uniqueness as seductive perfume. In 'American Beauty`(movie) the hero's quest to become special and unique ends up in a short clarifying moment, before he is killed. In 'Fisher King`, and in almost any other film dealing with the urge to become unique or significant, the 'solution` is finding one's love and becoming a good citizen who helps others. It's very fine old medicine against rebellious itches and the symbols are quite seductive. Yet people don't become unique just by doing this. They just fulfil an urge to love and to be loved, and then conform to the moral ideal of being a good citizen. Sad to say, but there are mechanisms in our societies, now and in the past, which prefer citizens who conform to specific priorities and values; docile, mediocre people. Even the methods used may remind us of some old systems: bread and circuses, plus the modern brain washing; entertain them with illusions of uniqueness and significance. In this respect, it seems that capitalist democracy is, like other civilizations before it, torn apart by the ancient conflict between the Apollonian and Dionysian poles and forces. Without stressing the Apollonian motives in our lives, it is hard to see how people can become unique or significant.

The mental cancer called greed:

Greed, covered as the uninhibited pursuit of economic expansion and welfare, is the hallmark of our modern society. It is inherent in our 'growth economy` concept and in the 'self-realization` ideology. Like everything in excess, it makes lots of people act in an obsessive-compulsive manner. A joke I heard once told by the rabbi of Copenhagen illustrates this point. Three pious Jews—one from Poland, the second from Holland, and the third from America—meet and started bragging about the merits of their respective rabbis. The Polish Jew tells of his rabbi, 'One day a devouring fire broke out and threatened to burn down the whole city. And do you know what our rabbi did? He went into the middle of the street, where the fire was ablaze, and roared, 'Fire to the right, fire to the left,' and by doing it, he saved the city. `

'That is a very great miracle indeed, ` said the Dutch Jew, 'but listen to the great miracle my rabbi performed. One day the sea broke through the dikes. Great waves of water gushed through and threatened to drown the whole country. And do you know what my rabbi did? He went to the scene, stood firmly in front of the huge waves of water, and roared, 'Water to the right, water to the left,' and by doing it, he saved the country. `

'Amazing, ` said the American Jew. 'You have very powerful rabbi, but listen to the amazing miracle my rabbi achieved. He went on a plane from New York to Chicago, and just before the Sabbath commenced, he got a telephone call from some influential connection, telling him he could earn much money if he concluded a deal right now in New York. What could the poor rabbi do? It was now the holy Sabbath, where a Jew is not allowed to travel or work. Then he stood up and roared, 'Sabbath to the right, Sabbath to the left.'

I cannot warn people strongly enough regarding the dire psychological, spiritual, and societal consequences of being preoccupied by Mammon and the 'golden calf. ` It corrupts the human soul in the most insidious manner. The Western society is indeed invaded by the virus of greed—that is not to be confused with the wish for a decent, sustainable life.

The failure of Western upbringing:

In my childhood and youth, I retrieved the joy of singing. Wherever and whenever we had the opportunity to learn new songs, we did so. We sang about the Volga and the open spaces of Russia, about how everything on earth is perishable but that the melody will live forever. We sang of how human life is a narrow bridge over the abyss and that the most important thing is not to feel anxiety or despair. We sang about how times change and years pass by, beauty blossoms and beauty withers. And I waited and longed for, but what is it I was waiting and longing for, I did not know. We danced, danced in circles, in rows, in pairs, the Arabian dances and the Israeli hora, and we persisted until we became breathless and exhausted. Time and again, our songs, dances, and play, without alcohol or free love, intoxicated us. Alcohol was out of the question and love, in its physical manifestation, had to wait until we were mature, so we learned in the hard way self-discipline, focus, and postponement of needs and pleasure. All of this had become an essential part of my melody. We ate a basic and balanced diet, with lots of fruits, vegetables, and milk, and not that much meat. As we were working and training in the open with lots of fresh, dry air, there was nobody that became obese or was plagued by allergies. When I compare my health when I was young to most Danish youth I meet today, it stands very clear that modern life takes its heavy toll on their health as well as their mental alertness. We learned to be prudent and part of prudence was reflecting on your actions, knowing or foreseeing your disposition and trying to generate balance between extremes. Self-correction began with self-knowledge, we were taught. Excesses were bad. We learnt already then that many youths wanted freedom to be slaves of their impulses. We knew that instability and shifting emotional states and attitudes caused by drugs and alcohol, ruined people's will and reduced their judgment and understanding. So I did not use drugs or got into the habit of drinking alcohol. I drink wine only occasionally, and three glasses at a time is enough for me. So, what have I missed following the path of temperance when my health is good, my brain- fresh, I am curious and inquisitive, and my spirits high? There is no wonder that the kibbutzim had accomplished these results in those years; an engaging ideology and faith combined with a complementing upbringing in small enclosed social settings could yield these results. If you judge this upbringing from the point of view of what we all became, it was a great success. None of the children I grew up with from my kibbutz, locals as well as immigrants, became a criminal or hooligan. Many hundreds of children turned out to be decent, hardworking, contributing grown-ups. Many years later, it occurred to me how big a treasure we had been given, watching in dismay lots of people who had not learnt to control their whims/impulses and who suffered as a result of this lack of self-discipline. It had become a different 'up the hill` task to bring up your children in a modern mass society, in a big city for example, where freedom to practice individualism, materialism and hedonism is the ruling measure. I know what I am talking about because I had to bring up my children in such context and helped countless parents manage this task with their own children. In my family (Danish)We would not accept drinking every second or third day as many Danish teens did. We would insist on our children doing their homework, getting up in the morning and managing their duties. I ´brainwashed` them against smoking and drug use and succeeded. I ´brainwashed` them against the seductive force of the mass media and infotainment industry in making children as well as grown-ups follow hedonistic values and glittering´, false success` criteria. I ´brainwashed` them against the mass cultivation in our societies of the trivial story, scoops, clichés, and sensations of voyeurism, narcissism, exhibitionism, and excessive pornography. I tried to help them build up a mental bulwark against all these modern, self-defeating seductions, which reduce our lives to chasing satisfactions and nothing more. I tried to rear my children to think critically and independently, not to savor uncritically all the ´fairy tales` modern societies spin around youth regarding their potential ´self-realized life. ` Through my work with humans in distress for the last twenty years, I have come to realize how poorly people think in term of problem solving, especially in difficult times for them. And I realized that with this direction Western societies followed, children's problems would grow significantly.

The Two Garbage Cans as Your Combat Outfit

Believe it or not, but even if you cannot see it, I bear with me two portable and invisible garbage cans under my arms, wherever and whenever I go. The first one is designed to contain, dispose, and forget all the nonsense, NBB (nonsense baffles brains), the endless repetitions and half-stupid comments and statements people—and the mass media—produce abundantly all the time. Be it on direct contact, lectures, the radio, TV, or in the newspapers, I just place it in this garbage can after sorting it as useless 'garbage. `. I called this can, Trivia. Talking to and with people on a personal-social level is not going to get this label because in this case, my relations with them plays a significant role in my assessment unless they become a constant pain in the back. But if I am to attend a lecture or a course that I find boring or repetitive, I would probably find my way out, and the garbage can will fulfill its function. This garbage disposes propaganda and brainwashing seductive norms and values, which I know are damaging to me and to most other people. Do you need some examples? All commentary criticizing my right to be who I am are disposed by this can. Norms and values bound to self-realization, and self-preoccupation for its own sake, end in this garbage can. Norms promoting greedy consumption, power shopping, omnipotence, exhibitionism, fanatism, be it religious or secular, and the false wisdom of market forces end also in this can.

The second garbage can is to contain, and dispose of, some people whom I do not wish to waste my energy on after realizing that they are a ´pain in the neck` and are not respectful in their contact with me or with others. These two garbage cans are being constantly emptied, like in a computer where you click Erase or Delete, so therefore, they are very light to carry around. They serve two purposes: (1) not to give any of these comments or remarks the possibility of derailing my attention, energy, and focus, and (2) to prevent people who are not respectful from getting close to me, not because they are always nasty people, but because they demand too much of my precious energy and focus by making me be on guard in relation to them. What makes me so sure that I select only useless ´garbage` and not a well-founded critique or good people who just failed once? Well, for the first, because I know who I am and have accepted myself as good enough judge to make a distinction between nonsense and essential things, between people failing once and people who repeat a pattern. I am willing to listen to critique of what others think I do wrong to assess its validity. If it makes sense, I will take it in; but if it does not make sense, it will end up in the first garbage can. Once I know who I am beyond changeable moods, fortunes, and circumstances and people wish to know who I am, they have to be both patient and positive. If they persist on exerting pressure on me or to define who I am, they end up rather quickly in the second garbage can. There is no other way to learn to know me than being respectful, patient, and accepting me and my way of revealing myself. In my life, I have experienced only a few times when people did not respect these premises and the outcome was . . . You may by now guess rightly.

Modern spiritual escapists:

The Illusion of Attaining ´Flow` to Avoid Existential Despair: Have you read the story of Herman Hesse Siddhartha? It is about a young prince in India who is looking for enlightenment. He tries almost everything in life to free himself from his ego and desire and to attain the cosmic unification of things, which is embodied in the Buddha's nirvana state of mind and the cosmic sound of ´Om.` All his life he spends searching for it, enjoying, suffering, despairing, and lusting. Only at last, when he is old and earns his livelihood as ferryman, this ´Om` resounds in his heart and mind. He becomes a Buddha. Om is much about flow feelings, when a person has learned to detach himself of his ego binding, of his desire, pride, anxiety, greed, and of transcending the ´self, as to experience a timeless harmony. Many times, I have talked to people (among them psychologists as well) who in their desire to transcend their ´ego, ` greed, and despair and become ´selfless`, joined different meditation courses and ´retreat seminars` under the guidelines of some gurus. Some of them had done ´so well` that upon coming home to their beloved ones, they were not in tune with them any longer, still hovering in their special state of mind. Once I talked to a psychologist, a mother of two young children, who was convinced that the right thing for her to do was to stay in retreat in a monastery for two years to deepen her state from the last retreat. ´What about your children and your family that you had committed yourself to? What about your responsibility over them? ` I asked her. ′I have also a calling I have to follow. This is my real destiny, and compromising on it is painful, ` she replied. It was obvious to me that her life with her family, friends, and workplace was not the place she wished to be in right now. She felt a kind of existential void in her own life, which she tried to fill up with a spiritual retreat into a monastery. I told her, ′You strive to become selfless, but may become—being unaware of it—selfish in a disguised manner. Leaving your children may help you break your own bonds, but it is still a selfish act because giving birth to them, you became selfless by committing yourself to them, knowing very well that they needed you. This is, in my view, your primary stage to train yourself in being selfless. Once they grow up, you can broaden your experience. If you will follow your desire to retreat into a monastery for the next two years, you may lose your children, your husband, and even your friends, but more than this: you will lose much of yourself. You may pay a staggering price for trying to deny your selfishness hidden in selflessness. It may cost you your sanity. ` She fortunately backed out and later thanked me for my frank and brutal advice.

I remember attaining flow, already as a child, playing in the sandbox. I sat there, building my castles, tunnels, palaces, the walls, working in the wet sand, working with the transient elements of life, yet being engulfed by the sense of eternity. Is it not this flow in our creation that opens for us this porous membrane between the transient and the eternal? Later in my life, I retrieved these feeling by engaging in something of utter importance for me and for others, which always implicated unfolding efforts and focusing on the struggle to accomplish what I found significant.

became a clinical psychologist. We became friends and kept contact ever since to the day she died in November 2006. From the age of seventeen, she had been fighting and suffering from muscle atrophy and became dependent on respirators and other technological devices to survive. As years went by, her tongue swelled up, pressing her teeth aside, and the throat constricted, making eating and speaking daunting tasks. But she kept on fighting in the most admirable way in order not just to survive but to engage and contribute as well. She kept her job as a clinical psychologist up to her retirement at the age of seventy, inspiring and teaching many generations of new psychologists. She belonged to the little group of people who won my admiration because they had all shown such personal strength, stamina and engagement in times of suffering and prolonged adversity. I have always appreciated her views and listened to her. And yet, when she or other people I appreciated, did not agree with me or approve some of my ideas, I just shrugged my shoulders off and went on pursuing them anyway. I did not do it out of sheer arrogance. I did it because I knew I was not going to miss her or others just because we did not agree. I did it because I believed in my ideas, and by pursuing them, I did not damage anybody, so people could agree or disagree, and that was it. They had no reason to dislike me on this ground. But if they did, which was unlikely, I would pay the price of them disliking me. I would rather stick to my ideas and ′evolve my own garden` than lose my soul.

If you refine too much, you conclude nothing.

I remember once a rather funny, if not tragicomic, encounter with a thirty-eight-year-old man who contacted me because he had a peculiar problem. He always came late to his workplace and to his appointments, and at last, his boss got annoyed with him and told him he would be fired unless he got solved this problem. He wanted me to help him out with this problem. I asked him how long a time he ´practiced` this pattern of coming late. He said he had done it ever since he was a teenager. When had he first noticed he behaved in this manner? He told me that at the age of fifteen, he got some mental problems and was sent to a psychoanalyst in the city. In this setting, he realized after a while that he was coming regularly late to the appointments. ´What happened then? Was it commented? ` I asked. ´No, ` he said. ´The session lasted fifty minutes, and the watch was set by the psychoanalyst when the session was supposed to start. ` ´Did your analyst not comment at all on your delays? ` ´Not at all, ` he answered. ´And what about you, did you try to explain them to him? ` ´I did not comment on it either. I did not realize it as a problem. ` ´How long time had you gone to therapy? ` ´From the age of sixteen to last year, ` he said. ´Nineteen years? ` ´Yes, ` he confirmed. ´And in these nineteen years, you came late every time?' He nodded. I was both amused and stricken by the fact that such stupid therapy was still practiced by stupid therapists. ´Why did you stop having therapy with your analyst and decided to start in my clinic? ` I asked. ´Because he died last year, ` he retorted. Imagine this: two stubborn children—one is a trained psychoanalyst and the other one is my client—entangled in some kind of infantile and silly power game against each other for nineteen years? What I found to be morally unacceptable was that the one of them, the one who died, came to live very well on this unresolved problem of the other. The client's problem was solved very quickly by explaining to him the core of the problem utilizing his motivation and pointing to the fact that a well-lived life is essentially a matter of being self-determined and not a victim, pursuing positive reciprocity with people and choosing out of ´benefit-cost` considerations. If it was profitable for him to lose his job, to become a loser, and to end up with losing his faith in life, he could keep on coming late. On the other hand, if he saw the opportunities life could open for him by being focused, resolved, and self-determined, I would be glad to help him do just this. We solved this problem in less than four sessions, and he called me some years later to tell me that he had followed successfully my ´prescription` regarding his life, children, and his work. What I liked about him was that he was not embittered by wasting nineteen years and lots of money on playing ´two stubborn donkeys` with his analyst, but he assured me that this was the last time he had done it.

CHAPTER VI

I SPOT A MISSION: 2000-2012

Is our destiny fixed or mutable? The current state of our minds conceals our ultimate meaning.

The state of our humanity is extremely grim,
all the while people do vainly themselves trim,
obsessed by Maj flies` daydream!

Our Maj fly's destiny is tragic.
Those who accept it are stoic.
Those who deny it are comic.
Those who challenge it are heroic.

Human nature is our cage,
Which fosters our beastly rage,
If we to turn off this page,
We must against the cage
A revolt -stage!

We are its mind slaves that went astray.
We must pursue our evolving way,
If we wish on this earth to stay

The chronic constipation of the human situation:

'Humans' domineering application
is uttering ritualistic replications,
hoping that they are new creations.
Our deceitful minds' fabrication
gives us the kick of mental elevation,
while we`re in a state of stagnation!'

'Praise the creatures who bring our daily salvation!
They start their lives with bursting/flurry animation.
On their way, they are burdened by life's gravitation.
Yet they keep on believing in their own reincarnation.
Generations vanish, and there come new generations
but they hold on to their sacred ritualistic replication,
as sucking babies to their fingers for consolation,
forgetting their own one ultimate aspiration!'

There is the human inferno of sounds and utterances resulting in mass conditioning of human minds, so it is difficult to catch humanity` hymen for our ultimate meaning med our voyage through time, as the above mentioned cacophony erases it.

Has humanity an ultimate mission? of course; our further evolution, without which, our lives are but a blind alley.

Therefore:

'The cubes are cast:
We are not going to last
unless we pursue our evolutionary Must!'

Poshlost' is the Russian version of banality, with a characteristic national flavoring of metaphysics and high morality, and a peculiar conjunction of the sexual and the spiritual. This one word encompasses triviality, vulgarity, sexual promiscuity, and a lack of spirituality. The war against posh lost' was a cultural obsession of the Russian and Soviet intelligentsia from the 1860s to 1960s.

In the West and in my former country, Israel I see this tendency very clearly. While many dictatorships mass produce swarm humans, uncapable of thinking beyond their own conditioning, our societies mass produce dumbed down good life consumers.

At the same time, 'more of the same`, replicating big politics seems to accelerate the problems and the 'Age of Aquarius` is but a fantasy.

Meditation, Mindfulness, Love and Compassion so strongly advocated are not universal cures for the human condition. They relieve pain but not evolve us further beyond sapiens complicated/conflictual nature.

I feel more strongly than ever before that we need to look for measures, beyond politics, religion and social education, which will change humans minds, mindsets, that is to say our conflicting nature, which is the main cause for humanity` downwards spiraling course.

'Call it a new race 'man-Plus's-call it what you will. The people who constitute this new race of men are not of recent arrival; They have been cropping up among men-Homo sapiens, that is-for hundreds, perhaps for thousands of years, but they are trapped in the human environment; they are trapped in the company of men, and they are molded by the company of men and by the human environment So you see, the process is quite certain`(The Trap: Howard Fast).

'The human being cannot live in a condition of emptiness for very long: if he is not growing toward something, he does not merely stagnate; the pent-up potentialities turn into morbidity and despair, and eventually into destructive activities.'

— Rollo May, Man's Search for Himself.

So, what are we, the wise ones to do?

The most rewarding effort for a wise man to engage in our time, in teaching Icarus` minded folk to get much 'stronger wings and brains`, to ascend higher-higher without being burnt and destroyed.

The wisdom, we have to teach is, as I view it, life affirming and sustainable global faith combined with science/technology pursuing/promoting our further evolution beyond sapiens` physical, mental and ideational limitations, which its focus is upgrading us to attain our ultimate meaning; To become Creators by our own right.

Scientifically, we enjoy a progress which can open within this century the possibility of enhancing humans` capabilities and thinking. Yet technologically and socially we run a risk of half success, considering our self- created global setbacks like pollution with the outcome of dumbing us down and make us sick, climate change, wars and conflicts and social disintegration, but have no other credible options, as our human nature has become our deadly foe.

I don´t count any longer on our free will as to motivate us to become far sighted and wiser and to create critical mass for radical change of our self- destructive behavior.

As a potentially advanced civilization we have five global priorities: climate recalibration, sustainability, fair share of resources on earth and our further evolvement, and ´to the stars with difficulties`. Right now, we are not capable to prioritize and operationalize them.

This, to make people aware that this is the direction we have to focus on in the coming centuries, will become my mission! This was meant to be my evolving Bustan` mission, but it took me many years to identify it…

Important historical/psychological observation in these years:

2001

January 15: Wikipedia is launched.

January 20:

George W. Bush is inaugurated as President of the United States.

January 26: An earthquake strikes Gujarat, India, on Republic Day, resulting in more than 20,000 deaths.

May 27: Dos Palmas kidnappings: Twenty tourists are abducted by the Abu Sayyaf Group terrorists from a popular island resort in the Philippines.

September 11: September 11 attacks: Nineteen Al-Qaeda terrorists hijack four planes, crashing two into the twin towers of the World Trade Center in New York City, the third plane into the Pentagon in Washington, DC, while the fourth plane is downed on the outskirts of Stony creek Township, Pennsylvania. 2,996 people, including 2,977 victims and 19 hijackers, die in the attacks.

October 7 – December 17: The United States invades Afghanistan and topples the Taliban regime, resulting in a long-term war.

October 23: Steve Jobs introduces the first iPod.

December 11: China becomes a member of the World Trade Organization.

December 19 — 20: During an economic crisis in Argentina, the government effectively freezes all bank accounts for twelve months which leads to riots and President de la Rúa's resignation from office. There are five ′presidents` in less than a month.

The al-Aqsa Intifada continues.

2002

January 1: The Euro enters circulation.

February 8: The Algerian Civil War ends.

February 27 – March 1: Riots and mass killings in the Indian state of Gujarat leave 1,044 dead.

March 14: SpaceX is founded by Elon Musk.

May 20: East Timor gains independence.

July 1: The International Criminal Court is established.

July 9: The African Union is founded.

September 19: The First Ivorian Civil War begins.

October 12: The 2002 Bali bombings killed 202 people and injured 209 more.

October 23 – 26: Chechen rebels seize a theater in Moscow. Amid this siege, around 200 people died.

November 16: The 2002-2004 SARS outbreak begins in Guangdong, China.

2001–2002 India–Pakistan standoff ends.

Israel starts Operation Defensive Shield in the West Bank in response to a wave of Palestinian suicide attacks.

Construction of the Israeli West Bank barrier begins.

America demands Iraq allow unfettered access to weapons inspectors.

The Guantanamo Bay detention camp is established.

2003

February 1: Space Shuttle Columbia disintegrates upon reentry, killing all 7 astronauts on board.

March 19: The United States invades Iraq and ousts Saddam Hussein, triggering worldwide protests and 8 years` war.

August 5: 2003 Marriott Hotel bombing kills 12 people.

August 27 – 29: The first six-party talks, involving South and North Korea, the United States, China, Japan and Russia.

November 3 – 23: The Rose Revolution occurs in Georgia.

November: The War in Darfur begins.

The Human Genome Project is completed.

The Second Congo War ends with more than 5 million dead.

The Second Liberian Civil War ends.

The last Volkswagen Beetle is made in Mexico, after 65 years in production.

Final flight of the SST (Supersonic Transport) Concorde.

2004

February 4: Facebook is formed by Mark Zuckerberg, Andrew McCollum, Eduardo Saverin, Dustin Moskovitz, and Chris Hughes.

March 11: Madrid train bombings killed 193 people and injured around 2,000, Europe's deadliest attack since Pan Am Flight 103.

September 1 – 3: On September 1st (first school day in Russia), a group of Chechen terrorists held students, parents, and teacher's hostage in Beslan school, in North Ossetia–Alania. During three days under attack, 334 people died.

November 7 – December 23: The Second Battle of Fallujah occurs. It is the deadliest American battle since Vietnam, killing 95 troops.

November 18: Massachusetts becomes the first U.S. state to legalize same-sex marriage.

December 26: Boxing Day Tsunami occurs in Indian Ocean, leading to the deaths of 230,000.

NATO and the European Union incorporates most of the former Eastern Bloc.

Spirit and Opportunity land on Mars.

Orange Revolution in Ukraine.

First surface images of Saturn's moon Titan.

2005

January 9: Second Sudanese Civil War ends.

February 14: YouTube is founded by Jawed Karim, Chad Hurley and Steve Chen.

February 14 – April 27: Cedar Revolution in Lebanon triggered by the assassination of Rafic Hariri.

March 22 – April 11: Tulip Revolution in Kyrgyzstan.

July 7: 7/7 attacks on London Underground.

July 26 – 27: Floods in Maharashtra, India over 1000 people die.

July 28: The Provisional Irish Republican Army ends its military campaign in Northern Ireland.

August 18: Peace Mission 2005, the first joint China–Russia military exercise, begins its eight-day training on the Shandong Peninsula.

August 29 – 31: Hurricane Katrina kills 1,836 people in the Gulf of Mexico.

September 30: Controversial drawings of Muhammad are printed in the Danish newspaper Jyllands-Posten, sparking outrage and violent riots by Muslims around the world.

October 8: 80,000 were killed in an earthquake in Kashmir, Pakistan and Afghanistan.

Israel withdraws from Gaza.

Second Sudanese Civil War ends.

2006

January 25: Hamas wins the 2006 Palestinian legislative election.

February 22: 2006 al-Askari mosque bombing turns the escalation of sectarian violence in Iraq into a full-scale war (the Iraqi Civil War of 2006-2008).

March 21: Twitter is launched.

April 23: Spotify is launched.

July 11: Mumbai bombings.

August 11: Guimaraes oil spill.

September 19: A coup d'état in Thailand overthrows the government of Prime Minister Thaksin Shinawatra.

November 21: Comprehensive Peace Accord ends the Nepalese Civil War.

December 30: Execution of Saddam Hussein by hanging.

2006 Lebanon War.

Mexican Drug War begins.

Somalia War of 2006 begins.

The Baiji, the Yangtze River dolphin, becomes functionally extinct.

Israeli soldier Gilad Shalit is abducted by Hamas.

2007

January 9: Introduction of the iPhone.

January 25: A civil war escalated in the Gaza Strip throughout June, which resulted in Hamas eventually driving most Fatah-loyal forces from the Strip. In reaction, Palestinian president Mahmoud Abbas dismissed Hamas prime minister Ismail Haniyeh and dissolved the Hamas-ruled parliament.

March 4: First Ivorian Civil War ends.

April 16: Virginia Tech shooting.

August 15: Anti-government protests in Myanmar suppressed by ruling junta.

December 13: 27 EU member states sign the Treaty of Lisbon, with the treaty coming into effect on December 1, 2009.

Spike in food prices and subprime crisis help trigger global recession.

2008

Tesla Roadster launched in 2008, the first mass production lithium-ion battery electric car.

May 2: Cyclone Nargis kills 133,000 in Myanmar.

November 4: Barack Obama is elected to become the first black President of the United States.

November 26 – 29: 2008 Mumbai attacks.

The Gaza War begins.

2008 South Ossetia war.

Kosovo declares independence, though it is not recognized by the United Nations.

Iraqi forces crack down on Muqtada al Sadr's Mahdi forces in Basra and Sadr City.

The Large Hadron Collider is completed as the world's largest and most powerful particle collider.

Stock markets plunge around the world, signaling the start of the Great Recession.

2009

January 3: The cryptocurrency Bitcoin is launched.

June 16: Formation of BRICS economic bloc.

September 26: Typhoon Ketsana kills 789 people in the Philippines.

The Gaza War ends while Gaza blockade continues.

The Sri Lankan Civil War ends.

Election protests begin in Iran.

The Second Chechen War ends.

Boko Haram rebellion begins in Nigeria.

2009 swine flu pandemic began in North America.

2010

January 12: A 7.0 magnitude earthquake in Haiti kills 230,000.

February 18: 2010 Nigerien coup d'état.

March 29: 2010 Moscow Metro bombings.

April 10: The President of Poland, Lech Kaczyński, is among 96 killed when their airplane crashes in Smolensk.

April 20: The largest oil spill in US history occurs in the Gulf of Mexico.

May 31: Gaza flotilla raid.

July 22 – August 10: 2010 Colombia–Venezuela diplomatic crisis.

August 23: Manila hostage crisis.

November 23: North Korea shells the island of Yeonpyeong.

A military crackdown occurs in Thailand.

The threat of Greece defaulting on its debts triggers the European sovereign debt crisis and Republic of Ireland's financial crisis.

Arab Spring starts.

Kyrgyz Revolution of 2010.

The iPad is introduced.

Instagram is launched.

2011

February 22: Christchurch earthquake kills 185 and injures 2,000.

March 11: A 9.0 earthquake in Japan triggers a tsunami and the meltdown of the Fukushima Nuclear Power Plant.

May 2: Osama bin Laden is shot dead by United States Navy SEALs in Pakistan.

July 9: Independence of South Sudan.

July 22: 2011 Norway attacks.

August 6 – 11: Riots flare across England.

October 20: Muammar Gaddafi is captured and killed during the Battle of Sirte.

World population reaches 7 billion.

Arab Spring: revolutions in Tunisia, Egypt and Libya follow, as well as uprisings in Yemen and Bahrain, and protests in several other Arab countries.

Syrian civil war begins.

Second Ivorian Civil War.

Second Ivorian Civil War ends with the arrest of former president Laurent Gbagbo.

Iraq War ends.

Bombings occur in Russia and Somalia.

Floods in Pakistan, Thailand and the Philippines kill roughly 2,500 people.

NASA launches spacecraft to visit Jupiter and Mars.

2012

May 7: Vladimir Putin is elected president of Russia for the third time.

July 20: 2012 Aurora, Colorado shooting.

October 22 – November 22: Hurricane Sandy causes $70 billion in damage and kills 233 people.

November 6: Barack Obama wins second term as President of the United States, defeating former Massachusetts Governor Mitt Romney.

November 26 – December 8: UN Climate Change Conference agrees to extend the Kyoto Protocol until 2020.

December 4 – 9: Typhoon Bopha kills over 1,600 in the Philippines.

December 14: Sandy Hook Elementary School shooting.

Conflict begins in the Central African Republic.

Israel launches Operation Pillar of Defense against the Palestinian-governed Gaza Strip.

The US rover, Curiosity, takes a selfie on Mars and finds evidence of an ancient streambed of water on the Red Planet.

Northern Mali conflict, the MNLA declares Azawad an independent state.

In this period, the idea of the collective, socialistic kibbutz is being buried down and my kibbutz resembles most of all in its functioning a little town.

What did happen with human nature, being reflected by the above- mentioned world` events? Nothing. It stayed stable, partly beast and partly humans.

My story: Baseless hopes on the verge of illusions and delusions-Waiting for Godot! (Godot: a play where people wait for somebody who never arrives!)

In 2000 I grasped that hope underlying most of our convictions and aspirations, being blended with both illusions and delusions, is simply not enough any longer to save us from our own folly and vices in a growing unsustainable, warming up and polluted world, which we are generating.

Hope comes as the last out of Pandora box, but we need the light of farsighted wisdom, as the darkness of folly-creamed with baseless hopes- is in us all the time!

Otherwise, there are dystopias which are awaiting us in this stage of our development. The best known are Orwel´s and Huxley`: ´What Orwell feared were those who would ban books. What Huxley feared was that there would be no reason to ban a book, for there would be no one who wanted to read one. Orwell feared those who would deprive us of information. Huxley feared those who would give us so much that we would be reduced to passivity and egoism. Orwell feared that the truth would be concealed from us. Huxley feared the truth would be drowned in a sea of irrelevance. "Orwell feared we would become a captive culture. Huxley feared we would become a trivial culture, preoccupied with some equivalent of the feelies, the orgy porgy, and the centrifugal bumblepuppy. As Huxley remarked in Brave New World Revisited, the civil libertarians and rationalists who are ever on the alert to oppose tyranny 'failed to take into account man's almost infinite appetite for distractions.' In 1984, Huxley added, people are controlled by inflicting pain. In Brave New World, they are controlled by inflicting pleasure. In short, Orwell feared that what we hate will ruin us. Huxley feared that what we love will ruin us` Postman (!985.)

[This excerpt from Amusing Ourselves to Death: Public Discourse in the Age of Show Business (Penguin Books, 1985, pages XIX-XX) has been published by Delancey Place, `A brief daily email with an excerpt or quote we view as interesting or noteworthy`.]

I realized that unless we find a way of making people wiser, as to create a critical mass to change our current, consumer/exploiter mentality, we are up for apocalyptic trouble in this and the coming centuries.

Slowly it became clear to me, that dreaming of ascending is not escapism or the enemy of reality; it's our blessing compared to our all too present ′power monger, divisive, greedy short -sight. This greedy, power monger, divisive short sightedness is highly contagious, being passed on from generation to generation through our traditions, religions, ideologies, and life views. It is a curse stemming from our very nature!

It became clear to me, that there is a mighty taboo in our lives, our tacit conspiracy to ignore who or what we really are and can become. For thousands of years the religious anthropocentric conviction made us believe that we were the center and purpose of creation. It turned out to be wrong.

The prevalent sensation of oneself as a separate ego enclosed in a bag of skin, strongly promoted in our time (′individualism`) has caused much alienation in our minds towards ourselves and our planet, indicating that this view of ourselves and our potentials is somewhat also wrong.

As is so often the case, what we have suppressed and overlooked is obvious. The Germans call it a Hintergendanke, an apprehension lying tacitly in the back of our minds, which we cannot easily admit, even to ourselves. We are partly blindfolded survivors, who can either evolve and become Creators or destroy ourselves.

All those people who can identify the current feeling of "Hintergendanke" regarding humanity's present state and future perspectives, and who wish to find new ways of evolving are on my wavelength.

while working with all kinds of clients and watching the mental state of the populations in Europe and USA I started asking myself: If it is so good- our psychological massive help and prophylactic work- why more and more people suffer of mental problems.

Then in the 198eeth, I read some of Lester Brown assertions on the worsening state of our planet and our responsibility for this. Lester Brown was an icon of several movements: the green revolution, population control, sustainable development, and environmental conservation. He founded two think tanks, the World watch Institute and the Earth Policy Institute.

I became aware of his writing on Climate change and global sustainability already in the 80eeth, but it took me time -10 years- to fit it into my view of humanity declining mental health, global, cognitive decline and our limited mental capacity to deal with global issues. Then around 2000 I became good at predicting future events, due to my understanding of the complicated and contradictory human nature.

I became aware of the mental pitfalls of humans` brains and mindsets:

Collective fanatism /swarm behavior, dichotomous prone faiths and ideologies and lack of critical thinking have been plaguing us throughout our history and constitute mortal dangers for our future journey.

Could it be that God/Nature created a human brain hooked on rigid, untested convictions, which infect humans` swarms, forming hereby deluded reality? Probably.

It became apparent for me that we are partly beasts, partly potential angels:

We heal and kill: Health care, sanitation and food supply have become better in our time, while air pollution, overweight, lifestyle ailments, drug abuse and mental illness have taken a very heavy toll on many millions of humans` health and life expectancy.

It became apparent for me that our affliction: Cognitive dissonance is the king of our reality:

The state of having inconsistent thoughts, beliefs, or attitudes, especially as relating to behavioral decisions and attitude change.

Cognitive dissonance is mantal defect all humans and societies suffer of in varying degrees. In its core lies the blind and automated defense of the integrity/status and self - view of people and nations. ´I am more right, wiser, better and therefore have the right for my actions/attitudes` is its software

Some examples of cognitive dissonance include:

- Smoking: Many people smoke even though they know it is harmful to their health. ...
- Eating meat: Some people who view themselves as animal lovers eat meat and may feel discomfort when they think about where their meat comes from.
- Being human rights/open debates/ peace loving adherents and enforcers in their own countries, while being war mongers and power/greed followers in the world, starting many conflicts.
- Claiming to act freely and yet accept being puppet on a string in relation to a big power.

As long as humans and societies will be under the control of this self- destructive mode of thinking, we will keep stumbling around in our efforts to be become wiser as to manage world affairs.

2000: Who am I?

When I became fifty-five years old, I threw a big party. One of the guests held a speech about the creation of the world from the point view of an ancient Persian tale. When God created the world, he formed three types of human beings. The first type was the camel human beings. They were strong, resilient, hardworking, and determined. They walked long distances, in a long row, bearing their burden. The second type was the bird human beings. They were light and not at all hardworking, but on the other hand, they could raise themselves up from the life mud and dirt and see great horizons and perspectives opening for mankind. The third type was sort of a mixture, kind of orchid bird: they were strong with small wings that could not bring them up to see great horizons. They could run very fast but would not bear a thing, and in a moment of danger, they could bury their heads in the sand. The speaker turned to me, after describing these three human types, and asked me in rhetoric style where I would place myself. A pause, and then I answered, ´If I was to decide, I would be alternating between a camel who can work hard and determined with patience and determination and a bird which could fly up and get both oversight and the splendid, breath-taking landscapes and visions that can only be seen from this perspective`.

2001: I reached the following terrifying conclusion: This century as well as the next ones will be crucial for the survival of advanced, ever evolving and sustainable civilization, without which the human world will disintegrate and fall apart.

There are many predictive suggestions regarding what we may expect within40- years:

2 degrees Celsius above the preindustrial mean temperature may mean 40 feet higher sea level within one hundred years:

The ice sheets will melt quickly, and that the world will need to ramp up its climate efforts to avert disastrous sea level rise.

I must shoulder the responsibility of both the canary bird in the mine and the guide out of the collapsing mine… It will cost me disapproval, belittling and ignorance at the beginning, but it is a MUST.

Voltaire gave me the last kick in his saying:

´Our wretched species is so made that those who walk on the well-trodden path always throw stones at those who are showing a new road. `— Voltaire

2002: If binary thinking/vanity are the rules, and propaganda /brain washing enhance them, citizens become zombies, not enlightened thinkers.

Humans fall into their binary thinking/ Vanity vortex,

reducing hereby the functioning of their neo cortex I must engage myself in this mission of explaining that investing in wiser people is the only long- term viable solutions for our plights, which are mainly due to our contradictory nature.

I must engage myself in this mission of explaining that investing in wiser people is the only long- term viable solutions for our plights, which are mainly due to our contradictory nature.

To become a good thinker beyond the conditioning mainstream/ Group Think constraints you must have varied/contrasting life experience, close contact with nature, some child` experience with children's games which develop social skills and responsibility for the common good, where Talk and Walk supplement each other. You must be free of greed and vanity, the cancer of modern civilization. You must be able to free yourself from human common dichotomous thinking and swarm semi- automatic behavior and use critical thinking to fight conditioned convictions and Mundus Vult Decipi. You must command knowledge of human history, human` nature and its mental pitfalls!

We are slaves of dichotomous thinking, of blindly trusted life narrative/convictions and their byproduct-vanity, and of debilitating short sight.

´Knowing is not enough; we must apply. Willing is not enough; we must do`

--(Attrib. to) Johann Wolfgang von Goethe (1749-1832)

In 2003, working with people for many years and observing the human nature and condition and the slow deterioration of the global climate, I walked on the dusty path at the age of almost fifty-five toward the place where my Bustan flourished once, many years ago. Darkness came tiptoeing on the hills, and the first stars were flickering and blazing up in the sky, inviting and enchanting. I thought, Soon Orion, the Great Hunter, will dominate the sky overhead. Do people sense, looking at the night sky—which became invisible in towns and cities around the world—that we are a part of something incredibly awesome and wonderful, a quest more marvelous than most of us imagine? ´Look up at them, ` I whispered to myself and pointed up toward the glimmering stars. ´They are also a part of it, ` I said to myself. ´To the stars, through difficulty, is the essence of our evolving journey. Never mind the details right now. You will work them out later!" I kept talking to myself. 'Just remember that occasionally, the fundamental laws of the human life universe, as we know them, seem to be momentarily suspended. And not only does everything evolve right, but nothing seems to be able to keep it from going right. In the same spirit of semi miracles, we can make ourselves, fusing what we are with what we wish to be and into what we must become. I am not sure why it must be so. But it is, and it helps me to focus on it!'

Against the darkening sky, the warrior part of me talked to the other comfort-seeking part, 'Where are you hiding, Benjamin? How long time will you hide from your responsibilities and mission? Will you walk here on earth like most of us who want to make a difference in this human world but remain what they least of all wish to be—ordinary, temporary guests in this world? Or will you reply to this nagging question with 'Here am I to serve our grand purpose!"

The question haunted me for some time. And then the warrior won, and I came to cross a threshold by accepting that a precondition for making our world sustainable and flourishing again was our further evolvement. We had to evolve beyond sapiens as we were not wise enough to nurture the gift of earth-Bustan- which was granted us. It was a painful recognition, but from it I could—at last—move to ask a down-to-earth question: how to make it happen.

First step was to acknowledge the fact that mainstream psychology does not help us a bit regarding our global difficulties, although its focus the human nature/psych.

Upon realizing this, I had to find the courage, determination, and focus to challenge and defy the mainstream psychological thinking.

I went on extending mainstream psychology from dealing mostly with individuals, groups, and organizations, to deal with our history, politics, lifestyle, economy, demography, and ecology do to us on a global scale. I added to it other crucial aspects to our well-being like modernity and its stressors, the deterioration of global ecology, consumerism as a lifestyle and meaning, unsustainable global economy and demography, and even unsustainable spirituality in our global focus.

Both these disciplines must be included in the evaluation of what makes us thrive or wither and in the cure of these malaises if we were to reduce humans' misery and enhancing our and nature` well-being.

2006: I learn to think strategically and evolving:

The Persian Sufi philosopher Rumi told the following story that clearly illustrates my view of the impact of human stupidity on us: In a lake there were three fish, one wise, one half-intelligent, and the third, stupid. Some fishermen came by with their fishing nets. The three fish got frightened. The wise fish evaluated the situation and decided to leave the lake immediately, seeking the safety of the ocean. It didn't find it opportune to consult with the others, for they were very attached to their lake, and would no doubt weaken his resolve to flee. The two others viewed the lake as HOME. The wise fish was convinced that their attachment and lack of knowledge would keep them there. The wise fish told them 'I'm leaving! ` It struggled along and, like a deer being chased by the dogs, suffered greatly on its way, but finally made it to the safety of the ocean. The half-intelligent fish thought: 'My guide has gone. I should have gone with him, but I didn't, and now I have lost my chance to escape. I wish I'd gone with him`. He mourned the absence of his guide for a while and then decided to pretend to be dead. Maybe that would save his life. And he did so, floating on the surface of the water. He was picked up by his tail by a fisherman who spat upon him and threw him on the ground. He rolled over and over again and slid discreetly into the lake. Meanwhile the dumb fish was agitatedly jumping about, trying to escape the fishing nets. Using his agility and being confident of his cleverness, he was sure that he would escape. But alas, a net caught him, and as he was put on the frying pan. A thought rushed through his head: 'If I ever get out of this, I'll never live within the confines of a lake again. Next time-the ocean! I'll make the infinite into my home`. In this metaphorical story, the wise fish is strategic in his view and execution of his plan. It creates new perspectives and possibilities for itself. The half-intelligent fish is a shortsighted tactician without a clear overview and grand scheme, and its attitude is very risky in dangerous times, as the story points out. And the dumb fish, well, it pays the price for being dumb in a dangerous time. I wonder if you can see some parallels to our time's predicaments and how people, institutions, governments, and agencies view and ignore them.

2008: Are we sapiens at all? Both the deception and the revelation!

Look at the shadowy side of humanity: There are so many Jihadists, ruthless capitalists, inflaming populists, reckless hedonists, and naïve anarchists. They are all perverted human beings to certain degrees.

Take a long-term perspective regarding global sustainability into account: the industrial giants of the 19th century were not called 'robber barons` for nothing. Great entrepreneurs succeed by breaking the old rules and pursuing crazy, greedy and unsustainable vision, invariably undermining the truth of our evolving journey. This Glod calf′ vision can't be applicable in regard to our deadly challenge; fighting global pollution, climate change, and the depletion of the planet's resources. In this area, we don't have the benefit of the doubt to play with cheaters or wait for their betterment. Cheating is what may put our civilization down.

I concluded that Homo sapiens are driven by mental hardware, which I dub as Stupidligence.

We are Homo Stupidligence both as social and political animals, because we alternate—without being in control of it—in our behavior between deeds of brilliant intelligence and self-destructive deeds of utter stupidity; between being aware of our mental limitations yet denying our own folly when it suits us; and between what we say we will do to better life on earth, and what we actually do. We are burdened by the following interconnected mental problems, which define Homo Stupidligence:

1. The short-term gain, long-term pain: A cognitive-emotional dissonance when we deal with the long-term global future. Generally, humans will choose the short-term benefit even though it results in severe long-term problems. The ongoing economic and financial crisis (2008-2013) due to our reckless greed and speculations and lack of prudence, is a clear example of peoples' and nations' shortsighted behavior resulting in much pain.

Likewise, it is reflected also in the way we treat our health. More and more people are harmed by hormone-like drugs that exist in our foodstuffs, beverages, shampoos, and creams. At the same time, the agricultural sector increases its use of pesticides, antibiotics, and agents to promote quick growth. The explanation: we have to feed more and more mouths, as the population grows. But if the cost is that we will feed humans like the animals we feed on, and eventually, with the growth of population and the climate change (generating draughts and flooding worldwide), many of these people will die of starvation anyway, then what is the long-term gain?

These are a few examples of the combination of cynicism, laissez-faire, covetous goodness, and reckless greed amounting to shortsighted stupidity, which is characteristic to Homo Stupidligence.

2. The tragedy of the commons: This means that each individual person will aim at gaining his own short-term goals and interests rather than the long-term interests for the common good, and thus eventually create major collective catastrophes. In the sixties Garret Hardin recognized this psychological mechanism and its scary but inevitable effect and recurrence.11 In our civilization, we have degenerated into a "serve your-self" mentality. Unrestrained, we consume the globe's limited resources just like pigs in a pigsty. When it comes to tangible and independent action, people be-have in a greedy and ruthless way regarding our common future; we cut down trees in the Amazon, exhaust and pollute our drinking water reserves, poison our oceans, and burn oil and coal as never before. Only a minority of the population is willing to sacrifice their own individual interests and comfort for the common good of our future generations.

We saw troubling examples of the validity of this mechanism at the Climate Conferences in Copenhagen, Cancun, Durban, and Qatar, where the interests of national states triumphed and superseded a sustainable solution for the common good.

3. The ego trippers' cultivation: Most of the people on this planet truly believe that they will end up in some kind of Paradise, reincarnation, or other "arrangements" which will infinitely preserve their spirits or minds or render their souls a kind of eternity. This conviction, which is rooted in our denial of our temporariness and insignificance, is in fact self-promotion and ego tripper cultivation. This illusory conviction has resulted in countless tragedies and holy wars through-out human history.

4. Self-deception: We possess an impressive talent for legitimizing our absurd thoughts and actions to our-selves and consequently, we voluntarily wander into traps and blind alleys.

This is the foundation and fountain for all religions, which billions of people accept. This is how we create meaning and cope with our own faults, unpredictability, and the meaninglessness of life. This approach to life, being biased by illusion and delusion, is not compatible with the complex and menacing reality we face and have created as well. Had my family members in Poland not put their faith in God as a guarantee for justice on Earth and as the force to salvage them from the Nazis, they stood a fairer chance to survive than following like sheep.

Sorrowfully, most people follow this self-deception to some extent!

5. We are incurable cheaters: People have always lied and cheated. And business people may have lied and cheated more than most: in a survey of American graduate students, 56 percent of those pursuing an MBA admitted to having cheated in the previous year, compared with 47 percent of other students.

6. And more and more people distrust businesses thanks to scandals and broken promises.

Many social psychologists contend that the vast majority of people are prone to cheating. They are more willing to cheat on other people's behalf than their own.

People routinely struggle with two opposing emotions. They view themselves as honorable. But they also want to enjoy the benefits of a little cheating, especially if it reinforces their belief that they are a bit more intelligent or popular than they really are.

Customers like to think well of themselves; but they also like small bribes. The key is to convince them that an in-document is not really a bribe. So, for example, drug reps make doctors feel beholden by inviting them to give lectures in golf resorts or by offering to fund their terribly important research.

Doctors naturally think their later decisions are taken entirely with their patients' best interests in mind; in fact, they may be kidding themselves and cheating their patients.

Can something effective be done about dishonesty? I doubt it, and particularly on a global scale in connection with, for example, polluting business. The prospects for profit will prove to be much stronger a motivation for Homo sapiens than self-restraint and practicing honesty.

We can hope for the best, but must prepare for the worst, as human beings have a remarkable talent for getting around rules—including the rules they try to impose upon themselves. And new technologies introduce new opportunities for cheating; just look at the e-mail that slips through your spam filter. Moreover, the line between succeeding by cheating and succeeding by serving customers is not always clear, unless we

7. Conspicuous Consumption: Homo Stupidligence is subjected to seduction by conspicuous consumption. The Western civilization and much of the rest of the world are based on us being indulgent, conspicuous, dumb consumers, regardless of the negative consequences to our life conditions and health. Pollution, diet, and lifestyle cause conditions and ailments like obesity, asthma and allergies, diabetes, hypertension, depression, and other mental problems, all exploding Western health budgets.

This phenomenon was brought to light by the Economist Thorstein Veblen in his book The Theory of the Leisure Class. It is characterized this way: a) people buy and use status symbols to draw attention towards themselves and to project wealth and success and surpass others. b) People with this behavior demonstrate indifference towards waste and pollution. c) Its basic mechanism is primitive ape imitation of the aspired norms/group and on the competition to belong with and even outshine, and thereby dominate, the others.

We are used to throwing away useful items and instead buying new prestigious items. This environmentally damaging behavior and "monkey see, monkey do" attitude is wide-spread and most of us can recognize it in our own behavior, but we have hard time controlling and suppressing it. This behavioral pattern of Homo Stupidligence—conspicuous consumption—is now threatening our very future existence.

8. A Babel Tower's state of mind: There is a Jewish saying that ′Where there are two Jews, there are three synagogues.` The state of mankind nowadays is worrisome, because we lack a global direction, mission, and vision, which could make us evolve in a sustainable manner. We have a civilization standing on clay feet, and it is just a matter of time—at most a century—before it will collapse. This endeavor of trying to feed, clothe, educate, and give shelter to 9.5 billion people in 2050 is a metaphoric repetition of the Babel Tower narrative, but this time, it will be Nature, not God, which will brutally dismantle this ′tower.`

The trivial and dumbing noise pollution by the mass media is also a major contributor for promoting and enhancing this state of "Babel Tower" in our time.

You need only listen to a news or debate program for a single evening—especially leading up to an election—to realize the hypnotizing and stupefying effects of this deluge. With such a flow of banalities and non-essential information there is no wonder that the saying "Nonsense baffles brains" be-comes a terrifying reality in a human world, trying to build again a Babel Tower.

9. A search for ultimate life meaning and its pitfall:

Homo Stupidligence seeks transcendental meaning in life but takes the road of escapism towards it. They choose either the religious faith in the Almighty God, who grants this meaning for them, or the individual path, where the focus is on their lives as the Northern star for pursuing this meaning. In the meantime, our world becomes more and more chaotic. Has it anything to do with this slippery search for ultimate meaning with our lives? Obviously, since we need it to navigate our way into a promising future. These two sources of life meaning—the religious and the individual—are basically devoid of long-term perspectives regarding the further journey of our species. Therefore, unless they are supplemented by an all-ruling, viable, and down to earth grand vision regarding advanced intelligent life's ultimate life meaning, they will become redundant even though many will still stick to them to the bitter end.

10. Accomplice behavior:

We contain a propensity to become active or passive accomplices of ideological-religious communities, associations, and criminal groups. This can lead people to commit unimaginable acts of cruelty and folly, to become passive, placid, and non-cooperative in the face of immense danger. While the Nazi criminals executed their orders out of conviction, many ordinary Germans sent countless people to death by becoming passive accomplices to the Nazi regime. Countless people in the modern world send, through their reckless consuming lifestyle, countless numbers of future people into their death, by tipping off the global climate. Both groups would claim that they did not know that their actions or inactions could lead to a brutal outcome.

11. Excessive behavior:

It is a common observation that everything in the human realm decays and dies out, and that this process can be enhanced by human excessive behavior or addictive-compulsive behavior. We often accelerate this process by our excesses.

We become first aware of this malfunction when it has dire consequences on us or on others. As I view most hu-mans as functioning most of the time on a semi-conscious level (according to fixed patterns of thinking and behavior), it is very likely that many things in their lives turn out to be addictions and compulsion.

Homo Stupidligence has, literally, a strong addictive propensity for impulsive greed, power, and other excessive behavior (alcohol, drugs, medicine, sex, etc.), which suppresses long-term thinking and actions. These excesses become destructive without "everything in moderation" and prudence.

To sum it up: The 'Homo Stupidligence syndrome` mani-fests itself in functioning on a semi-conscious level for most people, originating from our unrecognized folly, and results in institutional stupidity with worldwide consequences for our societies and future civilization.

This syndrome has brought about 'The Stupidligence Anthropocene`:

I dubbed our era 'The Stupidligence Anthropocene` after realizing the magnitude of the ill consequences human activities have had on our environment and our reluctance to deal with them effectively. We stand right now at a historical juncture, where humanity's technological progress, its reckless consumption of the planet's resources, irresponsible pollution of its life conditions, its uncontrolled propagation, and its denial of the severity of these self-created problems to our future existence, deserves to be called 'The Stupidligence Anthropocene`.

The Creators are our evolving destiny:

'You have your way. I have my way. As for the right way, the correct way, and the only way, it does not exist.`

— Friedrich Wilhelm Nietzsche

It does exist: It is our evolving journey to ensure our-in ever transforming essence- our longtime survival and mastery. If we keep following parole: If kept following Nietzsche perspective, it will end up with our global doom.

The only way is the way for our long- termed survival and further evolvement into our horizons, vistas, the stars ever mastering and expanding beings; The Creators. This truth I am certain of, as all other relative ways will lead to our extinction and thus Oblivion. With such futile end- our extinction- there is no meaning to all which we do and utter.

Lots of people try throughout history with different ways to better humans, humanity and the world. They have used vast arrays of spiritual/educational /modeling tools/methods, but all their efforts have been like a drop on the sea. We keep being self- destructive.

These well- wishing people have never throughout history succeeded to generate a collective mind alternating Critical Mass among us, as to reduce/weaken our short sighted, beastly and greedy part of our nature.

Therefore, I concluded that only long- term efforts-stretching over hundreds of years, maybe even one thousand years- to upgrade our cognitive/mental and emotional nature is the only tool/method which would work to save us out of our own self- destructiveness, which leads to our oblivion.

2006-I define what I wish to be and why.

In May 2006, I visited my childhood pals in Israel after a long time of not meeting each other. We were all sixty years by now, and the get-together was nice yet also "spiced" by the recognition that the passing time has left some unmistakable marks on our bodies, faces, and souls. Such an encounter brings certain mood up in me, be it ´falling leaves` mental autumn, or some melancholy realizing that a travel comes close to its end. I try to keep this mood at bay by reminding myself of all that life had granted me, including mental alertness, unbound curiosity, a provocative and exploring mind; that my legs, lungs, and heart can, without great exertion of power, manage half a marathon; and of the exciting challenges I plan on taking on. I remind myself of all the provocative and defiant thoughts I am going to put forth, never to surrender to the murmuring voices of groupthink or of ´closing time` mental old age. In my mind, I have a moral obligation to focus my mind on some worthwhile and operational goals greater than ´here and now` and my narrow sphere and insist on achieving them. In such moments, where I meet my old pals, I come to repeat to myself my battle cry, which is taken from the poem of Alfred Tennyson about the legendary Odysseus. Here are some of my favorite lines: ´Death closes all: but something ere the end, some work of noble note, may yet be done, not unbecoming men that strove with Gods . . . . . . Come, my friends. 'Tis not too late to seek a newer world . . . We are not now that strength which in old days Moved earth and heaven; that which we are, we are; One equal temper of heroic hearts, made weak by time and fate, but strong in will to strive, to seek, to find, and not to yield`.

On the other hand, I meet more and more people I knew, who never heard this battle cry, who lived for the sake of living without any high motives or noble purposes. One of them getting dement, showed me his dairies and they are all filled up with accounts of where he travelled, ate, mated, met other people and much lamenting about the political situation, which according to his, went from bad to worse. He was clearly an hedonist type, like many other Israelis and foreigners I met in the city of Copenhagen throughout the years: All very common, looking for being free for obligations to others than themselves, being foodies, self- focused. Is this a man?

We are not doomed to become mentally meek, rigid, and resigned and self- focused pleasure seekers. We are not destined to become conformists, but we are very much prone to this process due to the way our minds work. We seek often security and certainty and group identity in the known rather than challenge and struggle in the domain of the unknown. Our minds start to react in an overcautious manner regarding attaining megalopsychia, already when we are over twenty to twenty-five. Pleasure seeking is a sure lane. Instead of assessing the risks involved in daring something new, the conditioned minds send alarming signals to these people: Do not try to become a wiser Icarus. People like those who resemble them in wits and capacity. What if you fail? What if people will find you silly? Or what if you die somewhere else trying something great instead of in your bed?

This is not being a special man, who defies the odds of revolting for something better than the existing, especially in the face of mortal danger. It is being an ordinary man looking his eyes and his mind for a luring danger. Looking for `Challenging life premises you will find your security` keeps your mind young and agile, while without this warrior mission you become mentally old as you lose the very elements of what made us what we are: explorative, creative, defiant, challenging, ever-expanding and evolving creatures.

2006:

One Sunday afternoon in December, the opening lines in the movie The Lord of the Rings surfaced in my mind: `The world has changed. I feel it in the water. I feel it in the earth. I smell it in the air. Much of that which once was, has been lost`.

Yes, the world has changed radically in people's awareness in the last two years. On Sunday, the tenth of December 2006, I went running around the lake. The sun was bright, the air fresh and crispy, and the temperature was at around 10°C. I did not need my gloves. In the same afternoon, I went on a walk with my wife, and the sun was as bright and beautiful and the air—crispy, and it was nice yet so unusual. Never before had I experienced such a warm December in Denmark. By then, I knew that 2006 had been the warmest year ever since we started to register global temperatures. The consensus among most scientists regarding this new phenomenon, climate change, has emerged, and the culprit for the change was clearly identified: human beings' economical activities. Therefore the tenth of December, which was so seductively beautiful, was also an undisguised warning for us. The world has changed; climate change caused by human activity now became irrefutable fact and perhaps irreversible as well. That is why the lines from the movie came up into my mind as the script on the wall from the Old Testament. If we cease for a while to justify our follies and our ′irrefutable` ideologies in a laughingly vainglorious manner, we will see clearly why our world has come to this point (of no return?). Our global climate has tipped because people in general have been ignoring the ear-deafening whistle of impending necessities that now face us headlong, threatening our very future. I have no doubt in my mind that history will judge us and our civilization in the following manner:

1. The era of unprecedented excesses and lack of checks and balances in areas ranging from global ecology, economy, consumption, lifestyle (including massive transportation of people and goodies resulting in, among other things, the spread of diseases worldwide), values and the total lack of control of global demography
2. The era of unprecedented technological and scientific breakthrough, innovations, and development
3. The era of unprecedented mass facilitation of both information and NBB, where people could become much more informed and enlightened than ever before on all matters including global affairs while the industry of ′mayfly talkativeness` has become a way

of living for countless 'parrot' human beings that confound the citizens' minds and undermining the fruits of enlightenment

4. The era where our latent institutional stupidity has manifested itself in horrifying and ingenious manner regarding management and navigation of world affairs and our common future
5. The era in which there has been a growing consensus on the value of human life (through human rights and improvement in health care and education) while the same value has been undermined by overpopulation, massive pollutions of our environments, and unsustainable ecological and economic policies. I dub our time as the Age of global necessity because our development has brought us to a very crucial junction in our short history, and unless we address the necessities facing us, our civilization will sooner than later crumble down. Mind you, there will probably be some survivors left after a global crisis, but for what human costs and what kind of a brutal world will they live in? All the prayers in the world regardless of religious affiliation, all lotus positions, yoga positions, or rituals aiming at reaching a higher awareness, all compassion and offering the 'second cheek' a la Jesus, love and happiness a la Dalai Lama or 'freedom, ' and 'self-realization' patented by the Western world, blended with the 'sublime wisdom' of the market forces, have not motivated us so far to act in a concerted manner to promote our long-term interests. Unless we are forced to it by sheer necessity, which we first identify qua our nature, facing the abyss, humanity will delay using the needed remedy to ward it off.

The Age of necessity implies working on long-term goals to reestablish sustainability between human beings and earth and its diverse life, and the work must be done on all levels—individual, group, society, and global. Furthermore, it implies working globally to improve and evolve ourselves beyond our mental and biological constraints by trying to form a global policy that fulfills these necessities. The Age of necessity will require our best and some 'up the hill' efforts regarding our minds, time, and energy. We have faced natural catastrophes, devastating human crisis (like epidemics), aggressors and unimaginable atrocities, disasters, and challenges before and yet prevailed, but this is the real big trial, which will demand our very best and protracted efforts. The Age of necessity implies a paradigm shift regarding our longstanding goals and the grand meaning with our lives. The main ideologies of our time, socialism, the capitalistic system, and the religious ideology are bad guides to follow, if we are to survive, thrive, and evolve into the future.

There are two main modes to relate to our existence and observe our reality: The first is the factual and the second is convictions' based approach. Since most people need to believe in some great transcendental force granting meaning to their Maj fly lives, it is hard to build a bridge for people with these differing thinking modes.

In a new paradigm, these ideologies will be, therefore allowed to exist as a personal /social need, but without having a political influence as to dictate a political direction. Ergo, their believers will be submitted to follow the grand outlines of the new, sustainable, and evolving vision.

2007:

Self- knowledge and getting older:

When I came to Denmark, the Danish language did not make any sense to my ears. There were no clear sounds I could really catch up, discern from each other and hold on to withhold. It was like undistinguishable vocals. The Danish mentality was entirely different from what I was used to, and nonverbal language was impossible to interpret. Therefore, every time I had to say something in Danish, I became pretty uncertain. After a year or two of frustration, I made a strategic decision. I said to myself, ´Black is beautiful`. I am as I am, and they will have to take me and accept my broken language and terrible accent. From this moment on, things started moving forward and upward. I even became fond of making speeches in Danish, praising shamelessly my exotic accent as a breakthrough in the recreation of this old language. I faced the enemy—my doubt to open my mouth and hold speeches in this extremely difficult language—and prevailed. This was an experience that deepened my self-knowledge.

In the summer of 2007, I held an improvised speech in a surprise party for a friend who became sixty. He was moved by the speech and, shortly afterward, began talking to the guests about my attributes. Admittedly, I am used to some of these surprises, but when he praised me for being humble, my wife and I looked at each other and smiled broadly. Then I broke in and told him, smiling, that this compliment of me being humble held only to my clothes, food, and the apartment in which we lived, while the rest of me as humble I had a hard time recognizing. There was great laughter. There is no reason to pretend; I am not a model of humbleness when it comes to virtues, but I don´t boast, show off or blow myself up with false significance. My morning prayer is: Put your finger into a glass with water and draw it back. The hole which you left is how important you are. I am not important, but my deeds may be...

I know that I am only worth what I try to contribute to the long term common well of humanity and man. This is also a piece of self-knowledge!

As I grew older, I found out that what threatened me most was forgetting who I really wanted to become. To remind myself this, I wrote to myself a little ´poem` which ends up in the following way: ´I think I choose to become a ´foolish´ visionary. Rather evolutionary than revolutionary! Of all the choices, it is the least scary! ` Having a greater goal than sustaining yourself and your family and succeeding in your time and place to gain status or riches, can make you more resilient toward frustrations and setbacks, which our focus on our micro reality exposes us to.

My View of God:

Religion and religious faith are interwoven into human minds, telling us partly of who we are and mainly of who we wish to be. 'Religion has everything on its side', says Schopenhauer, 'revelation, prophecies, government protection, the highest dignity and eminence . . . and more than this, the invaluable prerogative of being allowed to imprint its doctrines on the mind at a tender age of childhood, whereby they become almost innate ideas. '

I personally believe in God seated in my mind and heart not as a formal or external one. I am convinced that we invented God and the story of God because our awareness cannot tolerate a life without a meaning that does not transcend our biological existence. And it is good because it makes us aspire to become much greater and better than we are, to evolve. Our invented God and the story about Him have formed and influenced us to a great extent, as I pointed out in my book; The Fifth Narrative, because great narratives influence us as well as we influence them. In the long run, we will, if we give ourselves a chance to survive, transform ourselves to Creators, which is our utmost purpose and meaning in our existence.

Do you remember Martin Buber tale-mentioned her before- on a Chassidic rabbi who was imprisoned for suspicion of conspiracy against the regime? The commander of the prison visits him and wishes to catch him in religious contradictions. He asks the old saga, 'How come God asked Adam where he hid himself after eating from the Tree of Knowledge: 'Where are you, Adam?' If this God knows all, as you Jews present Him, why does God ask this question?' The rabbi changes not only the context of this discussion but also its focus by telling the commander that God is all-knowing, but the question should be understood as God's inquiry to all Adams who have existed since the first Adam: 'Where are you in your life? Are you hiding from yourself and me? How are you shouldering your responsibility to find the way of meaning within your life? '

And the rabbi ends the discussion, telling the commander, 'And you are forty-six years old. Where are you, Adam?'

Adam tells God, 'I am hiding, ' so he knows he is hiding, escaping his responsibility. Acknowledging this, he has made the first step toward an awareness of finding his way—responsibility for our evolving journey towards becoming Creators. I, who tasted the fruit of knowledge, like most of us have done, am also tempted to escape from my own personal responsibility of doing more than just living my own life, consume, and daydream. My inner God asks me time and again, 'Where are you, Adam? ' because I am tempted by convenience, comfort, mayfly scoops and trends, and the illusions of being unique without doing anything unique and lasting. I am too tempted by TV programs that waste my time, the pleasures of life, obsessive rituals, transcendental, endless religious and semi religious hyper hopes and who knows what more. Transformed into my language, God in my mind asks, 'What do you do with your life and responsibility right now, Benjamin? Are you hiding from it? Are you hiding from yourself and from the only mission that can lift you beyond your mortal cage? `

I know what my God in my mind talks about, and I know what kind of mission He refers to, and I am thankful because He reminds me of my obligations. Yet, sometimes I do escape and hide because I am just as weak as any other human being, and being a human being is being like a little ant with dimmed awareness of its limitations. Therefore, my God in my mind whispers into my ears, ′Remember Jacob's struggle with the angel. ` ′And Jacob was left alone; and there wrestled a man with him until the breaking of the day. And when he saw that he prevailed not against him, he touched the hollow of his thigh; and the hollow of Jacob's thigh was out of joint, as he wrestled with him. And he said, let me go, for the day breaketh. And he said, I will not let thee go except thou bless me. And he said onto him, what is thy name? And he said, Jacob. Thy name shall be called no more Jacob, but Israel: For as a prince hast thou power with God and with men, and hast prevailed. (Old Bible).

The struggle Jacob had with God's messenger at Jabbok was not initiated by Jacob, but by God, who wanted to test Jacob's resolve, faith, and commitment. And Jacob prevailed and was blessed. Being challenged to show what we can and taking the fight against our own demons, fears, self-repression and slave mentality, bring the best out of us as evolving intelligent beings. My God tells me time and again, ′Do not be afraid, Jacob-Adam, to challenge me if your challenge is life affirming, sustainable, long term, and evolving. Trust me by challenging me!'

What am I transforming into: A visionary or a fraud?

Now, gentlemen, let us do something today which the world may talk of hereafter. —Admiral Collingwood (1748-1810) before the Battle of Trafalgar, October 21, 1805,

Imagine that you are on a journey as fateful and inevitable as the one the hobbits Frodo and Sam were forced to take in Tolkien' saga, The Lord of the Rings. Frodo has in his possession the One Ring, which must be destroyed to prevent the evil forces from taking over the world. He is on his mission out of sheer necessity, realizing that the hobbits' way of life and the civilized world are in mortal danger. If he fails, both are doomed.

Your journey as Homo sapiens is somewhat different, yet both fateful and inevitable if you are to survive the next stage in the history of intelligent life. Your journey is different in the sense that it is not aimed at preserving the old world and you in your current mind, with its intricate conflicts and excesses. This mindset is doomed, regardless of what you wish. The only good thing you can do for it is to transform it. The aim and meaning of your journey is to reshape and reform wisely our minds and our world and simultaneously transform yourself your fellow intelligent beings. In this transformative journey, you are the creator of the coming changes, including transforming yourself as well. What does it mean? It means that on this particular journey, we are not going to keep being what we were at the start, yet with your active help and engagements, your great-grandchildren will salute you for taking on this visionary journey and grand task. You will become, in their eyes, the legendary pioneer who thwarted humanity of its self-destructive tendencies and spearheaded it into its only ultimate mission: to survive, prevail, and evolve.

I do not know what your personal destiny will be, but one thing I know: the only ones among us who can be truly content are those who have sought and found how to serve humanity's long-term aspirations and grand goals. Years ago, I tried to condense in the following little verse my life view.

What Am I to Choose?

´If I am to become a servant of God, what are the odds of finding my own evolving road? Many servants of God who went astray, I tended and helped and showed them a way.

If I am to choose the dung beetles' goal, living alone on oversight blocking dung balls, can I ever find beyond them worthy mission or calling?

If I to become a flurry mayfly, unaware that tomorrow I will surely die, unknowing of possibilities that ahead of me lie, can one die for not asking, ´Where to? And why?`

If I wish to become trivial news—quacking frog, will I fill people's minds with clarity or fog? Will my ceaseless talk avoid becoming mental smog?

If I choose to become a leisurely sofa sitter, how long will it take for this ´sweetness` to turn bitter and for my life's perspectives to become littered?

I think I choose to become a ´foolish` visionary. Rather evolutionary than revolutionary, because of all the choices, it is the least scarry!'

A mutant?!

Something happened to me. I can see a hundred, a thousand, or even a million years ahead. It can snap a glimpse of the potential future to come, and I can even envision the creation of a super-continent some 250 million years from now. I can see the horrible conditions on Earth one billion years from now, as the sun starts her death struggle by expanding and heating Earth. I can see, but I cannot strategically plan any reliable contingency. I tell myself that if intelligent life like us is to survive when Earth becomes unfit for habitation due to human activities, we have to colonize our solar system as the second step after trying to reset the global climate. They have to supplement each other. We need to reach to the stars. That will take much longer than to reach the moon and Mars, but can we last until then? It is a terrible feeling sometimes to have in this sense because it has its overview but lacks yet strategic thinking and operative contingencies. I, who all my life combined my overview with appropriate and resolute actions, am disturbed by this impotence when it comes to saving humanity from its own misdeeds.

But in the meantime I can do my best on pointing these dangers and how we can flee our cognitive/mental/emotional cage`(current human nature) to face them head on.

The mental capacity of human minds is good at catching the fleeting, the passing moment, the mundane, and speculative transcendence, not at seeing its evolving potentials, so I feel alone in this respect!

It is not because some people cannot oscillate between the mundane and transcendent potentials we possess, but they stop often there as they don´t dare thinking beyond sapiens limitations. Ideas as pursuing our evolving potential and thereby overgoing our current species mental capacity is almost a sacrilege for them.

They often claim that we can manage our future challenges-including our self- created ones-with the intelligence and overview we already possess.

Why most people seemed blind to these dire prospects and our mental limitations?

Rejection of dire reality in the making is a very common escapist flight for sapiens and most people use it profusely. Other realize it by still thinking: After me -the deluge!

They think; Espere, which in Spanish word covering two meanings: ´waiting` and ´hoping`.

Espere Is an Attitude most People tend to follow when the task /challenge ahead seems overwhelming.

Espere without some long-term and life-evolving planning or bright prospective is demoralizing for the human spirit, and therefore, spiritual guides and political leaders—lacking them—feel compelled to grant these hopeful masses some meat to chew on. Since Jesus, who could transform water into wine, lots of imitators and charlatans claimed to be able to do the same. Many of them have been politicians and religious leaders with their entourage of propagandists and experts in mass brainwashing.

Believe me or not, but I have become rather good at predicting the near human future. This future is going to be murder in the rest of this century and beyond, mainly because we don´t seem to learn much from our history and deny our complicated, contradictory nature, and thereby ignore our growing global predicaments which interrelate with each to accentuate the coming crisis. I assume that as long as man has the same nature and brain/limited wisdom to think long-term, man will keep stumbling over his own feet, even to the points of decay, degeneration and chaos. He may stop short of total destruction of himself, but the price will be staggering for his lifestyle and billions of lost lives and. Nature will survive, but at what costs?

I foresaw the mounting mental problems hitting young children and adolescents, who were brought up with the ideology and practice of self- gratifications of all their whims and lusts, without any collective vision to pursue and work for. Compared with my background, where sublimation of our sexual drifts and other impulses was the thing to strive for, as it channeled our energy into working for something greater than our impulses the common well of society, thereby becoming tough and focused with clear cut identity, the children in the West seem confused about their identities and purpose in life due to pursuing their gratifications, personal careers and ′see me` vane show off. This ego focus does not lift people up over their petty life and ordinariness. And even worse. It turns people into compulsive, brain washed consumers, thus becoming the vermin of the world.

I reasoned that if we are the vermin causing nature and its sustainable balance to go awry, we must find a way to reset it by putting force new priorities and values which will, over centuries, change human global behavior. This project cannot be done only by political means. It implies making humans better long- term thinkers, much more amiable and benevolent and resistant to their impulses, whims, and the market′ seductive forces.

In 2008, In a burst of inspiration, I completed in verse my idea regarding our ultimate meaning as an Evolving, Advanced Intelligence:

′ Beware human being:

> **You stand on your destiny′ crossroad.**
> **The first road steers to your demise,**
> **following your automatic mind` code.**
> **on the second, you`ll evolve into Semi God`**

As:

> **′The ultimate human Meaning and Must,**
> **is in defying the destiny of animated dust.**
> **Challenging the constraints of life's Animator,**
> **to evolve and ascend and become a creator.**
> **Pursuing this road, you will become a creator.**
> **Rejecting it, you`ll become your destiny` traitor`-**

From this point of time, started my count down for crossing my mental Rubicon, the vision was slowly forming in my mind.

What are the Long-Term Consequences of This New vision?

It removes the authority of religions and cognitive capitalism, consumerism and other dichotomous, manipulating Isms'.

It is not meant to reject them altogether but to view them as private matters of belief, without any political influence or channels to brainwash children/ people mind`s with.

This vision stresses that Homo sapiens have played out their role in intelligent life's further evolvement and should be upgraded soon, to avoid our self-destructiveness.

This vision advocates phasing out the role of Homo sapiens in the next 400-1000 years to come while bringing into the arena a new, upgraded, and wiser beings stemming from, of us, who will be able to stop humanity's compulsive excesses and self-destructiveness.

This vision supports genetics editing, robotics, AI and other technologies to help the future.

Enhanced humans to think and execute far sightedly and long term, to live free of human demons and delusions and self- delusions, and to steer safely the upgraded humanity toward new and exhilarating horizons and vistas. This is the evolutionary essence of my forming vision. It is the best bet I can conceive to escape our own creating hubris and therefore it is most compassionate toward sapiens, granting us the best chance to evolve and prevail.

My vision is based on the following facts:

1) Life is basically harsh and unjust (which brings the question of a benevolent God into the open). Lots of innocent children, youngsters, grownups, and animals never get a chance to grow up to maturity or get a chance for decent life, because they are being killed, maimed or become severely or chronically sick. This is life on earth! If there is a God involved directly in the affairs of humans (as most religious believe, be them Christians, Muslims and Jews), He can't do much to reduce our terrible sufferings. Such God can at the best be a source of comfort and (false) hope for the many.
2) Homo sapiens are fundamentally advanced social animals for good and bad. We contain noble and generous sides but also sinister and vicious sides, due to the fact that we are evolved animals on a low level of development and awareness, equipped with old fashioned brains. Many people contest these limitations of our brains by claiming that it is not a matter of brain power, but that we lack right guidance in using it. Philosophical schools and religions have tried to put guidelines but so far in vain regarding changing the populace′ behavior.
3) Human beings are often driven by their shortsighted self- interests, greed, Mundus Vult Decipi (self- deception), unchallenged convictions and faith and much less so of hard facts and farsighted wisdom.

4) In the human world everything is temporary, including our religions, values and ourselves as species, a fact that most humans are inclined to ignore.
5) Sapiens is but a unit in the potential evolving process of advanced intelligent life, not the crown or the glorious end of it.
6) The potential ultimate meaning with our existence is to further evolve as to become masters of our lives and death and expand to far away environments in the Universe and steer the process of our further evolution.

A question may come from you, reader: Why did you feel compelled to undertake such immense task as writing a vision for future advanced human beings? Isn′t it megalomanic?

No! I am not megalomaniac at all. It was as simple as this; The task was there and had to be addressed immediately so I decided to take on the challenge!

When you make up your mind to design a future vision for self- destructive humanity, full of hollow self- praise and self- deception, you know you will run into all kinds of resistance, rejection and degrading. And I did!

Lots of people attacked me for being a day dreamer, for stirring a controversy/claiming absurd ideas, being unrealistic and ill prepared for designing such a vision. Friends ridiculed me, fusspots attacked me and my wits and some I knew well, tried to mentally stab me in the back- Et Tu Brutus- in these years? But I avoided their fatal poison by developing a mental defense called mental Teflon. Their venom could not harm me. Instead, I mused in my mind:

Do you wish peace and justice on earth?

> You may foolishly wish, pray, and hope,
> but peace/justice on earth are a NOPE,
> as long as your stupidity we can′t stop!
>
> Are we not willing to further evolve?
> So, our predicaments we cannot resolve.
> If we to retain our partly lizard brain,
> we will end up in history's drain.

How can I remain truthful for my vision/mission and the struggle it demands and for how long, if all around me are diehard followers of expediency, faithful followers of religions and ideologies, the human parrots, and self- focused peacocks?

You go and go, witnessing apathy, greed, selfishness, and just ordinary stupidity each day. Not counting the lies the mass media feeds us most of the time, it's all a bit bewildering.

And then some people try to do something noble and worthwhile. Meanwhile, government officials, wealthy businesspeople who need all the good PR they can get, and even ordinary people are just clueless, careless, acting dumb. It's a travesty.

Therefore, I followed Rabi Nachmann` advice: This world is a narrow bridge, and the most important thing is, that you don't frighten yourself!

I followed too, an old Chinese proverb: `If you aspire to reach the stars, you can't be sure that you will accomplish it in your lifetime, but it may help you to get your feet and mind out of human life` mud`

it does not matter what people think of me in this respect if my contribution can become beneficial for humanity` best long term` evolvement. If not, so I did not harm anybody.

I know the psych of the common people well: At first, they reject, secondly, they fight the ideas and when circumstances show the vision′ validity and usefulness, they will slowly adopt it in parts as their own But it won't be in my lifetime. I won't be thanked for it in my lifetime, and it is alright.

What is our most formidable woe in our further future journey?

on human stupidity, the major enemy of evolving humanity: What are the factors contributing to it?

Stupidity, so rife among humans, is caused partly by genetics, epigenetic, organic defects and by massive indoctrinations of both children and adults. Annulling the natural selection regarding our procreation and thus giving birth to lots of babies with severe defects on top of them these abovementioned causes make human stupidity becomes more widespread in modern times.

At least seven more specific aspects in our lives contribute to dumb people down in our time:

1) The consuming/individual-centered ideology (cognitive capitalism) dumb people down by turning them into obsessive, nonreflective consumers.
2) The resurgent fundamentalist religions and ideologies turn billions of people into unreflective worshippers, lacking the capacity to think beyond the boxes of their doctrines. I reckon that most religious people do reflect within their box; some are extreme in their opinions and certain needs, which lead them directly toward fundamentalism, but are they a majority? I don't know for sure.
3) Overweight and obesity are associated with many ailments and also with mental decline. As nearly half of humanity is overweight, it is a probable source for slowly dumbing us down.

4) Massive pollution in our cities and countries destroys our health and dumbs us down (especially children and youngster in the process of growing up). I don't know for sure if it is increasing, decreasing or stable.
5) The rise of CO2 in the air seems also to impair our mental capacities, making us dumber. New research shows that as the human-caused climate crisis worsens, one of the symptoms of our increasingly sick planet may be dumber and dumber humans. The new research paper, written by a team of scientists from the University of Colorado Boulder, the Colorado School of Public Health, and the University of Pennsylvania (16*), suggests that the gradual rise of CO2 levels in Earth's atmosphere could cause cognitive decline in humans as a whole. Studies have shown that too much CO2 in the air can trigger cognitive issues, decreasing the ability of a person to focus and hinder learning. 266 Benjamin Katz This research indicates that if temperature will rise in the end of this century by 4 degrees Celsius, which is very likely, it may affect up to 50 percent of our mental capacity because of huge concentrations of CO2 in the air.
6) Growing mental problems and fragility worldwide because of our stressful and straining lifestyle, including alarmingly growing loneliness, do affect our mental agility and capacity. Modern societies are characterized by booming loneliness, which is strongly connected with high risk for being plagued by dementia. Participants in research who reported greater feelings of loneliness were more likely to develop dementia over the next ten years. Individuals who feel lonely are likely to have several risk factors as dementia, diabetes, hypertension, and depression and are less likely to be physically active. Mentally burdened people don't think very well and almost always lack overview regarding their lives and reality. They tend to doubt, ruminate, and think in circles as they are tied down mentally by their unresolved problems.

Mogens Kischi

7) Our annulling of the natural selection in our own procreation and the massive saving of life of many babies with severe mental and physical defects add also its heavy toll to the global growing stupidity.

If you add on top of these causes, the probable fact that due to growing overpopulation in a future world and the need to cut down on eating meat, big contributor of CO2 and methane, people will eat mainly vegetarian and vegan diets, which is associated with reduced mental capacity. These diets are known to dumb humans down in the long run. It seems as we are ending up in a trap, which we can only come out of by cutting drastically on our consumption, production, and population and upgrading ourselves beyond our debilitating shortcomings. Have we got a better alternative? Can you imagine the impact of even dumber humans than we are in future civilization, while we didn't act to prevent this catastrophe.

The American dream has become a nightmare for the global community.

In 1949 Arthur Miller- a play writer- presented; The death of a salesman.

Death of a Salesman themes revolve around self-identity, unrealistic expectations, and powerlessness. The play addresses a man's struggle with not being able to live up to his own expectations and dealing with this through conflicts, flashbacks, and hallucinations during his final day.

Miller knew that not everyone had equal opportunities to succeed. What does it mean to live in a society that promises a lot but guarantees nothing? Miller wrote Death of a Salesman with that question in mind. It's a play about the struggle for success and disappointment of the American Dream.

If a person focuses on earning lots of money and gaining some fleeting status, public exposure or fame, he lives his life′s purpose in vain!

The American Dream right there is all about money. American don't have sufficient societal safety nets - it is earning enough or bare exist. To pursue higher interests, one must have food, shelter, some education, etc. In a capitalist society these things are not a given. And if born poor, one has to climb the ladder and sometimes reinvent the wheel. In doing so, ambition/money become the focus.

Yet, the cheating propogandists of this dream, tell you that if you `wish it -you will get it, as you are unique`.

This is the great cheating of liberal ideology to the mass society` folk: Telling them that they are unique for and can achieve whatever they wish, is a politically directed audacity.

The fatal ailments of liberal democracy were in Arthur Miller` time and are still now: reckless Greed and vanity, Ego trip, narcissistic culture and show off and much hollow talk about rights and almost no enlightenment of citizens or teaching them critical thinking beyond their sweety, hyper tolerant and flowery, socially/materially none temperance, neither collective contributing narrative. In the real test of our time-saving the climate and creating a better, wiser and just civilization- this ideology has failed miserably, as it did not focus on the defects and excesses of our Human nature.

Democracy in its current state is a projection of who we are, when we lose the sight of collective necessity and the restraint of our vanity and greed...

I have encountered countless materially, sensually and other addictive hoarders in the West, many of them singles. The consuming, narcissistic prone system has promoted this compulsion in them, and as a result, what kind of life is it, being a prey of ones´ compulsion and self- focus?

What seems to be a crucial problem for Democracy right now is the passivity of its citizens. Western Democracy has fluctuated between two cycles. One is a period with public engagement fighting for important issues - revitalizing it, the other, a period which has grown up in the last 30 years, is dominated by lobbyists and the pressure of interest groups, not public participation in the decision process.

These cyclic periods in the history of American democracy have taken place in this order: from 1890 to 1920 there was a period of engagement, another one took place under president Franklin D. Roosevelt in 1933-1944, the New Deal, and a third period of democratic revival took place in 1961-68, fighting racial discrimination under Kennedy and Johnson.

In between these periods, the democratic process receded.

In the last 15 years, the political picture has been depressing: Both the Republican and the Democratic parties have let the financial lobbyists get tremendous influence on the making and forming of laws. When the two parties become so dependent on the same money sources, there is a real threat to both democracy and pluralism.

Malcolm X said once (free citation): ´There is only one party in America, the money party. It has two wings, Republicans and Democrats.'

The different political analysts and spin doctors try to cover the fact of homogeneity, but much of the public recognizes it and draws back from the political process. Where the public still has its force is in the Gallup polls and its emotional impact on policy makers.

Being too dependent on the sway of the public and interest groups, and thus on shorttermed consensus solutions, Democracy undermines itself by becoming too petty and trivial.

Dealing with long term challenges and problems and engaging actively in the political process is what will make Democracy prevail. Focusing entirely on immediate, practical and short-term problems like rising fuel prizes, may become its kiss of death.

Information glut: Does it numb us?

Winston Churchill once said ´The empires of the future are the empires of Mind` (Speech at Harvard, 6 September 1943, in Onwards to Victory (1944) p.238) T. S. Eliot wrote in his poem The Rock ´Where is the wisdom, we have lost in knowledge? Where is the knowledge, we have lost in information` (The Oxford Dictionary of Quotations: Oxford University Press, 1996. p.270-3)

The information glut is over us: more than 50,000 books are published annually in the USA alone. The Internet is everywhere.

Media moguls promised that every home would have access to hundreds of television channels. And on the same time are we flooded by the social media` channels. The World Wide Web coalesced in 1992 and now has billions of web sites.

Every day many people fight the battle of Too-Much-Information. Most of them just retreat away from this unmanageable deluge.

Does all this glut make us wiser or on the contrary, does it make the world look more and more incomprehensible?

Knowledge and wisdom are manifestations of overview, of being able to discern between essential, secondary, and nonessential matters, of being able to perceive, react to and influence shifting and complex contexts. It doesn't seem that we are on the right track. On the contrary, the information glut seems to lead us to a fragmented overview, to collective dumb down and thereby political idiocy, without long term strategy.

Many people become either confused, anxious and depressed or withdraw themselves into little private sphere, where security and routine are the gravitational forces of their lives. The price for doing this is compulsion, a narrow mind, and lingering feelings of something essential being lost: a life with undiminished curiosity, challenges, vision, mission and passion. We are in a numb state of mind in these respects.

The mass media which is called the 4th power (executive, legislative and judicial are the other three) is acting as a traitor in this respect, selling us the narrative of the powerful and the rich. A totally free press is one of the cornerstones of democracy, but it almost does not exist any longer. These trends made me turn my back on democracy as our future savior.

A democratic narrative not having a transcending vision greater than acquiring immediate needs, which can't show us a way to a wiser human being and civilization, is in danger of being exhausted.

Changing its focus from telling the story of indulgent consumerism and a Dream Society to enhancing values like global co-operation, responsibility and accountability is our greatest challenge and its our only chance of revitalizing our civilization.

What can we learn from the collapse of past great civilizations regarding our most influential Narratives? That greed, self-indulgence, the lack of unifying and engaging vision, restraining moral norms, values and goals, bring civilizations down. The well dressed and fed, self-indulgent citizen of our societies would do well to remember this lesson.

Fighting windmills or real dangers:

I don't wage a battle against windmills. I am engaged in a real, existential battle for the sake of humanity. This year has been the warmest in 125,000 years. Draught is hitting many regions in the world as Iraq, Syria, and Iran, indicating massive hunger in the future.

When I wrote my vision, I calculated that with the stubborn, and short-sighted human nature, it will take some harsh global catastrophes to make growing numbers of people realize that the party on the Deck of Titanic is over and it is time to find the best long- term way to survive and recover. I knew then as I know now that our generations are mentally and cognitively: After me -the deluge.

I dubbed Homo sapiens as Homo Stupidligence, being highly creative and resourceful on the one hand-technologically, scientifically and even partly socially- but dumb, short-sighted, and self- destructive on the other hand (wars and conflicts, being unsustainable and greedy). My vision is based on the growing misery in the world side by side with technological advances that can make us in the long run circumvent our mental pitfalls, so we can establish a sustainable, fair, and evolving civilization. I gave this process 400-1000 years, from 2050, to come to fruition.

I calculated that from around 2050 my vision would make sense for growing numbers of people. It happens already now (2010), so the battle is not against windmills, but against human pervasive stupidity.

It is no satisfaction for me that my predictions regarding the negative development of the world were proven correct.

It pains me to see the worsening state of humanity and it strains also some relations, as friends considered me for years to be pessimistic or worse-misanthropic, and now they stand and watch with dismay, how right I was all throughout the way. No, it is not a good feeling, and sometimes I am a bit afraid of myself and my predictive capacity.

Soon my beloved continent will be on fire due to religious, cultural frictions between Muslim minorities and the local inhabitants. It is inevitable.

The point is that the stupid European politicians did not learn psychology and don't understand what Compatibility means. It means that inviting lots of Muslims to Europe with a different mentality, social and family culture, and religion, which prevents them from thinking critically and out of the box, is a No-go. They are not compatible with what Europeans are and wish to be.

The dreams of Multikulti were but an infantile illusion. See what happens in Sweden, France, Britain, and in Germany.

Yet, there must be an aspiration to come beyond this mental blockade of different mentalities and religions: we all have to nurture the birth of the Creators after the era of the mutant. We, the children in my kibbutz were supposed to be the children of the sun. We failed miserably because it was too early to form us as wise and noble creatures, without changing our genetical blue print and enhancing our mental capabilities with AI, but the aspiration is there waiting for us to take on the challenge one day, when the technology will be available.

What is, then, sapiens` main conundrum?

It is that we- or most of us- don′t live in peace with reality as it is.

Reality as it is reflected by the natural world and the universe is not based on moral, good or bad and it is neither benign nor malign. Nature′ main rule is survival by transmitting ones′ genes to the next generations and by eating all which is audible. Beyond this, nature contains no transcendental meaning in its repertoire. It is indifferent for such noble aspiration. We seek, due further development of our brains/awareness, a meaning beyond our short physical lives. For this reason, we -or most of us- believe in just, omnipotent and benign father God. We do so even when we see that nature acts on a different level than human moral justification. Out of our enlarged awareness, like with Pandora box, came our potential to form our reality to the better, but also to fabulate on it to such an extent- due to our self- deceptive capacity and fear of the void-as to make most of us to ritualistic /compulsive escapists from the real reality.

We have to go back to the drawing table and accept nature as lacking a meaning beyond itself. Then accept that we need a meaning beyond nature, all the while that we are dependent on it to our sustenance and survival. Then place the efforts of attaining such a meaning not in God` hands and his multiple servants and story tellers, but in our hands through our further evolutionary push. By doing so, we will move away from being escapists into being Creators who form more and more their own journey and destiny, within nature.

What will be humans` life value from my vision point of view?

Humans are in certain way like coins; different sizes and values. Human values are measured by their long-term contribution for humanity.

There is not any formal current measure of the value of human life, but our numbers increase more and more-by 2050 world population will be 9.8 billion people- and more and more of us are useless in their lives. We destroy life conditions on earth more and more and suffer and die more and more due to our pollution and lifestyle, which means that the general life value of man-being useful for both humanity and our further evolvement-is falling.

I designed a crude measuring means to evaluate the life value of a person in the future, where sustainability, our further evolvement beyond our mental limitation and fair global share of resources will be the dominating policies.

This Life Value will be of religious ideals, of humanistic overblown ideals, of consumer mentality` seductions and anarchistic self-focus.

This Life Value will be based on the evaluation of human worth through his engagements in his social nexus (reference group, society), in his environment (sustainable local and global ecology) and in his efforts to improve and evolve humanity and the human mind.

It entails living up to certain duties and obligations are required to attain it-Life Value- as practicing both individually, socially and globally ecological footprint quota. Living up to tits criteria, people will be rewarded and their status enhanced.

Life Value is thus bound to human impending necessity to both survive and evolve on long term′ basis

Human Life Value is based on what I consider as four Necessities:

1. The first necessity is working for a new Humanism. Our Hyper humanism does not make us willing to sacrifice what is needed to create the best future prospects for coming generations. It causes, by its shortsighted policies, (commercialism, religionism and greed are substantial parts of it!) dangerous divisions in humanity and thus fertile soil for future sufferings. In this sense it doesn't promote Life Value at all.

Life Value implies the creation of a new humanistic view based on long term and farsighted strategies - values and actions aimed at reducing self-made long-term human sufferings.

Humanism based on Life Value will grant people rights up to the point of not destroying human life and life conditions for the coming generations. This humanism will be less individually fixated and more committed to the planet's long-term well -being and humanity's future prospects.

2. The second Necessity is maximizing our survival chances by establishing s framework for a fairer, resource distributing global civilization than the current one. Without the establishment of a fair resources distributing global civilization, we are doomed to an ever-lasting, nasty and bloody life on Earth.
3. The third Necessity is that we become much wiser and farsighted:

Not all the forces which can hurt us can be avoided at the present time. Catastrophes like earth quakes, storms, volcanoes, mud slides, flooding, lethal micro-organisms causing widespread infections, asteroids hitting our planet, a burst of gamma rays frying life on earth, are beyond our power to stop right now. Even our own folly in operation (showing itself in self- destructive behavior) is beyond our control at the present time. Becoming wiser and more farsighted may help us to do a better job regarding these threats.

4. The fourth necessity is our further evolution as a species. Life without evolution is rendered pointless - a dead end. Our awareness, borne by our minds′ evolution, makes it self-evident for many of us that our further evolution (and refinement) is the real key to maximizing both our survival chances and the possibilities of attaining transcendental Meaning and Significance.

By lifting ourselves out of our stumbling essence, we may grant ourselves the chance of becoming more advanced intelligent beings than we are right now and thereby pursue our real ultimate meaning.

Will the introduction of such life value be easy? Not at all, taking into account our divisive nature.

According to Machiavelli, the best way to control human populations is by separating them into two-or more- distinct boxes. These boxes can be religious, they can be political, they can be ethnic, they can be color coordinated (red vs blue), they can be economic. The nature of these boxes is actually irrelevant, as long as it ensures division and ongoing.

You tell half the people their Box A is the good box, and that all the problems in the world are caused by people from Box B. Then you tell the other half of the population from box B, the same thing on those from Box A. Then administer propagandists for each box to reaffirm the manufactured prejudices of its inhabitants.

Tell these inhabitants that they belong to the right box, and they should be proud of it. Make them feel like they have a monopoly on morality and truth, appeal to their need to feel self-righteous, and make it clear that those from the other box are the antithesis of all that: immoral and living a lie.

Employ symbols and turn them into forms of idolatry. Invent terms designed to dehumanize anyone who attempts dissent (racist, misogynist, unpatriotic, heretic, baby killer, welfare parasite, uneducated etc...).

What you are left with is a divided population that will fight against itself on your behalf, and can be easily manipulated into doing whatever it is you desire. You can abuse your power as much as you please and get away with it, as the population will be too distracted by their conflict with the people from the other box to notice or even care.

This division lies as innate disposition in us.

This disposition will make it hard to introduce life value, but as our survival will depend on doing so, a bitter struggle will surely ensue, before it is widely accepted.

10 common mental traps which reduce most of us into self- destructive Homo Stupidligence:

1) Most of us posssess Gods` holes in our brains; ´I believe because it is absurd and anti-factual. `
2) The Talk versus the Walk´ gap. Most people promise to do things much more than they really do.
3) Most people main thinking mode is the primitive dichotomous thinking; Bad-good, right -wrong, best-worst etc.
4) Most people blame very often faults and failures on others than themselves: The blame game trap.
5) Most people possess clear disposition for being war mongers.
6) Most people are short sighted.
7) Most people focus on their self- interest and are driven by a strong greed` disposition.
8) Most people suffer of the Pecking Hens syndrome. They cannot se a danger coming as they are preoccupied by their immediate, minimal focus.
9) Most people are infected by magical thinking which implies their overestimation and vanity.
10) Most people suffer of a mental filter in their minds, which conceals from their awareness, the above-mentioned mental traps, which reduce dramatically both their minds capacity, problems solving potential and their overview of their world/reality.

The five blind men, touching an elephant from different angles and thus creating, each one, a wrong impression of it, don′t put together their puzzle pieces into a whole reality, because their brains prevent them from doing just this. This is a part of the human condition.

Three lies are often used to intimidate the visionary people among us:

1. You can't foresee the future. A statement that is not true at all. To foresee the future with probability, you need to know much about human nature, history, politics and be equipped with good brain power to discern complexities, vagueness and wisdom and far sight to act in evolving manner.
2. Everything is changing, and therefore it is hard to predict precisely. Yes, it does, but we can conclude from many facts and trends—like completing a jigsaw—some accurate assessment of the future to come, as we can partly steer in the direction in which we wish our lives/future to go.
3. Old people yearn for the past and find faults with the present—ergo, they are negative in their forecasts. This claim has not been tested or verified, and when the global situation is getting worse, can it be an indication for the future to come or not?

The ten commandments of the vision for advanced future sapiens

1. Be forever evolving beyond Homo sapiens mental constraints. Prune/ upgrade people's minds as to become wiser and more farsighted than current Homo sapiens are able to.
2. Be ever sustainable (in population, production, pollution, and consumption).
3. Be fair and just in regard to treating people and sharing fairly the global resources among people on earth.
4. Work for the pursuit of ′to the stars with difficulties.'
5. Be prudent, decent, compassionate, and caring at the right time/place.
6. Be ready to defend yourself and your vision/mission if met by threats and acts of violence/war.
7. Accept all kinds of faiths and beliefs as long as their believers accept the principle of global/local sustainable lifestyle and the need to evolve further and away from sapiens crude mindset.
8. Work to prolong significantly active human life and reduce the impact of ailments on future beings.
9. Reduce the reign of greed, power lust, deception, self-deception, and show-off in you and among your evolving people.
10. Work for eliminating wars and violent conflicts in the world.

10 commandments for you, personally:

1) Don′t overindulge.
2) Don′t over consume. Commit yourself to pursuing an ecological footprint quota.

3) Don´t destroy yourself and others by being abusive.
4) Don´t pollute your world as to make it unsustainable.
5) Don´t bring children into the world being incapable of nurturing them to become life affirming people.
6) contribute to the long-term wellness and progress of humanity.
7) Accept commitments serving the long- term wellness of evolving humanity as a precondition for being granted rights
8) Cultivate Humanism based on the principles of changing contexts, commitments qua rights and global sustainability as its foundation.
9) Believe in whatever you wish to but note that it is your private faith, and it should not to become a political force.
10) Fight wherever and whenever the destructive manifestations of human stupidity on our minds, bodies and deeds destroy our and other living things life conditions

CHAPTER VII

BECOMING A MUTANT: 2013-2024

The wisest folk, who into their minds zoom, find a concealed control room, with two buttons in it: Further evolve. Yourself doom

In our global behavior we are reckless dilettante.

To survive, we must reach the stage of a mutant!

How did I learn to harness humans′ mental senescence, and to reverse humanity` growing Demeans.

How? By first and foremost at acknowledge that Human nature is a fusion of a beast, intelligent animal, and a potential noble being; compassionate, loving and farsighted wise.

An ordinary human being is burdened by its inclination to greed, short sight, pretension, vanity, self- deception and most of all: escapism from his reality.

It is high time to replace it with more noble one.

How? By becoming mutant, both cognitively and mentally, the first stage for upgrading us into becoming Angels, one day.

How can people become mutants?

Today you embark on a glorious, evolving mission,

away from Sapiens` contradictory nature` submission!

They fight to free themselves for sapiens prevalent thinking mode: Dichotomous thinking mode (Good-bad, right -wrong, superior -inferior etc.), from sapiens mental defects as greed, power lust, vanity, righteousness and self- pretense, short-sight, divisive disposition and discrepancy between sapiens` Talk and Walk (what he/she claims to do on the one hand and what he /she actually does, on the other hand.

People who are becoming mutant endorse the introduction and practice of obligatory individual-social and global ecological footprint quota, which include areas as pollution, production, consumption, and population. They endorse the view that our ultimate meaning with our species′ life is evolving further beyond sapiens divisive minds, as to become harmonious Creators by their own right.

They focus mainly on realizing enduring solutions for the sustainable survival of the evolving humanity, as the only effective remedy against Sapiens` zigzagging and self- destructive course.

Shai Gabai: The mutant watches Homo Stupidligence!

History:

2013

February 15: An undiscovered meteor strikes the Chelyabinsk oblast in Russia, with an airburst injuring thousands and damaging many buildings.

July 3: President of Egypt Mohamed Morsi is deposed by the military in a coup d'état.

August 21: A chemical attack in Ghouta, Syria is blamed on President Bashar al-Assad.

November 8: Typhoon Haiyan kills nearly 6,150 people in Vietnam and the Philippines.

November 21: The Euromaidan protest begins in Ukraine.

The French military intervenes in the Northern Mali conflict.

Terrorist attacks occur in Boston and Nairobi.

Conflict begins in South Sudan.

2014

February: Euromaidan protest in Ukraine sparks a revolution and the overthrow of Viktor Yanukovych, leading to Russia's annexation of Crimea and the war in Donbas.

March 8: Malaysia Airlines Flight 370 disappears from radar while on route to Beijing from Kuala Lumpur. There were 239 people on board.

May 22: A coup d'état in Thailand overthrows the caretaker government.

August 9: The shooting of African-American teenager Michael Brown by police leads to violent unrest in Ferguson, Missouri.

November 12: The Rosetta spacecraft's Philae probe becomes the first to successfully land on a comet.

December 16: Terik -I Taliban Pakistan kill over 130 students in Pakistan.

The worst Ebola epidemic in recorded history occurs in West Africa, infecting nearly 30,000 people and resulting in the deaths of 11,000+.

The Yemeni Civil War begins after the Houthi takeover in Yemen.

Uyghur genocide in Xinjiang begins.

Indonesia AirAsia Flight 8501 crashes into the Java Sea, while Malaysia Airlines Flight 17 is shot down over Ukraine and Air Alegria Flight 5017 is downed in Mali.

Israel launches an assault on the Gaza Strip in response to tit-for-tat murder-kidnappings, leading to the deaths of 71 Israelis and 2,100 Palestinians.

ISIL begins its offensive in northern Iraq, leading to intervention in Iraq and Syria by a US-led coalition.

Second Libyan Civil War begins.

2015

January 1: Five former Soviet Union countries form the Eurasian Economic Union.

January 3 – 7: Boko Haram perpetrates a massacre of over 2,000 people in Baga, Nigeria, and allies itself with ISIL.

April 2: Al-Shabaab perpetrates a mass shooting in Kenya, killing 148.

April 25 – May 3: The death of an African-American man, Freddie Gray by police leads to violent unrest in Baltimore, Maryland.

July 14: Joint Comprehensive Plan of Action agreement reached, setting limits to Iran's nuclear program in exchange for sanctions relief.

September 30: Russia begins air strikes against ISIL and anti-government forces in Syria

November 30 – December 12: 195 nations agree to lower carbon emissions by negotiating the Paris agreement.

A series of terrorist attacks occur in Paris.

A series of earthquakes in the Himalayas kills over 10,000 people.

Liquid water is found on Mars.

First close-up images of Ceres and Pluto.

China announces the end of One-child policy after 35 years.

European migrant crisis.

The Supreme Court of the United States determines that same-sex couples have a constitutional right to marry.

Volkswagen emissions scandal.

2016

March 9-15: Artificial intelligence program AlphaGo defeats top Go player Lee Sedol in a series of 5 games, winning 4 out of 5 games.

March 20: Barack Obama becomes the first U.S. president to visit Cuba since Calvin Coolidge in 1928.

April 3: Panama Papers, a leak of legal documents, reveals information of 214,888 offshore companies.

May 9: Rodrigo Duterte becomes President of the Philippines, and initiates a controversial drug war.

June 12: A shooter kills 49 people at a gay nightclub in Orlando, Florida.

June 23 – July 13: The people of the United Kingdom vote to leave the European Union; David Cameron resigns as a result, and Theresa May succeeds him as the second female Prime Minister of the UK.

July 4: Juno enters orbit into Jupiter.

November 4: The Paris Agreement, signed by 195 nations to fight global warming, formally goes into effect.

November 8: Donald Trump wins the 2016 presidential election, in an upset against Hillary Clinton, the first female to be nominated for a major party.

The United Nations lifts sanctions from Iran in recognition of the dismantling of its nuclear program.

ISIL claims responsibility for a series of bombings in Brussels, a massacre at Istanbul's Atatürk Airport and car ramming attacks in Nice.

The Colombian government signs a peace deal with FARC to end the Colombian conflict, despite narrowly losing a referendum.

US troops withdraw from Afghanistan after 15 years.

2016 attack on the Saudi diplomatic missions in Iran.

An outbreak of the Zika virus is linked to a cluster of cases of microcephaly.

2017

January 20: Donald Trump is inaugurated as President of the United States.

January 21: Millions of people participate in the Women's March in response to the inauguration of Donald Trump.

May 22: A terrorist bombing attack at an Ariana Grande concert in Manchester, England kills 22 people and injures over 140.

June 2: 36 people are killed in an attack in Resorts World Manila.

August 11 – 12: Charlottesville, Virginia becomes the site of a far-right rally protesting the removal of Confederate statues throughout the US. During the event, a white supremacist rams his car into a crowd of counter-protesters, injuring 19 and killing one.

October 1: 60 people are killed in a mass shooting at a music festival in Las Vegas.

October 14: A bombing in Mogadishu, Somalia kills 587 people and injures 316. It is one of the deadliest terrorist attacks in modern history.

November 5: 26 people are killed in a church shooting in Sutherland Springs, Texas.

North Korea tests a hydrogen bomb and conducts a series of ballistic missile tests. The United States responds with a wave of export sanctions.

ISIL launches simultaneous attacks in Tehran, destroy the Great Mosque of al-Nuri in Mosul, Iraq, and kill 311 in Egypt, but is declared defeated in Iraq by the end of the year.

A military operation targeting Rohingya Muslims in Myanmar is declared ethnic cleansing by the UNHCR.

This year's Atlantic Hurricane season features Hurricane Harvey, which kills 107 and becomes the costliest hurricane in US history, as well as Hurricane Irma, killing 134, and Hurricane Maria, killing 3,059.

Allegations of sexual abuse against film producer Harvey Weinstein leads to a wave of similar accusations from within Hollywood and other areas of primarily the English-speaking world.

2018

Turkey invades northern Syria, while 70 die in a chemical attack, triggering a missile strike against President Bashar al-Assad's regime.

Twenty-year Eritrean–Ethiopian border conflict formally ends.

Yellow vests movement becomes France's largest sustained period of civil unrest since 1968.

The Sunda strait tsunami kills 426 and injures 14,000 and the 2018 Sulawesi earthquake and tsunami kills 4,340 and injures 10,700.

China–United States trade war begins.

First post-ISIL election in Iraq.

The Trump administration reimposes sanctions against Iran.

The first monkeys are cloned, and first genetically modified humans reported, in China.

The northern white rhinoceros becomes functionally extinct.

2019

January 3: Chang'e 4 becomes the first object to land on the far side of the Moon.

January – June: A series of suicide bombings occur in Sulu, Philippines.

April 10:

The Event Horizon Telescope takes the first ever image of a black hole, at the core of galaxy Messier 87.

December 18: US President Donald Trump is impeached by the House of Representatives for abuse of power and obstruction of Congress.

Christchurch mosque shootings kill 51 people, while a suicide bombing in Iran kills 41, and a series of bomb attacks in Sri Lanka kills 250.

ISIL loses the last of its territory.

Wildfires spike in Brazil, while Australia endures the most widespread brush fires in its history.

Isabelle Holdaway is the first patient to receive a genetically modified phage therapy to treat a drug-resistant infection.

The 2019–2020 dengue fever epidemic begins in Southeast Asia.

Bashar al Assad launches multiple offensives in Northwestern Syria; Turkey launches an offensive into northeastern Syria.

More than a hundred people are killed after police and Janjaweed attack protesters in Sudan.

The United States blames attacks on ships in the Gulf of Oman on Iran, escalating tensions in the Persian Gulf.

More than 50 prisoners are killed in a series of riots in Amazonas, Brazil.

Israeli Prime Minister Benjamin Netanyahu is indicted on charges of bribery, fraud and breach of trust.

2020

January 2: The Royal Australian Air Force and Navy are deployed to New South Wales and Victoria to assist mass evacuation efforts amidst the 2019–20 Australian bushfire season.

January 3: Qasem Soleimani is targeted and killed at Baghdad International Airport.

January 8: Ukraine International Airlines Flight 752 is shot down by Iranian Islamic Revolutionary Guards Corps (IRGC) shortly after taking off from Tehran, killing all 176 on board.

January 16 – February 5: Donald Trump is acquitted by the United States Senate in his first impeachment.

May:

Protests in Belarus against the Alexander Lukashenko regime begin.

May 25: The murder of George Floyd sparks protests across the United States and the world.

June 30: China's National People's Congress grants itself sweeping powers to curtail civil liberties in Hong Kong.

July 10: Turkish President Recep Tayyip Erdoğan orders the Hagia Sophia in Istanbul to be reverted to a mosque following the annulment of a 1934 presidential decree that made it into a museum.

July 30: NASA successfully launches its Mars 2020 rover mission to search for signs of ancient life and collect samples for return to Earth.

August 4: An explosion caused by unsafely stored ammonium nitrate kills at least 218 people, injures thousands, and severely damages the port of Beirut, Lebanon.

August 25: Africa is declared free of wild polio, the second virus to be eradicated from the continent since smallpox 40 years previously.

September 16: A United Nations Human Rights Council fact-finding mission formally accuses the Venezuelan government of crimes against humanity, including cases of killings, torture, violence against political opposition and disappearances since 2014.

September 27 – November 10: 2020 Nagorno-Karabakh war between Armenia and Azerbaijan.

October 29: The International Organization for Migration (IOM) confirms the death of least 140 migrants who drowned off the coast of Senegal on a vessel bound for the Spanish Canary Islands.

November 3: The 2020 United States presidential election occurs. Despite the pandemic, early voting and other factors result in the highest voter turnout since 1900, and a record of over 155 million votes cast. Although Joe Biden is declared the winner on November 7, Donald Trump leads an unprecedented effort to prevent official recognition of his defeat, culminating on January 6 the next year.

November 3: The Tigray War begins in Ethiopia.

The COVID-19 pandemic, which began spreading late in the prior year, spreads from China to the vast majority of the world's inhabited areas, infecting at least 81 million and killing at least 1.8 million people in its first year.

Fears of COVID-19 cause the Dow Jones Industrial Average to fall ten percent in one week, its largest drop in history, triggering the COVID-19 Recession, the worst economic crisis since the Great Depression.

The United States signs a tentative peace agreement with the Taliban.

China and India engage in border skirmishes, the largest escalation between the two powers in 50 years.

China launches Chang'e 5 and becomes the third country after the US and the Soviet Union to return samples of the moon.

2021

January 6: Supporters of President Donald Trump, gathered after a rally led by him, attack the United States capitol, leading to five deaths.

January 10: Kim Jong-un is elected as the General Secretary of the ruling Workers' Party of Korea, inheriting the title from his father Kim Jong-Il, who died in 2011.

January 13: In Lyon, France, the first transplant of both arms and shoulders is performed on an Icelandic patient at the Édouard Herriot Hospital.

January 22: The Treaty on the Prohibition of nuclear weapons, the first legally binding international agreement comprehensively to prohibit nuclear weapons, comes into effect.

February 13 – 17: Winter Storm Uri becomes the costliest winter storm in North American history, costing $200 billion and 237 lives, and triggering the 2021 Texas power crisis.

February 18: NASA's Mars 2020 mission (containing the Perseverance rover and Ingenuity helicopter drone) lands on Mars at Jezioro Crater, after seven months of travel.

March 21: Clashes in Apure between Colombian FARC dissidents and the Venezuelan Armed Forces cause at least six casualties and displace 4,000 Venezuelans.

April 15: Scientists announce they successfully injected human stem cells into the embryos of monkeys, creating chimera-embryos.

April 19:

Ingenuity becomes the first vehicle to fly in the atmosphere of another planet.

April 28 – May 1: A border clash between Kyrgyzstan and Tajikistan leads to 55 deaths.

May 6 – 21: Hundreds die in conflicts after Israel evicts six Palestinian families from East Jerusalem.

June 13: Benjamin Netanyahu, the longest-serving prime minister of Israel, is voted out of office; Naftali Bennett and Yair Lapid are sworn in as Prime Minister of Israel and as Alternate Prime Minister of Israel, respectively.

July 7: Haitian′ President Jovenel Moïse, is assassinated in a midnight attack by unknown mercenaries.

July 18: An international investigation reveals that spyware sold by Israel's NSO Group to different governments is being used to target heads of state, along with thousands of activists, journalists and dissidents around the world.

August 9: The Intergovernmental Panel on Climate Change releases the first part of its Sixth Assessment Report, which concludes that the effects of human-caused climate change are now "widespread, rapid, and intensifying".

August 15: Kabul falls following the 2021 Taliban offensive, as the Islamic Republic of Afghanistan collapses, and the country is governed thereafter by the Taliban as the reinstated Islamic Emirate of Afghanistan. The War in Afghanistan thus ends after 20 years following the withdrawal of U.S. and coalition troops.

September 15: A trilateral security pact between Australia, the United Kingdom, and the United States is formed to counter Chinese influence. This includes enabling Australia to build its first nuclear-powered submarine fleet.

September 16: Inspiration4, launched by SpaceX, becomes the first all-civilian spaceflight, carrying a four-person crew on a three-day orbit of the Earth.

October 3: The International Consortium of Investigative Journalists and assorted media partners publish a set of 11.9 million documents leaked from 14 financial services companies known as the Pandora Papers, revealing offshore financial activities that involve multiple current and former world leaders.

October 6: The World Health Organization endorses the first malaria vaccine.

November 16: Russia draws international condemnation following an anti-satellite weapon test that creates a cloud of space debris, threatening the International Space Station.

December 9: A truck crash in Chiapas, Mexico, kills 55 migrants who were being smuggled in it from Guatemala through Mexico to its border with the United States.

December 16 – 18: Typhoon Rai lashes into Visayas and Mindanao, killing 409 people.

The COVID-19 pandemic continues, infecting more than 220 million and killing at least 3.6 million people in its second year. The true totals of infected and dead are estimated to be much higher.

Coup's d'état occur in Myanmar, Mali and Guinea.

Russia begins a military buildup on the Ukrainian border, warning NATO not to intervene.

197 nations sign the Glasgow Climate Pact, agreeing to limit the use of coal, and the Netherlands legally mandates Royal Dutch Shell to comply with the Paris Agreement.

2021:

How do we resolve intractable international problems? The lesson of UNRWA

UNRWA's textbooks promote hatred and incitement against Israel and the Jews. In 2018, President Trump suspended funding to the agency. In 2021, UNRWA's director-general confirmed for the first time that there was a problem, but in practice no change was made and UNRWA's curriculum still treats Israel as an enemy, promotes "martyrdom" and claims that "Jihad is the way to glory". The absurdity in UNRWA is much deeper. The agency has 5.6 million registered refugees, an unimaginable number. Suppose there were 800,000 refugees in 1948, how is it possible that the number increased sevenfold, when the population aged and died? It is mathematically impossible, but it is part of a mechanism that ensures that the number of refugees will increase and ensures that the issue will never be resolved and the need for UNRWA will be maintained.

There were many attempts to get to the root of the problem and publicize it in the US, but only in 2021, when the Trump administration was preparing to vacate its place, outgoing Secretary of State Pompeo put an end to the secrecy and tweeted: 'UNRWA is not a refugee agency. The estimate is about 200,000, or less, Arabs displaced in 1948 are still alive and most of the others are not refugees according to any reasonable criteria. Taxpayers deserve the right to know the basic truth: most of the Palestinians under the authority of UNRWA are not refugees, and UNRWA is an obstacle to peace. The US supports peace and of the Palestinians, but UNRWA does not support any of them, it is time to end UNRWA's mandate. ` Pompeo basically confirmed that of the millions identified as 'Palestinian refugee` by UNRWA, less than 200,000 meet the criteria international organizations for refugee status and apparently the number that meets the criteria for refugee status is less than 30,000. For the first time a senior American official revealed the numbers, before that, administration after administration, both Democratic and Republican, allowed UNRWA to perpetuate the lie. The lie is also a significant obstacle to solutions to the problem. The Office of the United Nations High Commissioner for Refugees has a mandate to pursue sustainable solutions for refugees, through voluntary return, integration in the host country, or resettlement in a third country. UNRWA, on the other hand, has no such mandate. The agency admits that it does not have the authority to pursue long-term and sustainable solutions for refugees, including resettlement in third countries. UNRA has encouraged generations of Palestinians to settle in the hell of the refugees, when they are stuck between a possible new life, and the 'right of return`, which was promised to them by radical factions committed to eternal war with Israel. It is clear to the Palestinians, who admit this in private conversations, that the right of return is not realistic, However, it was and remains one of the main stumbling blocks in future peace negotiations. Instead of helping to solve the problem, UNRA exacerbates it.

2022

January – September: Coups d'état in Burkina Faso.

January 4: China, France, Russia, the UK, and the US—all five permanent members of the United Nations Security Council—issue a rare joint statement affirming that "a nuclear war cannot be won and must never be fought."[6]

February 24: Russia invades Ukraine, escalating the Russo-Ukrainian War, causing a refugee crisis and tens of thousands of deaths on both sides.

April – November: Pakistani constitutional crisis and attempted assassination of Imran Khan.

June 12 – September 12: Heat waves in Europe kill tens of thousands.

July: Oder environmental disaster.

July 11: James Webb Space Telescope takes Webb's First Deep Field, oldest and highest resolution image of the universe to date.

July 22: Chinese paddlefish declared extinct.

August 4: China conducts its largest ever military exercise around Taiwan in response to a controversial visit by Nancy Pelosi.

August 28: Floods in Pakistan trigger an economic crisis.

September 27 – 30: Hurricane Ian impacts Cuba and the US, causing catastrophic damage to both nations, killing at least 157 people, 16 missing, and leaving millions without power, including the entirety of Cuba.

October 6: 36 people are killed in a shooting, stabbing, and vehicle-ramming at Nong Bua Lamphun, Thailand.

October 29:

Severe Tropical Storm Naglaa lashes throughout the Philippines, leaving 160 people dead.

At least 158 people are killed and another 197 injured in a crowd crush during Halloween festivities in Seoul, South Korea.

November 2: Ethiopia–Tigray peace agreement.

November 15: The world population is estimated to have reached 8 billion.

November 30: OpenAI launched ChatGPT, an AI chatbot.

December 7: Self-coup attempt, impeachment and arrest of President Pedro Castillo sparks protests in Peru.

December 9: Qatar corruption scandal at the European Parliament.

December 13:

National Ignition Facility achieves first fusion ignition.

2023

January – October: 2023 Israeli judicial reform protests.

January 19: 2023 French pension reform strikes.

February 6: 2023 Turkey-Syria earthquakes kill nearly 60,000 people.

February 21: Cyclone Freddy kills 1,400 in Malawi and Mozambique.

April 4: Finland joins NATO.

April 15: War in Sudan.

May 11: The Covid-19 pandemic is declared over.

July 26: 2023 Nigerien coup d'état.

August 30: 2023 Gabonese coup d'état.

September 8: 2023 Marrakesh-Safi earthquake kills nearly 6000 people.

September 10: Storm Daniel becomes the deadliest Mediterranean storm in history, with over 4000 deaths in Libya.

September 19 – 20: 2023 Azerbaijani offensive in Nagorno-Karabakh.

October 7: Hamas attacks Israel; start of the 2023 Israel-Hamas war.

On the 7.10.2023 Hamas from Gaza invaded the southern part of Israel proper, and within 24 hours killed more than 1200 Israelis, raped, and maimed many others and destroyed kibbutzim close to the border. This resulted in a mini regional war between Hamas, Hezbollah in Lebanon, and the Houthi folk in Yamen. Iran, USA and England were also involved in this fray. When I write these lines -on 2.2024- the war is still going on and risks getting escalated to full out war between Lebanon and Iran on the one side and Israel and USA on the other side. It turned out that at least 12 employes of UNRWA in Gaza Joined in the attack on Israel on the 7.10.2023.

In the meantime, all sides try to gain something out of this bloodshed. The Palestinians want their state, but not just their state. They also want to take over Israel proper and the abolishment of the Jewish state. Others believe- probably naively- that moderate Palestinian state is a possibility. The idea of ′ Free Palestine is worth less than a dime, being utterly unrealistic, due to the animosity and deep suspicion between the involved parts, due to the ideologies of both Hamas and Patah and their bad record of granting their people any freedom, due to treacherous Arabic world and due to lack of Western powers` capability to guarantee such accord. It is an escapist` fake solution right now!

I view this situation as hopeless as so many bloodthirsty idiots are involved in it beside many other useful idiots who believe in peaceful settlement right now.

In the war in Ukraine the same human idiocy manifests itself without a willing to compromise. On the same time climate change ravages much of the Middle East, turning it into a time bomb.

What do these events and our other failures reveal about us? Yes, we are back to where my journey started: Human nature is partly beastly and as long as we don´t transcend it, we bring us closer for our extinction.

In its latest version of an annual report on armed conflicts, the British think tank the International Institute for Strategic Studies (IISS) paints a gloomy picture.

The report, released last week, has recorded at least 183 regional and local conflicts in the world within the past year (calculated May 2022 to June 2023).

According to the report, this is the highest number in three decades and 28 percent more than the previous year.

The world saw a gradual decline in the level of conflict in the years after the end of the Cold War, but that the trend really turned around 2010-2011 after the Arab Spring.

Something that also appears from data from the Institute for Peace and Conflict Research at Uppsala University in Sweden:

- There has been increased instability with a generally negative development, where wars in Africa weigh heavily in the statistics. We know that one of the causes of conflicts is other conflicts, because there is a spill-over where conflicts move from one country to another.

Since there were 183 armed conflicts going on in the world in 2023, we should focus on the real cause for them; the fucked up Human nature including short sight.

Ignorant, prejudiced (often Antisemitic) and foolish people concentrate on Palestine conflict as the sole reason for preventing a better, peaceful world. Now the facts: An authoritative new study finds there are 183 regional and local conflicts underway in 2023, the highest number in three decades.

It's Not Just Ukraine and Gaza: War Is on the Rise Everywhere.

http://www.bloomberg.com/.../it-s-not-just-ukraine-and...
http://www.bloomberg.com/.../it-s-not-just-ukraine-and-gaza

In the new report from the IISS, it appears that 14 percent more have died in armed conflicts compared to the year before, while the number of violent incidents has increased by 28 percent.

The authors behind the report describe a world ´dominated by increasingly difficult conflicts and armed violence`, with territorial disputes, internal terrorism and an increased number of criminal and armed groups being part of the cause.

2024

It is already clear that 2023 was the warmest in our history. Humanity just lived through the hottest 12 months in at least the last 125,000 years.

Scientists have compared this year's climate-change fallout to "a disaster movie" — soaring temperatures, fierce wildfires, powerful storms and devastating floods — and new data is now revealing just how exceptional the global heat has been (CNN,9.11.2023).

From a climate perspective, 2024 is beginning in uncharted territory. Temperatures last year broke records not by small intervals but by big leaps; 2023 was the hottest year ever recorded, and each month in the second half of the year was the hottest—the hottest June, the hottest July, all the way through to December. July was in fact the hottest month in recorded history. Already, experts predict that 2024 is likely to be even hotter. But these heat records, although important milestones, won't hold their title for long. "Getting too excited about any given year is a bit of a fool's game, because we're on an escalator that's going up.

On 6.1.2024 the CNN published a report on the dire state of India: ´ By 2050, India will be among the first places where temperatures will cross survivability limits, according to climate experts. And within that time frame, the demand for air conditioners (AC) in the country is also expected to rise nine-fold, outpacing all other appliances, according to a recent report by the International Energy Agency (IEA).

India emits nearly 2.4 billion tons of carbon dioxide (CO2) a year based on data collected by the European Union – contributing about 7% of global emissions. The United States, by comparison, causes 13% of CO2 emissions, despite having a quarter of India's population.

This raises a question of fairness that climate scientists have often asked: should people in the developing world shoulder the cost of reducing emissions, despite being among those least responsible for rising greenhouse gases?

At the COP28 climate talks in Dubai that concluded recently, India wasn't among the list of countries that signed a pledge to cut their emissions from cooling systems.

Nonetheless India, one of the world's fastest growing economies, is on the front line of the climate crisis. And it finds itself in a tough position. How can it balance its development while ensuring environmental protection?

Prospects for the near future:

Catastrophes are hitting mankind:

1)Crucial ocean current system could be on course to collapse with catastrophic impacts on global weather | CNN(2,2024: https://edition.cnn.com/2024/02/09/climate/atlantic-circulation-collapse-weather-climate/index.html).2)

Forskere slår alarm: 5 meters havvand stigning i vente - Avisen.dk(researchers with Stark Warning: 5 meter of oceans rise in the near future(2.2024: https://www.avisen.dk/forskere-slaar-alarm-5-meters-vandstigning-paa-kort_755749.aspx).

By 2050 will half of the global population-almost 5 billion out of 9.8- live in tropical climate. By 2070 the climate will be unbearable for as many as 3 billion.

And on the same time, Homo Stupidligence keeps nurturing hyper hopes for technological breakthrough,which would save us, like the old delusions of believers throughout our history of God saving us with a miracle :

"If you could meet your grandkids as elderly citizens in the year 2100…you would view them as being, basically, Greek gods…that's where we're headed."

--Michio Kaku (1947-)

How can we sum up, the magnitude of humanity growing self -destructiveness in the last years?

´What a terrible era in which idiots govern the blind`-William Shakespeare, Julius Caesar.

´What a terrible era we live in, in which the idiots and the blind leaders push humanity towards ecological/nuclear disaster! ` -B.K

There were alarming signs in the global village, and most people ignored them. I could not, as I knew what they mean for our future.

To start with, we -as species got dumber in this century, partly due to pollution and lifestyle (ailments and abuse) and partly due to bigger C02 concentrations in the atmosphere. High levels of carbon dioxide reduce the capacity of humans to think complexly, which affects their ability to rcspond to situations.7. Apr. 2022.

In 2023 the level of CO_2 in the atmosphere reached record high in humanity` history, 422 ppp. while the march of global human folly became more and pronounced.

This was alarming, as resolving our global self- created problems demand more wise brain, not lesser one. I did read many research showing that human average IQ were falling sharply in the last decades, but became convinced about it, when antisemitism broke out due to Palestinians /Israeli Gaza war. I became certain that the exploding Black- White emotional reactions towards the Jews and Israel (antisemitism)- one of many armed conflicts in the world without s clear solution- correlated well with what the research had shown: global growing idiotism.

On top of all the above- named bad news, there are other negative global developments:

The massive rise of brain damage, cognitive decline, and neurological disturbances among the population:

There is strong evidence that beside becoming generally dumber, the number of people being hit by neuro degenerative ailments are exploding in these years.

Is the global IQ decreasing?

Researchers across the globe have been tracking an apparent decline in human IQs, starting around the turn of the millennium. Theories abound as to why scores are dropping, but the smart money says our cognitive skills may have plateaued, teetering into an era of intellectual lethargy.29. mar. 2023

How much has the IQ dropped in the West?

Research published online in the journal Intelligence on Thursday claims the IQ of people in Western nations has fallen by an average of 14.1 points over the past century. Scientists in Europe used visual response times recorded in Western studies from 1889 to 2004.

14.1 IQ points an average human lost in this century, and it becomes self- evident that it has a profound impact on our behavior, when you watch the stupid verbiage which comes out of our politicians`/influencers mouths.

Environmental factors:

´It's not that dumb people are having more kids than smart people, to put it crudely, ` Roge burg told CNN. ´It's something to do with the environment because we're seeing the same differences within families.'

Environmental factors include differences in the way young people are educated, increases in time spent online, changes in nutrition and less reading overall and not at least massive pollution disturbing children cognitive and hormonal development. Many neurobiologists and psychologists suspect that digitization and changes in the media landscape could have a negative impact on IQ scores. Increased screen time and constant accessibility via smartphones have been proven to reduce our ability to concentrate. Our brains are simply overtaxed. And external biological factors could also have an impact on intelligence, such as the exponential increase in fossil fuel production and the everyday use of plastic.

Pollution of all kinds, bad diet (processed food, diet drinks etc.), density of population(thus transmitting virus and bacterial infections causing brain damage), all kinds of alcohol-drugs. Medicine and eating abuse, obesity, sedentary lifestyle, and bad sleeping habits.

Can air pollution cause neurological disorders?

Air pollution was significantly associated with an increased risk of hospital admissions for several neurological disorders, including Parkinson's disease, Alzheimer's disease, and other dementias, in a long-term study of more than 63 million older U.S. adults.20. okt. 2020.

Does air pollution cause cognitive decline?

Emerging studies suggest that exposure to air pollution may be associated with cognitive impairment, with reported effects ranging from impaired neurocognitive development in infancy and childhood to higher rates of cognitive decline and dementia in later life.27. Jan. 2022.

Links Between Air Pollution and Mental Health Symptoms.

A large study of people in the U.S. and Denmark found that exposure to air pollution ′is significantly associated with increased risk of psychiatric disorders,` including depression, schizophrenia, bipolar disorder and personality disorder.12. Apr. 2023

How does air pollution affect you intellectually?

They found evidence that exposure to air pollutants may lead to depression, anxiety, psychoses, and perhaps even neurocognitive disorders, such as dementia.6. Jul. 2023

Does air pollution cause ADHD?

Evidence suggests that high pollution levels are a risk factor for autism spectrum disorder, learning, neuromotor, and language deficits, and ADHD.15. dec. 2022

Can breathing in air pollution change your brain?

Air pollution is known to directly interact with our brain cells in the short term, altering the way they communicate with each other, particularly in the regions that control our emotions.

This could partly explain why some people who are exposed to high levels of air pollution experience anxiety and depression.15. jun. 2023

Does air pollution affect memory?

Researchers from the University of California, Irvine have found that exposure to traffic-related air pollution in Irvine led to memory loss and cognitive decline and triggered neurological pathways associated with the onset of Alzheimer's disease.11. maj 2023

Physical ailments due to pollution and modern lifestyle:

Air pollution is considered as the major environmental risk factor in the incidence and progression of some diseases such as asthma, lung cancer, ventricular hypertrophy, Alzheimer's and Parkinson's diseases, psychological complications, autism, retinopathy, fetal growth, and low birth weight.

What physical effects does pollution have on people?

Exposure to air pollution can affect everyone's health. When we breathe in air pollutants, they can enter our bloodstream and contribute to coughing or itchy eyes and cause or worsen many breathing and lung diseases, leading to hospitalizations, cancer, or even premature death.

What are the effects of pollution in the modern world?

Long-term health effects from air pollution include heart disease, lung cancer, and respiratory diseases such as emphysema. Air pollution can also cause long-term damage to people's nerves, brain, kidneys, liver, and other organs. Some scientists suspect air pollutants cause birth defects.

How modern life affects our physical health?

As a result, we have become more susceptible to a range of health issues associated with a sedentary lifestyle, including obesity, weaker bones and muscles, and poor blood circulation.22. feb. 2023

What are the health problems caused by modern lifestyle?

Health problems associated with the modern lifestyle include obesity, diabetes, heart disease, cancer, and gastrointestinal diseases. Balancing health and lifestyle are important. A healthy lifestyle can be adopted with a healthy diet, mental well-being, and physical activity.21. dec. 2022

Fertility: Sperm count

A new analysis of 25 studies of pesticides shows a clear connection, researchers say. A prolonged decline in male fertility in the form of sperm concentrations appears to be connected to the use of pesticides.

Mental health state and modern lifestyle:

Is rising mental health issues a global phenomenon?

In 2019, a study in The Lancet reported that some 12.5% of the global population would have an issue with their mental health at some time in their life. In March 2022, the WHO reported that worldwide, anxiety and depression increased by 25% in the first year of the pandemic.24. mar. 2022

Are mental health conditions increasing worldwide?

Mental health conditions are increasing worldwide. Mainly because of demographic changes, there has been a 13% rise in mental health conditions and substance use disorders in the last decade (to 2017). Mental health conditions now cause 1 in 5 years lived with disability.

How does modern lifestyle affect mental health?

Overuse of technology is a significant add to stress. People who are more active on social networking sites have comparatively higher stress levels. Substance abuse is also another cause. People who drink and smoke regularly are more prone to suffer from mental illness like depression, anxiety etc.29. apr. 2019

Is modern society making us depressed?

Contemporary populations may now be more susceptible to depression because of greater inequality, low social support, intense individual competitiveness, and increased social failure (Gilbert, 2006). Onset of a major depressive episode often coincides with stressful life events (Kendler et al., 1999; Nesse, 2000).12. jan. 2012

How does today's society affect mental health?

In today's fast-paced world, it is easy to feel isolated and alone, which can contribute to mental health issues such as depression and anxiety.19. mar. 2023

Now, as the trend goes in our dumb down′ direction, and our ultimate meaning- our further evolvement- implies nurturing wiser and more mentally balanced beings than we are, where does it leave us? AI technology and genetic engineering, both approaches which can give a boost for a wiser human, can they help dumb people? I doubt it, as dumb people feedback reasoning is probably more fixed and conditioned than in more intelligent and flexible minded people. This fact can mean that humanity will evolve in different tempi.

The Macro impact of our modern life:

The rats` Paradise observations:

"Behavioral sink" is a term invented by ethologist John B. Calhoun to describe a collapse in behavior which can result from overcrowding. The term and concept derive from a series of over-population experiments Calhoun conducted on Norway rats between 1958 and 1962.[1] In the experiments, Calhoun and his researchers created a series of "rat utopias" – enclosed spaces in which rats were given unlimited access to food and water, enabling unfettered population growth. Calhoun coined the term "behavioral sink" in his February 1, 1962 report in an article titled 'Population Density and Social Pathology` in Scientific American[2] on the rat experiment.[3] He would later perform similar experiments on mice, from 1968 to 1972.

Calhoun's work became used as an animal model of societal collapse, and his study has become a touchstone of urban sociology and psychology in general.

In the 1962 study, Calhoun described the behavior as follows:

Many [female rats] were unable to carry pregnancy to full term or to survive delivery of their litters if they did. An even greater number, after successfully giving birth, fell short in their maternal functions. Among the males the behavior disturbances ranged from sexual deviation to cannibalism and from frenetic overactivity to a pathological withdrawal from which individuals would emerge to eat, drink, and move about only when other members of the community were asleep. The social organization of the animals showed equal disruption. ...

The common source of these disturbances became most dramatically apparent in the populations of our first series of three experiments, in which we observed the development of what we called a behavioral sink. The animals would crowd together in greatest number in one of the four interconnecting pens in which the colony was maintained. As many as 60 of the 80 rats in each experimental population would assemble in one pen during periods of feeding. Individual rats would rarely eat except in the company of other rats. As a result, extreme population densities developed in the pen adopted for eating, leaving the others with sparse populations.

... In the experiments in which the behavioral sink developed, infant mortality ran as high as 96 percent among the most disoriented groups in the population.

Density: How does density of population affect human wellbeing?

Using 54 studies published since 1990, the authors conclude that higher population density is associated with multiple kinds of cancer, chronic obstructive pulmonary disease, cardiovascular disease, asthma, and club foot. Conversely, they found low population density associated with diabetes.

What behavior does density influence?

Studies have found that high population density can lead to increased aggression, decreased cooperation, and reduced helping behavior. In environmental psychology, density can refer to the level of crowding in a physical space, such as a room or a building.

Life conditions on earth and rise of sea levels. Scientists claim that as we exceed the pre-industrial temperature by two Celsius grades, sea levels may rise by 40 feet. That is to say, that with global population close to or above 10 billion people in the end of this century, with growing consumption, pollution and production as a result of growing population, and with loss of areas to the sea and growing frequencies natural catastrophes, draughts and failed food supply, and with growing the density, we are heading for a lot of global trouble.

Stressful daily day life:

If you're constantly connected, you're going to feel anxiety… that can lead to other things like mental health and physical ailments.

Advances in technology have made our world faster and filled with more potential than ever. Our smartphones, computers, and TVs place endless information, instant communication, and constant stimulation at our fingertips. Fast transport, both locally and globally, allows us to travel distances in hours which would have previously taken days, weeks, or even months. These things make modern life exciting, but there are also downsides which can seriously affect our physical and mental health.

The food you eat can be either the safest and most powerful form of medicine or the slowest form of poison.

Unfortunately, most people do eat junk food out of habits and lack of money. The obesity` epidemy is the result of eating junk food.

Drug abuse is a widespread′ phenomena, resulting in both huge physical as well as mental ailments.

Ego cultivation is also a huge health breaking factor.

Most people in the West are brought up with the notion of almost limitless possibilities for them and with a sense of them being unique. When it comes to reality many suffer of this discrepancy and get depressed, anxious or narcissists.

My state of mind; Becoming a mutant

As I come close to the end of my road, the world has changed radically in terms of lifestyle and the impact of technology on human life. There are significant breakthroughs in the field of artificial intelligence that bring the age of the cyborg closer. There is a significant development in genetic engineering that can upgrade man both physically and intellectually emotionally, as to create a wiser, more mentally stable, and longer-lived creature than a common Sapiens. Today's world is on the brink of self -destruction due to a mounting global stupidity demonstrated daily, by the humanity which cannot cooperate for its long- term survival, and therefore we will most likely need these technologies to upgrade humanity, beyond this self- destructive, debilitating mental mindset.

I changed too, of course. From being a kibbutz member, who earned no money, living material humble life, I came to earn good money in Denmark, but I did keep up my modest lifestyle. I would not yield to our time` show off, exhibitionism, self- indulgence, spiritual self- realization trends and brands, and personal self-exposure. I consider this self- focus to be a distraction away from what we can and should become.

I wrote 15 books on this matter, and did not try to collect my revenues. The publishing houses earned good money on me, I know for sure, but it did not bother me. I had enough to live for, and greed was a corruptive force I tried to avoid. Hundreds of promoting agents contacted me and would work with me. I rejected them all because their promotion was only suitable for our Maj fly′ culture. My books have a much longer focus on humanity further journey. It does not belong to this ever novelty plagued time. I contributed my books as a guideline for a future less self- destructive and blind civilization. This is the way I think because I have mutated.

′I am ashamed being Dane` is an expression used by Danes, not agreeing with Denmark's policy or moral stance. I did not feel like this neither in relation to Israel nor in relation to Denmark. I was not personal responsible for their politics and could do nothing to change them. Yet, I have become ashamed of being current Sapiens-which is in fact being Homo Stupidligence- acting and reacting in exceedingly stupid and reckless manners. Why ashamed? Because here I threw myself and my energy many years ago, into the battle of changing sapiens self- destructive course, and so far, I have witnessed MORE of THE SAME reckless behavior.

I will keep on fighting for the cause of our betterment/further evolvement, but not as full-fledged Sapiens- or rather Stupidligence- anymore, for this current human state has become an infectious disease, destroying humans′ judgement.

So, I state bluntly my view of us:

Human: Here is your choice!

If you all your life cared only for yourself,
you wrote your life story on an ocean wave.
If you abused life conditions on sea and land
you wrote your life story on moving sand.
If you reacted as hateful, fanatic swarm,
you wrote your life on the blowing storm.
But if you invested in our evolving stock
your life will be written on a bed rock!

In a 1980 interview that remained unreleased during Stanley Kubrick's lifetime, he provides insights into one of the film's- A space Odyssey,2001- concluding scenes. This moment depicts Bowman in old age, post his journey through the Star Gate:

´The idea was supposed to be that he is taken in by godlike entities, creatures of pure energy and intelligence with no shape or form. They put him in what I suppose you could describe as a human zoo to study him, and his whole life passes from that point on in that room. And he has no sense of time. ... When they get finished with him, as happens in so many myths of all cultures in the world, he is transformed into some kind of super being and sent back to Earth, transformed, and made superhuman.'

We can guess what happens when he goes back. It is the pattern of a great deal of mythology, and that is what we were trying to suggest.

In Part Four, Bowman reaches Jupiter and locates a third monolith. The monolith opens a Star Gate and Bowman travels through vast distances of kaleidoscopic space-time. On the other side of the psychedelic trip, Bowman finds himself in a classy, neoclassical hotel room. As he explores the room, Bowman ages considerably until he becomes an old man on his death bed.

At the moment of his death, the monolith appears to him and transforms him into a creature that looks like an angelic fetus.. The newly born Star Child travels through space in a futuristic amniotic bubble without the need of a spaceship and returns to Earth.

In this book, I informed the reader on the process of pursuing the idea of a Creator (Star Child) by starting with the first evolutionary step: Becoming mutants.

The human world´ crumbling slowly down, made me decide that I don´t belong any longer to this self- destructive species unconditionally. As Homo Stupidligence is partly a beast and partly an intelligent Sapiens, I became half higher Sapiens and half new species, a mutant.

I made a clear point that our survival as both advanced intelligent or dumb species depends entirely on us accelerating the process of our own evolution. Either we choose to become wiser and more farsighted than we are now to meet the immense challenges of climate change, over population, dwindling resources and life endangering pollution…and not the least -our declining intelligence and foresight, or keep this so- called sacred status quo of being who we are. (which means, becoming dumber).

Yet,I am still partly Sapiens/ Stupidligence, when it comes to it.

In july,2019 I left my wife after many years of marriage, as I fell for another woman. The circumstances were not as banal as they may seem to be. When I left my home, I was turning soon 74 years old. I could all slowly feel that I lost my warrior energy and got bored by both my wife and our old friends and the cozy/petty talking Danish environment. All these people, including my wife were good, decent, and ordinary people, but I became afraid of wasting the rest of my life in their cozy, boring sort of ′mental elder home`.

I felt estranged with the Western consumer/hoarder′ mentality that was seducing us with plenty goods and the good lifestyle, and with `feel good pep talk on how unique we are and can become by self- growth and self- focus ((American pseudo dream).

I felt estranged with human nature, being so gullible and easy to manipulate. I became impatient with our distraction capacity: Why are we blind for the potential we were granted to learn to steer our own further evolution beyond the constraints which subject us? Why was it so difficult to lay aside our divisive pettiness and power struggles and focus on the essentials of our further evolving journey, which meant-to start with- collective and global working together on making us wiser?

So, I decided to start a new life, as not to sink down in the debilitating comfort craving, which kills the little star dust-To the stars with difficulties, as they are our cradle-, most of us possess.

I left and started a new life. The bet was again painful for all of us and I became a pariah, losing contact with almost all my extended family and with 6 old friends. This very day, in 2024, I have no contact with them, beside my old son and his family. My young son and his family broke up contact with me for three years ago, and being equipped with my Teflon shield, I accepted this fact without bitterness. This is a price a warrior must learn to accept for his struggles. I got new friends though, and have a girlfriend, her family and some of her friends- and live in peace with myself, yet still fighting hard for our transformation as species. Since 2019 I wrote no less than 4 books, excluding this one. The absence of My young son and his family and my wife- we did not get divorced, though- did not drain me or made me moody. I know that lots of people experience such breaks up. I just did it rather late but it did pay off. While keeping warm feelings toward my wife, I have to admit that for the rest of them- including my young son and his family- I have no real warm feelings. No love, no hatred, no bitterness, and no longing. It must be the Teflon reaction of my psychological make up, due to my Kibbutz` background.

Now in the beginning of 2024, over the age of 78 years, and still enjoying good health while writing these lines, I look at what I achieved as a passing by passenger and what I achieved taking up advanced intelligence` torch up and showing a credible-if not ultimate- way to its next epoch.

When looking at myself, I admit that as a human worm, I made mistakes and failed sometimes to be my best version, though I did not try to harm people on purpose. I learnt to protect the force in me, which brought about my global vision and mission. This meant that while being very loyal to friends, I disengaged emotionally from those who either turned their back on me or tested my patience by their presumptuous stupidity. I was willing to go to war against few others if I found the case to be in the category of Casus belli. I would fight for my family members, for good friends, for people who could not manage on their own and needed my support. I would fight for Israel` right to exist and for humanity right/obligations to evolve beyond its self- destructive stupidity on a global level. I would fight against antisemitism, against vicious propaganda, which dumb people down and makes them slaves of their inflamed emotions, and I would fight against giving religions/ current ideologies the right to be the primary guiding faiths for the masses, as they all accentuate negative aspects of groupthink and thus perpetuating conflicts.

And I declare openly that I no longer belong to this disturbed, bewitched species. I am a mutant, the first of his sort, hopefully a ´Bridge over troubled water` to a wiser, more balanced, and benevolent descendent of man.

15 years ago, I was in Jerusalem, visiting the wailing Wall at night, where I came upon a number of men wearing shawls, and clearly involved in worship; one of them, according to his uniform, an officer in the IDF, seemed to be in deep prayer, but as I approached him from his left side, his right hand went to the grip of the assault rifle which was hanging from a strap on his shoulder. So, he was fully present in both worlds.

This officer-like many of us- was present in both worlds, but not in my third one, which is giving birth to a new future civilization beyond sapiens contradictions. Being and acting in this third world or dimension is what can turn most of us into mutants.

What it means, practically, to become a mutant?

By now-2024 I have rejected more than 200 proposals from sleek and smart mangers within the book industry to make me-as they falsely claimed- famous and successful (The American false dream). Thcy all expressed so called keen interest to help me get the credit I´d deserved. They used flattery and would do so much for me and my books. Yet, I rejected them all, because I don't operate on this common, foolish premise of transient illusory fame and success. For me, it is selling false dreams for people, who are doomed to oblivion. My vision is the essence of what I achieved in my life, and I did it solely for the sake of evolving humanity on its course to partly extinction. I don't need fame, credentials, or money for this effort, as I am not any longer a common human being. This is being a mutant.

Why must a mutant tread carefully while pursuing our ultimate meaning?

Becoming a mutant was extreme difficult decision for me knowing that I chose to tamper with both human's mindsets and destiny. My experiment may fail, but if it succeeds, it will be the most important historical/evolutionary event determining our long-term survival. As I see it, if we keep being the same and doing the same, due to our conflicted nature, the monstrous side of us will erupt again and again as to end up our voyage in destruction. By breaking away from the human state of not being truly humans and not truly beasts, we have our best chance to realize our potentials as to become angelic like. When I speak of such transcended state, I talk on a goal, an aspiration far beyond our current accomplishments. Such true humans do not exist yet, only in a coarse form/essence. But we must go humbly and slowly in this direction, humbly, because those who will evolve, will be wiser and better than us, and slowly-because we enter a perilous labyrinth, being creators of our own design.

Mutants must be aware of the danger of being hunted down by many homo Stupidligence in the future:

Mogens Kischi

I hereby give a stark warning to my potential mind children: Beware of Homo Stupidligence: They will try to destroy you!

Mark Clifton in his science fictional novel ′What have I done`? expressed this human′ lowness very sharply: ′ I looked into the past and I saw a review of the great and fine and noble and divine torn and burned and crucified by man. Yet my only hope of saving my race was to build these qualities, the fine, the noble, the splendid, into these thirty beings. To create the illusion that all men were likewise great. No less power could have gained the boon of quality for man with them.

I look into the future. I see them, one by one, destroyed. I gave them no defense. They are totally unprepared to meet a man as he genuinely is-and they are incapable of understanding.

For these things which man purports to admire the most noble, the brilliant, the splendid are the very things he cannot tolerate when he finds them.

Defenseless, because they cannot comprehend, these thirty will go down beneath the ravening fury of rending and destroying man always displays whenever he meets his ideal face-to-face.'

They will do it, try to destroy the new, advanced beings, because the new comers will be perceived as a mortal threat to them.

As Homo Stupidligence, you may feel that by departing the global arena as the prima ballerina, will leave much undiscovered and much unexplored and unfinished. You may think that there is no nobility whatsoever in its slow transformation, not of our own choosing. Yet it is inevitable if we are to prevail and take with us the best in us—by transcending ourselves—on a long-term basis.

Then, at last, the lights will go out for us, Homo Stupidligence, and a new era in the history of advanced, evolving intelligent beings will begin anew. And the sand or the water will cover us as the species we were but not our name, a worthy destiny of a great race giving place for the Creators` era to fully dawn.

How will this transformation of us take place:

What is my major motto right now?

Cato's words about Carthage were ;Carthage delenda est(Carthage must be destroyed)

My words on our most fatal foe: Stultitia (Folly, stupidity, silliness: Latin) delenda est!-

I am a visionary in a time where visionaries are not supposed to exist. I live in accordance with the maxim: Care about what other people tell you to think and you will always be their prisoner. **Therefor: My message coming out of a burning Bush:**

Humans; Keep on pursuing your evolutionary push!

Goal: No one can compete with Jesus who turned water into wine,

but trying to reduce global stupidity can be attainable goal...

Will gene editing ever be possible?

´Perception is awareness shaped by belief. Beliefs ´control` perception.

Rewrite beliefs and you rewrite perception. Rewrite perception and you rewrite genes and behavior… I am free to change how I respond to the world. So, as I change the way I see the world I change my genetic expression. We are not victims of our genes. We are masters of our genetics`-Bruce Lipto, cellular biologist.

As advancements in genetic technologies accelerate at an astonishing pace, the potential for gene editing to transform our world becomes closer to being realized. With the advent of revolutionary tools like CRISPR, scientists now possess an unprecedented ability to target and modify DNA with exceptional precision.

Can we genetically modify humans to be stronger?

By identifying and modifying specific genes related to muscle growth, endurance, or other physical attributes, it may be possible to enhance human strength. However, the ethical and safety considerations surrounding genetic engineering in humans are complex and require careful consideration.

In my opinion, Crispr and more advanced technologies in this area will be used to boost the expected intelligence of an embryo by a considerable amount.

Can genetic modification increase IQ?

With genetic engineering, it should be possible to manufacture a pretty substantial number of children with the potential intelligence of Goethe or Newton. It may also be possible to raise the average IQ of children by at least one standard deviation.

Will AI give us an evolutionary thinking push?

Just as ancient Greeks fantasized about soaring flight, today's imaginations dream of melding minds and machines as a remedy to the pesky problem of human mortality. Can the mind connect directly with artificial intelligence, robots, and other minds through brain-computer interface (BCI) technologies to transcend our human limitations?

Over the last 50 years, researchers at university labs and companies around the world have made impressive progress toward achieving such a vision. Recently, successful entrepreneurs such as Elon Musk (Neural ink) and Bryan Johnson (Kernel) have announced new startups that seek to enhance human capabilities through brain-computer interfacing.

How close are we really to successfully connecting our brains to our technologies? And what might the implications be when our minds are plugged in?

Will AI, based on factual analysis will be able to correct our faulty problem-solving process?

The monitor:

No religion, faith or political system/ideology can subdue the murderous beast´ impulses, seated in the brain folds of humans

Beware: we cannot stop wars, our greedy and reckless behavior, short -sight and the destruction of our environment, possessing sapiens conflicting nature!

Can a computer chip, external wisdom guiding monitor and genetic upgrading over centuries do the trick?

One of the applications which I envision for AI, is pointing out, based on facts and clear/ researched evidence, both environmental and verbal/ written pollution, so we can punish those who are responsible for them in the future. These AI monitors will be sort of filters against the deluge of nonsense, manipulation and sheer stupidity and lies, which pour over us. These monitors,,both personal and social and global will contend the far sighted wisdom and insights needed to teach humans to think in this manner and check, by using them, whether they think far sighted and wise. These monitors will be defended-as a unit for itself- against intrusion of commercial or other manipulating forces.

What year will AI surpass human intelligence?

t's taken more than four billion years for intelligent life to emerge by natural selection on Earth, but there are billions more years ahead in our planet's lifetime. Over that time, intelligence could develop in entirely new directions.

We human beings may be near the end of Darwinian evolution – no longer required to become the fittest to survive – but technological evolution of artificially intelligent minds is only just beginning. It may be only one or two more centuries before humans are overtaken or transcended by inorganic intelligence. If this happens, our species would have been just a brief interlude in Earth's history before the machines take over.

Many assume that human beings are the peak of intelligence, but it's possible that our species may represent a stage on the path towards minds that are more artificial. This could explain why the cosmos seems so empty of life like us. If an evolutionary transition to non-organic intelligence is inevitable across the Universe, our telescopes would be most unlikely to catch human-like intelligence in the sliver of time when it was still embodied in that form. It is perhaps more likely that the aliens would be the remote electronic progeny of other organic creatures that existed long ago.

That raises a profound question about the wider cosmos: are aliens more likely to be flesh and blood like us, or something more artificial? And if they are more like machines, what would they be like and how might we detect them?

In the classic movie: The Day The Earth Stood Still, one of the aliens is a robot - but still humanoid.

The prospect of inorganic alien intelligence raises some striking possibilities. If these beings are out there, they would act and think totally differently to us. They may not want to be detected. Indeed, their intentions may be impossible to fathom. To quote Charles Darwin, "A dog might as well speculate on the mind of [Isaac] Newton." However, we might deduce a few things.

For one, non-organic intelligence may have no use for an atmosphere, or the planet on which they originated. Interstellar voyages – or even intergalactic voyages – would hold no terrors for near-immortals.

Indeed, they may prefer to live in zero-gravity, because there you can make very large, very lightweight objects. If you wanted to build a huge, elaborate gossamer-thin structure to harvest energy, for example, it's easier in space than on a planet.

If they have silicon-based brains, they might realize they could expend less energy in colder regions away from planetary systems.

It's also not obvious that they would need to live in orbit around a star. Perhaps they'd have new ways of getting energy that we just can't envisage yet. If they have silicon-based brains, they might realize that the energy needed for processing "bits" is less at low temperatures, so they would expend less energy in colder regions away from planetary systems. They might even choose to hibernate for billions of years until the cosmic microwave background – the leftover radiation from the Big Bang – is further cooled by the continuing expansion of the Universe.

We look to the galaxies for life, but could AI aliens live in the cold in between?

They may not have the same base desires as us. We have evolved through Darwinian pressures to be an expansionist species. Selection has favored intelligence but also aggression. But if Darwinian pressures do not apply to these artificial entities, there's no reason why they should be aggressive. They may just want to think deep thoughts.

The fact we haven't seen any, and haven't been invaded by them, doesn't mean there's nothing out there. They may simply be more contemplative. We can't assess whether the "great silence" of the cosmos signifies their absence, or simply their preference.

We also can't assume that they'd even be a ′civilization`. On Earth, this term connotes a society of individuals: in contrast, ET might be a single integrated intelligence.

Pessimistically, they could be what philosophers call "zombies". It's unknown whether consciousness is special to the wet, organic brains of humans, apes, and dogs. Might it be that thoseelectronic intelligences, even if their intellects seem superhuman, lack self-awareness or inner life? If so, they would be alive, but unable to contemplate themselves, or the beauty, wonder and mystery of the Universe. A rather bleak prospect.

Alternatively, their more advanced intelligence could well allow them to understand crucial aspects of reality that we cannot, just as a monkey can't understand quantum theory. There could be complexities to the Universe that neither our intellect nor our senses can grasp, but electronic brains may have a quite different perception.

Elite researchers in artificial intelligence predicted that ′human level machine intelligence, ` or HLMI, has a 50 percent chance of occurring within 45 years and a 10 percent chance of occurring within 9 years.

Once this technology will surpass our intelligence, especially in complex, multi factorial/ contextual and farsighted thinking, they will assist us in our major, long- term decisions making, which we are not at all good at. In this field, I see clearly the benefit of advanced IA for the further progress of us.

Cyborg technology is also a very attractive option for enhancing humans` capacity to think wiser than we are capable of currently.

What is Advanced, evolving wisdom?

It means above all, farsighted, sustainable, socially just and ever evolving thinking and praxis of future humanity. It means evolved humans beyond sapiens limits, who will open for new vistas and horizons for exploring and challenging our physical and mental limitations and space.

It includes contextual thinking, rejecting fossilized stiff convictions/faith and outdated moral as a guiding star for future humanity. Its guidelines and practices will supersede all other ideologies, religions, and convictions.

It includes complementary thinking, where contrasts and differences can supplement each other in creating new mental and practical order.

It implies combinatory thinking, where elements for different disciplines and areas are being combined to create new attributes and original thinking.

It includes far sight and our ultimate meaning with our existence-becoming sustainable and expanding Creators.

It stands for re calibrating the global climate, population, consumption and production to maintain global sustainability. It means strong reduction of global population, consumption, pollution and production).

We need to follow a long-termed strategy for reducing drastically global population (max 3-4 billion) pollution, production, and consumption. If we don′t reduce them, we will choke our life conditions on earth.

We need badly more far sighted, advanced intelligent beings than the convictions prone humans we have in abundance today (who often are slaves of wishful thinking/compulsions and greed).

Therefore It stands for upgrading many of us- who are willing and capable- into becoming emotionally/mentally more stable (compared with the common mentally fragile sapiens), equipped with mindsets free of greed, short sight, war mongers attitudes,deception and self- deception.

It promotes human dignity based on granting rights qua demanding obligations from future beings to work for the common, long termed well of civilization.

It goes for abolishing the group of the very rich /powerful and reducing economic gaps between future human beings.

In the future we will upgrade the followers of this wisdom to become wiser, mentally more healthy, stable, long lived, and farsighted compared with the current common sapiens. We will grant them much longer and healthier lives and meaningful engagements by dedicating themselves to pursuing and realizing our ultimate meaning; Becoming Creators.

Only a global order based on Advanced, evolving wisdom can open for great collective deeds where people can feel that they contribute for something much greater than their mundane lives. Only by joining in this huge feat of expanding our capacities and mastery of our world and destiny can we grant people the solid notion of engaging in megalopsychia prone life.

This Advanced, evolving wisdom will not be rejected for a very long time, as it is a precondition for our future progenies` survival and further evolvement. If we won´t take it as a friend, we will suffer immensely and the survivors among us will then take it to them.

Modern technologies like CRISPR will facilitate this wisdom` promises.

By starting to focus on upgrading many of us beyond our debilitating shortcomings and ailments, it will get more and more followers. Its followers will focus on how to curb physical / mental sufferings in the world and boost future humans` capacity to think long term, far sighted and evolving. Suffering caused by mental disorders (like psychiatric ailments, depression, anxiety, chronic fatigues, autism, ADHD, and other ailments) will be reduced as to boost people capacity to think/act beyond their own current spheres.

This wisdom is not dictatorial, but it will weaken deceptive notions of baseless personal uniqueness, so prevalent among ordinary people in our mass societies, and presents instead, down-to-earth engagements on how to attain megalopsychia.

Being practiced properly it will reduce markedly human folly, mediocrity, and their negative omnipotent manifestations in our lives.

Wake up, reader, from your mental slumber and focus on your ultimate mission:

"Veni, Vidi, Dormivi": I Came, I Saw, I Slept, or Odysseus What happens to most people when they grow old and become frail and sick? They slowly or abruptly lose their social prestige and status, which is connected to their career or social status and thus often lose also much of their attraction and good spirits if they had had such. Luciano Pavarotti, who died in 2007, captured this mood of losing vigor, former status, and influence in the touching song ´Pourquoi me reveiller?`. He sings: ´Why do you awake me, O breath of spring? On my brow I feel your caresses, and yet quite is the time of storms and sorrow! Why do you awake me, O breath of spring? Tomorrow, into the valley, will come the traveler Recalling my former glory and his eyes will look in vain for my splendor They will find only misery and grief! Alas! Why do you awake me, O breath of spring?`

A poem so true about a man who wishes not to be disturbed in his sorrow, not to be awakened back to life, because what is left there of his former splendor and significance? All his greatness and brilliance are gone, so what is there to wake up to? Yet there is one great gift in life, you may receive if you are both lucky with your health and mind and are used to work hard for a good purpose. This gift is growing very old with the capacity and attitude to keep being proactive, engaged, curious and exploring, open-minded, trusting, skeptical, critical, and creative. It will keep you being attractive and capable of creating new nourishing contact throughout life. We are born and destined to become evolving and evolutionary warriors, not a pack of resigned souls. This is what I remind myself of.

In such moments, I come to repeat to myself my ′battle cry, which is taken from the poem of Alfred Tennyson about the legendary Odysseus. Here are some of my favorite lines: ′How dull it is to pause, to make an end. To rust unburnished, not to shine in use! As tho' to breathe were life! Life piled on life Were all too little, and of one to me Little remains; but every hour is saved from that eternal silence, something more, A bringer of new things; To follow knowledge like a sinking star, Beyond the utmost bound of human thought. Death closes all; but something ere the end, Some work of noble note, may yet be done, Not unbecoming men that strove with Gods. The lights begin to twinkle from the rocks; The long day wanes; the slow moon climbs; the deep Moans round with many voices. Come, my friends. 'Tis not too late to seek a newer world. Push off and sitting well in order smite the sounding furrows; for my purpose holds To sail beyond the sunset, and the baths Of all the western stars, until I die. We are not now that strength which in old days Moved earth and heaven, that which we are, we are— One equal temper of heroic hearts, made weak by time and fate, but strong in will To strive, to seek, to find, and not to yield`.

We are not doomed to become mentally meek, rigid, and resigned as we get `past our youth, but we are very much prone to this process due to the way our minds work as we grow older. Our minds often seek security and certainty in the known rather than challenge and struggle in new territories. It becomes comfort seeking and safeguards the person against ′taking risks` which slowly makes him favor rigid patterns. The mind starts to react in an overcautious manner. Instead of assessing the risk's magnitude and what is at stake, it sends warning signals to us: ′Do not do this. What if you fail, or what if people will find you silly, or what if you die somewhere else than in your bed?` This trickle of doubt and anxiety is our mortal woe because we become intimidated by his projective voice of all possible murky outcome connected with daring. Listening to this voice we become old in mind. And I can tell you that after observing so many people, I know that this danger is very real. The young curious and exploring Homo sapiens tends to become, as he grows older, tame, a shadow of himself, as he has lost his very living core: explorative, creative, and challenging mind. If we do not explore and ′conquer new territories and evolving capacities ` in our lives, we lose the battle against folly which is seducing us not to do so.

So how may a future civilization differ from and resemble ours?

The future civilization, which I envision hundreds of years from now, may look, albeit me, as following:

1) A new grand narrative for humanity, free of superimposing God and the lust for mammon and greed, is the backbone of this paradigm. It is designed to focus on grand, farsighted, and longstanding goals, a long-term mission and ultimate meaning that serve intelligent life's survival and evolvement.
2) Micro- and macro-dimensions in our lives: The micro reality encompasses our personal, interpersonal, social, occupational, political, and religious-spiritual spheres of existence. Macro reality encompasses our long-term, sustainable existence on the planet and our evolving journey as an intelligent species. By acting in relation to the macro level of our reality, people will find much more gratifying and enduring life meaning than any other ideology or religion can possibly grant them in the long run.
3) Homo sapiens must be upgraded because they are characterized by (a) behavior of "short-term gain, long-term pain; short-term resurrection, long-term self-destruction" and by (b) possessing a troublesome and unstable combination of intelligence and mind clouding stupidity. He is also characterized by (c) defective self- knowledge since it does not encompass the macro-dimension of his existence, by (d) a strong propensity for self-deception and wishful thinking, by (e) a strong propensity for greed and profit, by (f) excessive behavior, a lack of ´everything in moderation` and addictions of all kinds. The inevitable impact of these ´characteristics` can become his endgame.
4) The creators are a new species, wiser and more farsighted than HS, and therefore lead the evolving journey of intelligent life. The creator is supposed to clean up the mess after Homo sapiens. His ultimate goals are (a) transcending the mental limitations of both Homo sapiens and those enforced by nature and resetting the global climate back to preindustrial era, (b) creating a sustainable and evolving civilization, and (c) ´to the stars with difficulties. `
5) Life value will be for such civilization (a) the value granted human life only when people live in a sustainable manner and in accordance with the planet's capacity to renew itself and regenerate its life-giving resources and (b) the measure of their usefulness in a stable and enduring manner, to the long-term survival and evolving prospects of future generations and civilization. The maxim dynamic ´The first generation establishes something new, the second builds up upon it, and the third destroys it by friction and hatred` will not happen as the project of evolving, struggling to create something new and better will be the very essence of this civilization.
6) Global governance with dictatorial powers over essential issues like economy, ecology, demography, production, traffic, and defense. On regional level, democracy will be a part of the political fabric.
7) Hypotension regarding lifestyle, consumption, production, and transport/traffic. Free movement will be reduced strongly.

8) Borders will still be useful and will be enforced. Borders will be a necessity as to regulate the movements of people and goodies. As free travel over long distances and from continent to continent will be strongly reduced to reduce epidemics, pollution, and waste of resources, borders will be a necessity.
9) All production, including food, will take place-where it can be practiced- close to where people live as to save the cost of expensive transportation and increase independence of the local societies.
10) Mega cities' numbers will be reduced, and towns and cities will not exceed one hundred thousand humans. The measures are meant as to reduce loneliness and estrangement and encourage cooperation and solidarity among people.
11) Human commitments regarding the long-term common good of evolving humanity will precede human rights. Human rights will be dependent on fulfilling one's public duties.
12) Global population will be, over hundreds of years, reduced to upgraded humans of three to four billion on Earth altogether and some millions common sapiens.
13) Global sustainability in all essential areas will be the iron rule.
14) Fairness and justice will be the iron rule, and social or financial privileges/speculations/ elites will be curtailed.
15) Prudence, humbleness, impulse control, and long-term common needs will precede the individual needs.
16) Aspiration for megalopsychia (the greatness of the soul) via one's contributing deeds for the common well will be their cherished focus, and they will be rewarded and respected for this. I had some heated discussions with friends regarding the idea of evolving and transcending beyond sapiens, and some of them reminded me of Plato's allegory of the cave. Everyone thinks that THEY are outside this `cave` watching the others, that is, they are knowledgeable free people while all the others are the people chained to the wall of the cave, facing the blank wall, watching shadows projected on the wall. To get out of the cave, you must design and follow a route beyond sapiens' constraints and limitations; otherwise, you are in ′the cave` regardless of what you think/ imagine. Plato allegory is not a destiny. Knowing in the first place that you are in the cave and identifying its contours makes it possible to escape it. But you must know the dynamics between you and your cave, its spell on your mind, and what it hides from you on you. A person who knows that the only way to escape our ′cave` is to evolve beyond sapiens limitations has found an escape route out of it—the human mental traps, shortcomings, and blindness. In the last twenty years, many people contested my global vision regarding our inevitable upgrading, but none of them came up with another viable alternative vision on how to curb our self-destructive excesses. This aspiration/focus on evolving and upgrading is a part of the advanced evolving wisdom of tomorrow. The current view of wisdom is that it is the outcome of accumulative knowledge on oneself, the others and our world/reality in life-affirming manner performed by the mentally balanced, flexible-minded, and experienced human. Future evolving wisdom is based on the same premises, but the

knowledge in action here is long termed, life affirming, evolving, and sustainable, and the subject practicing this wisdom is ever-evolving intelligent creature, far beyond sapiens' limitations. The future wise, upgraded beings will know the truth regarding sapiens, lucidly conveyed in the following lines:

Basically, you are still but Universal Maj fly,
noisily you buzz, pretending to ascend high.
Before your day long life is gone and you die
you'll reject this truth with delusions and lies.
Silly Maj fly; stop your self-delusions' cries!
Your only escape from this destiny is a try
to evolve far beyond your encased Maj fly. —BK

When it all started…

Many years ago, in springtime full of fragrance, scents of mint and many other strange flavors of bushes and wild flowers, a little boy walked alone, asking himself once in a while upon passing a beautiful new flower, 'And what is this kind of flower, Benjamin?` And the boy held his breath a bit and then muttered to himself, 'A beautiful red flower.` And the next one was also 'a beautiful blue flower,` and the third, 'a beautiful yellow flower` and so on—a fine definition that settled in his mind the matter of the botanic. Many years later I and a friend walked on the same narrow dusty way, and the wildflowers were scarce. The horizon around us was framed by the almond trees in bloom on the small hills and the vague smell of pesticides. The scents and fragrance of yesterday were gone. From a distance, I could see some of the cypress trees around the cemetery, where most people whom I knew from childhood, including my parents, had been buried. Eddie, my friend, looked around him, squinted at the bright light, and asked me, 'Where is it, your childhood, lost paradise, pathfinder? ` I told him to be patient. In the east, the bluish mountains raised themselves against the blue sky as a crystal wall protecting a magic world behind them. The mountains, with their stern crags and inaccessible cliffs, brought back the magic of childhood when they were conceived by an imaginative child's mind as precious blue crystals, he could get half a kingdom for rescuing the beautiful princess. Far away to the west, I could sense the salty scent of the sea with its caressing blue waves, those waves who bore my little tanned bronze body, smiling and giggling with me. And the seashore, which was my good friend, with its fine white sand on which huge crabs ran to and fro, hiding in their holes. The seashore, where we collected the most beautiful shells and found amazing shells, which could whisper the tale of the deep sea and its treasures and how life was to evolve was hidden behind the hills. Now they were all gone. 'I know the way, trust me` I told him, sensing that he was a bit tense. Although it was springtime, he was sweating and panting heavily. We two have gotten a bit old, yet I felt as if I was a little child again coming back to my 'green, green grass of home. ` And down the path we went, Eddie beside me, and there, right there, my childhood Bustan, which once had bloomed there and formed my life, lay buried under the almond trees. I knew for sure that this was the right location since some of the old fences of thorny bushes were left there, those thorny bushes that each summer in our childhood had given us their sweet, thorny fruits. 'This is the site' I told him. 'And what am I supposed to think of it?' Eddie sighs. 'Here it all started for me anyway, Eddie. Here, on this spot, existed once a beautiful creation, a sustainable creation in the midst of the dry, arid landscape, and it evolved, and here it graced the landscape around it and talked with the flickering stars, and here it died years ago, but it can wake up again and wake up sleeping souls. Here it is!'

'Nice story, ' he sighed again, 'but then what? I wish to tell you straightforwardly, do not bullshit me with fairy tales as if they can help people or humanity. Life, for me, is the same as it always was, unruffled by events like this or others, indifferent to the joys and sorrows of man, mute and incomprehensible as the sphinx. But the stage on which this everlasting tragedy we call life is enacted, changes constantly and avoids monotony. This seems to be the real plot, but I do not see a designer for it. The world we live in moves, in my view, inexorably, assisted by our follies, toward its doom, and so do we.' I sighed. 'I have heard this before, Eddie. You do not need to be Eddie or a wise man to realize this possibility. I just came from the cemetery where I lay some flowers on my parents' graves. There I met all the people whom I knew so well. Many of them, like my parents, used their best years to accomplish things that were far beyond their personal interests and of utmost necessity in a much broader context. They immigrated to Israel in their youth. They started a new kibbutz society and founded the state of Israel. They were far from happy all the time, yet they made a difference in their own time and afterward, even though many people nowadays may question the nature and outcome of their accomplishments. They had experienced only one great tragedy in their lives, and this was the death of their families in the gas chambers, a tragedy due to lack of human compassion and foresight and due to human passivity in the face of mortal danger. 'In the cemetery, I greeted all the children and youth who died before their time because of ailments, accidents, or wars. I remember some of them, and the deep sorrow I had felt for them when they had lost their struggle against death. So, I know the lesson too, but I learned that life was not meant to give us meaning. This is an infantile thinking, a crying baby's imagination. We are supposed to grant our lives meaning, and we are the ones who have always done it out of physical, mental, and emotional necessity. When will you understand this simple truth? And we do it in utter defiance of life's ultimate silence, and this is how we form it. There is no other way! '

I sighed. We sigh because our difficulties and sufferings seem sometimes insurmountable. This sigh follows us as we realize that human life will always be influenced by troubles, difficulties, ambiguities, battles for survival, great visions, dreams, and painful stumbling. The sigh is created to relieve us in our interaction with that reality, which disappoints us time and again. We also sigh because we are not omniscient or omnipotent, and therefore, our lives cannot be a victory march of free, unbending will. We sigh because we keep stumbling over our own feet as if we were drunkards while ignoring the imperatives of our own times, even when the strategies to encounter them are visible. I sigh because we destroy our planet—our own Bustan—when we know all that is needed to know on how to make it sustainable, thrive, bloom, and evolve at the same time. ′You sigh, ` he commented. ′You know why, ` I uttered.

The sun was going down, coloring the sky with crimson, red, orange, and violet while we started our way back home. While walking on the hills, light and shadows were mingling on the field with its graceful wheat. ′So you had gotten a call many years ago? ` Eddie was mocking me again. ′No, I did not! ` ′Was it a mission?` ′Yes, it became one,` I retorted. ′And you too may join it now that you know its essence! ` ′Is God involved? ` he became suspicious. ′Not a bit! I just have had this notion of the Bustan, and later in my life, I was granted great possibilities to learn about human nature, aspirations, longings, and mental shortcomings. Out of all these, I distilled a vision in action. That is all to it. ` ′Working for a Bustan! ` he kind of stated. Darkness came tiptoeing on the hills, and the first stars were flickering and blazing up in the sky, inviting and enchanting. Soon Orion, the Great Hunter, will dominate the sky overhead. Does Eddie sense, looking at the night sky that we are a part of something incredibly awesome and wonderful, a quest more marvelous than most of us imagine? ′Look up at them` I pointed up toward the glimmering stars. ′What about them? ` ′They are also a part of it. ′To the stars through difficulty' is the essence of the evolving Bustan. ` He gazed at me. ′Never mind, ` I said. ′Just remember that every once in a while, the fundamental laws of the universe seem to be momentarily suspended, and not only does everything go right, nothing seems to be able to keep it from going right. In the same spirit of semi-miracles, we can make ourselves, fusing what we are with what we wish to be and into what we must become. I am not sure why it must be so, but it is. It helps to know this though. `

Against the darkening sky, two seemingly half-old people were walking in silence back to the parked car in one of these unforgettable starry evenings in the hidden story of mankind, when stars come so close. One of them said to the other, ′Where are you hiding, Adam-Eddie? How long will you hide from your responsibilities and mission? ` What did Eddie do? He just walked there, like most of us, who want to make a difference but remain what they least of all wish to be—ordinary, temporary guests in this world. Will he reply to this universal question and, thereby, resolve his utmost meaning dilemma? Let us hope that this question will keep haunting all the Eddies in this world, as long as they hide from themselves in a self-deceptive manner, ignoring their responsibility for themselves and for humanity. Let this question haunt you. as long as you keep being undecided as my friend Eddie. Where are you hiding, Adam-Eddie?

Last words:

The vortex of human vanity/self- deception is detected in the ocean′ drop, firmly believing that it can change the Ocean` composition. This is an illusion to avoid the pangs of existential loneliness.

I chose another journey to achieve the change of human civilization, mindsets and perspectives, and mine would take as long as advanced intelligent life` saga keep on existing.

As I was the only openly self- declared mutant, I was often lonely. Lonely in solemn, anticipating and planning manner. A loneliness tinged with grandeur. A loneliness which is burdensome, yet one craves it as one carves a course a species which has lost its way.

It is not the loneliness of people trapped within themselves and within their suppressive, sweet nothing conformism, the loneliness of people who said too often the wrong things, and come to regret that, but lack the courage to admit it, the loneliness of fear.

There is no grandeur in these kinds of loneliness, no purpose, and no vision. It is loneliness without meaning.

Yes, it hurts at times to be alone on a new paved way towards the stars, but it sure hurts much more to be alone at a party.

The time has come for H. Stupidligence
our evolving technologies to embrace…

Inspirations in Hebrew/English:

יצור אדם נולד- פרח,
בילדותו - זרח.
בבגרותו- אחר הבלים נכרך.
בהזדקנותו- מהחיים נחרך
ובמותו - זכרון היותו-פרח

A baby is born and blooms, in childhood she/he shines up.
In maturity she/he are seduced by distractions,
and in old age- is burnt by life. In death- the memory of her/him withers.

.ומסוכנים מסכנים, קטנים כתוכים נוהגים האדם בני רוב
בפנים זאת להם תאמר אם לך יהיה מר
-האנושות כפותה בו הגורדי הקשר זהו
וטיפשות עיקשות, אשלייה של בעבותות

Most people act as parrots, blindfolded and thus dangerous.
You invite trouble if you tell them this truth!
This is the Gordian knot, in which humanity is caught up:
In chains of delusions, stubbornness, and stupidity!

, לנוצץ לסגוד יעדיפו אדם בני
,רפש הוא אם אפילו
הנפש גדולת את לטפח מאשר

Humans will prefer to adore all which glitters,
even it is rubbish, then to nurture their soul towards greatness.

רפש שפע יש בימינו
,נפש לכל
קיבה לכל תועבה מזון שפע
חירות הנקראת יהירות שפע ויש

In our time there is plenty of rubbish to all souls in need of it. There is plenty of fast food to every demanding stomach and plenty of arrogance which is called freedom to do what one will…

יום אחר יום האדם אל אמונותיו הטפלות – נעקד
וכך הוא נתון כל ימיו באותו סד.
?!כשיחלוף מהעולם, האם יצא עולמנו נפסד

Day after day a man is willing to be crucified for his faith,
And in this manner, he is imprisoned by his conditioning.
And when he leaves this world- will our world miss anything?!

ממבול השטויות שאנו מפיצים יום יום,
סובלים רבים מתהליכים גוברים של שטיון .

From the deluge of verbiage people utter each day,
Lots of people become demented.

בימים של שפיכות דמים,
מתרבים בעלי הרחמים,
ועוד רבים מהם- צד אחד מגנים...
אך חפש בזכוכית מגדלת- חכמים?!

In days of bloodshed, the numbers of the so called merciful folk swell.
And the numbers of the denouncers swell even more,
But we need magnifying glass to find few wise people…

האם קיים אל מלא רחמים?
אם כך,כיצד בעולמו רבו הדמים,
המסוממים, נוכלים - ערומים,
תמימים ומטומטמים וכה מעט חכמים ?

Does a benevolent God exist?
So how come there is so much bloodshed,
so many fools, crooks, and deceitful folk?
So many easy to cheat and so few wise people?

שפע תקוות וציפיה בבובאטרון
והמתנה לבוא המשיח
הם נחמתו של השטן המדיח ...

Abundance of hope and expectations from Human` dolls theater-
kings queens and other show men and influencers-
all waiting for the coming of the Messiah:
the comforts granted by the deceiving Satan...

טרגדיה אנושית:
בימינו הזחוחים,
בהם אנשים מרוב חשיבות עצמית - מנופחים,
כל משתין בקיר הוא בעל פוטנציאל אדיר...
לנוכלים ולאיוולים יש בעלות על פטנט ארוך זקן:
להיות תמיד צדקן

A human tragedy:

In these days with so much promoted self- love
,where lots of folk brag about self- importance,
Everyone is full of immense potential.
and cheaters and fools have been granted patent on truth and moral.

חופש הדיבור בציבור
הפך לבירבור עכור
ובמה לסכל ולבור

Free speech in public, became a deluge of verbiage,
as it granted a stage for the fools.

הבה נחדל להלך סחור סחור;
האדם במיטבו הוא יצור אפור.
נטיותיו: גם לבן ,גם שחור.
לאלוהים בראשו יש מסתור,
ולחיית טרף,טמון בטבעו- בור.
על כן מתקשה הוא להפיץ אור .

Let us stop going around the bush:
A human at his best is a conflict prone creature.
His mental dispositions: Both black and white.
In his mind dwell both God and a beast, and
Therefore human´ light is grey toned.

הבו גודל לאנושות המודרנית - לישטין,
שיש בה אין סוף פרשנים
רעשנים,פטפטנים ומשפיענים

Praise modern humanity called Lishtin,,
which contains countless reality interpreters
noisy and talkative influencers

האדם להתניותיו הוא עבד כנוע,
למרות שמצבו זה עליו שנוא.
את תכלית קיומו הוא מוצא בשמיים
ועל זה הוא טוחן שפע של מיים

A human being is often a slave to his impulses
even though he hates this subjection.
The meaning for his existence he finds in Heaven,
and on this subject, he treads water…

בעולמנו המטופש,רבים הויכוחים,החיכוחים,
הסיכסוכים והניתוחים שכהרף עין הם נשכחים,
לעומת התפתחותנו למלאכים שתיזכר לנצחים

In our world, there are lots of conflicts,
debates and interpretations, which their roots are quickly forgotten,
but almost nothing of our potential evolution which may turn us into angels.

אם לא למדת את היסטוריית העולם והאדם,
כל חוכמתך היא להדם.

If you did not learn human history thoroughly,
All your assumed wisdom is nothing worth.

בני האדם הם טפיל נפוץ
אם לא יזכרו שהם אבק כוכבים,
הרוקד עם הטבע במחול אוהבים,
ישארו הם עד סופם -טפילים עלובים.

Human beings have become reckless parasite.
If they won´t recall that they are made of star dust
Which dances with nature a loving dance,
They will go down as infesting parasites.

מעשים טובים רק עבור האדם
שאינם כוללים את כל החי בעולם,
הם בחינת: לא היו הדברים מעולם!

Good deeds only for humans` sake,
which don´t include natures life
, bring us only to our doom.

אילו הייתי יצור עילאי,אורח פורח
הייתי מפטר את אלוהים הפוחח
שאת עבודת שיפור האדם -מורח
ושאת יעודו עבור בני אנוש זונח
מסיבלם וסכלותם הוא בורח.
על ארצם הייתי בסתר צונח

ומכיוון שהאדם הוא יצור סורח
בהרצאה על מידות טובות
לא הייתי פותח.
מוח חדש וחכם להם הייתי רוקח

If I was a earth visiting super being,
I would had fired their gods
who neither work for improving them nor show them
the right direction for attaining the ultimate meaning;
gods that have forsaken them

I would land unmarked on their soil,
but I would not try to persuade them to become
better or drop their gods,
but I would plant better brains in their skulls.

Insights in English:

′There are no angels among sapiens. All of us are, to certain degrees contaminated by life mud, but most don′t seem to accept this!

In humanity, there exist three groups:1) Innovators/originators (tiny) 2) Replicators (huge) 3) Nonsense′ uttering narrators(big). This is one of humanity` big conundrums.

When your moral is black- white, you have patent on right and wrong and you only see good and bad guys, watch yourself in the mirror: There stands in front of you a made of mud, dumb person.

This dumbness combined with self- glorification is the poison of humanity, as it falsifies of who we truly are and must evolve away from…

The feeling of self-importance is so ingrained in humans, that they are willing to pay a high price - sometimes even die, as the case is often with Holly wars - to keep this delusion.

Stupidity exposes itself very often with so called context free observations on the human condition. Lack of context focusing indicates convictions, which may serve some mental purposes, but not to promote wisdom and far sight, which are essential for our long-term survival. This is where stupidity appears in disguise as it encourages all kinds of escapism.

Can it be also the outcome of nurture?
No society wants you to be farsighted and wise.
Its interest is in you being semi -automated size.
For when you are wise, you see its deceit and lies,

while you beyond its dumbing down project up rise,
making you free of its debilitating- enslaving prize`-Benjamin Katz

The mass production of self- centered narcissists` in the West is interrelated with the general dumb down of the population. Lack of self- awareness resulting in constant projections of ones` own emotional/ social inadequacy/ recurrent problems, is typical for the narcissistic people.

Without self- awareness and learning by one's own faults, people tend to get dumber with growing age. The extent of one`s free correlates to ones` capacity to open up for fault correcting feedback, instead of projecting them consistently on others.

The major human mental defect and tragedy:

Human beings are plagued by delusions, illusions greed, short sight… and are not granted mental capacity to reign them!